International Politics and Civil Rights Policies in the United States, 1941–1960

In the period following World War II, the federal government devoted more time and attention to civil rights reform and legislation than it had since the end of Reconstruction in 1876. Despite the impressive literature that analyzes the modern civil rights movement, its connection to American foreign policy during and after the war remains largely unexplored. Focusing on this gap, Professor Layton shows that the revolutionary changes in world politics created by the war also created new opportunities and pressure points for reforming U.S. race policies. The Holocaust, the dismantling of colonial empires, the Cold War, and the establishment of the United Nations all contributed to a new receptivity to civil rights reform in both the executive and judicial branches of the federal government. And, as Professor Layton describes, civil rights leaders quickly recognized the opportunities presented by the new international environment and were able to use them in exerting their own pressure to enact domestic policy reforms.

Azza Salama Layton is assistant professor in the Political Science Department at DePaul University. Her articles have appeared in the *Arkansas Historical Quarterly* and *Proteus*.

International Politics and Civil Rights Policies in the United States, 1941–1960

AZZA SALAMA LAYTON

DePaul University

CAMBRIDGE
UNIVERSITY PRESS

PUBLISHED BY THE PRESS SYNDICATE OF THE UNIVERSITY OF CAMBRIDGE
The Pitt Building, Trumpington Street, Cambridge, United Kingdom

CAMBRIDGE UNIVERSITY PRESS
The Edinburgh Building, Cambridge CB2 2RU, UK   http://www.cup.cam.ac.uk
40 West 20th Street, New York, NY 10011-4211, USA   http://www.cup.org
10 Stamford Road, Oakleigh, Melbourne 3166, Australia
Ruiz de Alarcón 13, 28014 Madrid, Spain

First published 2000

Printed in the United States of America

Typeface New Baskerville 10/13 pt.   *System* MagnaType™ [AG]

A catalog record for this book is available from the British Library.

Library of Congress Cataloging-in-Publication Data
Layton, Azza Salama, 1956–
    International politics and civil rights policy in the United States,
    1941–1960 / Azza Salama Layton
        p. cm.
    Includes bibliographical references.
    ISBN 0-521-66002-5. – ISBN 0-521-66976-6 (pbk.)
    1. Afro-Americans – Civil rights – History – 20th century.
    2. Racism – Political aspects – History – 20th century.
    3. United States – Foreign relations – 1933–1945. 4. United
    States – Foreign relations – 1945–1989. 5. United States – Race
    relations. 6. United States – Politics and government – 1933–1953.
    7. United States – Politics and government – 1953–1961. I. Title.
    E185.61.L39   2000
    323'.0973'0904–dc21   99-24439
                                                              CIP

ISBN 0 521 66002 5 hardback
ISBN 0 521 66976 6 paperback

For my parents Kamal and Mona Salama
and
my son Matthew

Contents

Acknowledgments

Even though acknowledgments usually begin with the professional and end with the personal, I choose to begin mine in reverse. I dedicate this book to my parents and my son. Since I began graduate school in 1988 as a single mother of a four-year-old son, my parents have been leaving their home in Egypt for extensive periods of time to be with Matthew and me, to help us and provide us with unconditional love. Their sacrifice went beyond any cultural definition of parenthood. My success is theirs in every way. Matthew, thank you for your patience, kindness, and love. You gave me so much. No parent could wish for a better child or friend. I love you, son. Thank you, Donald Henderson, for your love, humor, and companionship. It is true, life did start at forty.

I want to thank Fran Buntman and Camille Busette for their friendship and constant encouragement. Fran heard a very early version of the ideas behind this work. When other "specialists" were discouraging me from pursing this project because "the United States feeds half of the world, therefore no one can pressure us," Fran pushed me forward. She read, edited, and edited again. Fran, I look forward to many years of friendship. Camille, your friendship and support are crucial. Thank you for being there for me. Your professional and personal dignity have always inspired me. Not only did your contribution make this work better, but your love and warmth provided me with the sister I never had.

One of the most exciting and challenging periods for me was the summer I spent at the National Archives. I had never left my son before. Tagrid Wahba, my dear friend of many years, extended her home and family to be my own in Washington, D.C. It was a home away from home. Without the hospitality of Tagrid and her husband Ron, I would have been unable to spend the many weeks I did at the Archives. When I needed office space in D.C., Lissa August provided me with that. Thank you, Lissa, for two decades of a lovely friendship and for your belief in me.

Thank you, Janet DiVincenzo and Tom Liao, for your friendship and for reading through my chapters. Thank you, Joan Yamani, Gary Freeman, Richard Kraemer, Cherly Malone, Cheryl McVay, and Suzanne Coldwell. Theda Skocpol, Richard Vallely, David Meyer, David Chappell, Charles Epp, Tom Jackson, Kelly Moore, Dwane Oldfield, Gilda Zwerman, and Esme Bhan were good friends to this project. I want to thank Mary Dudziak for sharing her ideas and unpublished work with me.

Many have asked me if I had considered specializing in Middle Eastern politics since Egypt is my native country and Arabic my native tongue. But how could I have done that when I had Walter Dean Burnham as my first teacher of American politics? Thank you, Dean Burnham, for fascinating me. I also want to thank the other members of my dissertation committee: David Prindle, Julius Ihonvbere, Ray Marshall, and Robert Divine.

This work was funded by grants from the College of Liberal Arts and Sciences of DePaul University and also by the university's Research Center. The Center for African and African American Studies at the University of Texas funded the last crucial year of my graduate program, while the Center's director, Sheila Walker, served on my dissertation committee. Thank you, Sheila, for your friendship and sponsorship.

To my friend and colleague Beth Kelly, thank you for your incredible generosity. Your editorial advice was crucial. Thank you for the many hours you gave me. I was fortunate to have completed this work in an intellectually and personally supportive environment. For this I want to thank my colleagues and the staff of the Political Science Department at DePaul University. Alex Holzman, my editor at Cambridge University Press, was a pleasure to work with. Thank you, Alex, for your encouragement, criticism, and friendship. I want to thank the anonymous reviewers who helped me refine this work. I also want to thank my copy editor, Andrew Saff, for his help.

For my conclusion I saved space for a very special person – a person who has inspired, influenced, and guided me. For six years, Doug McAdam encouraged me, reviewed and commented on my work, boosted my confidence, told me how important my research is, and restored my hope and faith in our strange profession of academia. Doug, I feel an incredible debt of gratitude. You have been my mentor and my friend. Thank you for holding my hand when I needed it most.

There are countless others I have not forgotten who have helped contribute to this project in numerous ways. I extend to all of them my humble thanks.

CHAPTER ONE

Introduction

If the United States merely wants to "dominate" the world, the atomic bomb and the U.S. dollar will be sufficient to achieve that purpose. However, the world cannot be "dominated" for a long time. If the United States wants to "lead" the world, it must have a kind of moral superiority in addition to military superiority.[1]

The racial strife in America is a disgrace to the civilized world, and if the United States wishes to preach the principle of justice and humanity to others [it] must first solve the race problem within [its] own borders.[2]

The inhumanity of racial arrogance seems to have become the privilege of certain people with blonde skins and the odd thing is that it finds apologists among American leaders who want to convert pigmented Asians to the American cult of democracy.[3]

In the two decades following World War II, the advances in U.S. civil rights were unmatched in American history. During Franklin D. Roosevelt's second administration, there were hints of a new receptivity to civil rights changes on the part of some within the federal government establishment. Simultaneously, civil rights advocates continued to pressure and mobilize supporters to end institutionalized segregation and racial discrimination. Nevertheless, these

1

pressures from below were insufficient to explain the qualitative shift in the extent and nature of federal attention to civil rights reform in the immediate postwar period.

To explain this qualitative shift, we need to examine the new Cold War pressures impinging on the United States – and especially the Executive branch – in the postwar years. The emerging Cold War pressures attendant to the superpower competition for influence in the postwar world order represented a sea of change in the federal approach to the "Negro problem." Domestic pressures had to be accompanied by international pressures. International factors and their impact on America's foreign policy interests swung the pendulum in favor of civil rights advocacy.

Why did the Executive branch of the federal government, in 1946, place civil rights reforms at the top of its domestic policy agenda? Why in the midst of an era marked by civil rights violations and colored by rivalry with the Soviet Union and a national phobia concerning domestic Communism that were used to justify repression at home against unions, universities, business, and even government sectors do we see improvements and a push by the Executive and Judicial branches for civil rights reforms for African Americans? Why did the efforts of civil rights groups produce few advancements under President Franklin D. Roosevelt's liberal progressive administration, yet we see groundbreaking initiatives in civil rights sponsored by President Harry S. Truman's administration? What was the critical motivating factor behind the speedy and comprehensive intervention by the Executive branch in an area historically and traditionally reserved for state and local politics?

The key to explaining why President Truman pushed civil rights reforms to the top of his public agenda following World War II lies, I argue, in the dynamic relation between domestic race policy and U.S. foreign policy interests. America's entry into global politics and the "complex interdependence" of international politics altered the bargaining position of African Americans and civil rights advocates and also that of Southern Democrats. Geopolitical realities provided new opportunities for civil rights activists at home and critics abroad to call for race reforms. The increasing international pressures on the U.S. government to "put its own house in order" pushed forward reforms that started with executive and judicial measures. International pressures injected confidence into African American aspirations. These pressures provided new opportunities for civil rights advocates and helped in the peaking and culmination of the civil rights movement and the passage of the long overdue Civil Rights Act of 1964 and the Voting Rights Act of 1965.[4]

Neither the reality nor the prospect of African American electoral power would have sufficed to produce the attention the Truman Administration devoted to civil rights reform. I argue that the unprecedented presidential racial policy activism following World War II was the result of changes in U.S. foreign policy in the context of a new geopolitical order. In addition, Truman's tenure as president coincided with an era, unmatched in history, of the centrality of race in international politics.

While President Roosevelt was politically secure with historically unprecedented margins of victory at the polls, in 1946 Truman was a nonelected president who enjoyed neither the popularity nor the electoral support of his predecessor. Roosevelt was a social and political liberal who cemented the New Deal coalition of the South and the North, labor and business, the "less fortunate" and the rich, and African Americans and whites. His New Deal reforms successfully lured the black vote away from the Republican Party – the party of Lincoln, the emancipator. But with the exception of Executive Order 8802, which established a Federal Employment Practices Committee (FEPC), Roosevelt's accomplishments in the arena of civil rights may be described as political rhetoric lacking in substance.[5]

In contrast, Truman, a Missourian who showed signs of racism in earlier years,[6] began his presidency by appointing the first civil rights committee in U.S. history. His action was the first official assault by the Executive branch on black oppression. By proposing an end to racial segregation in schools, housing, and public facilities, equal access to jobs, and equal voting rights, the 1946 Civil Rights Committee established a national agenda that the black civil rights movement would seek for the next twenty years. Truman also issued two landmark executive orders in 1948 prohibiting discrimination in federal employment and desegregating the armed forces. In 1951, he established the Committee on Government Contract Compliance to prevent employment discrimination by private employers with government contracts.[7]

What explains Truman's crusade in the mid-1940s when "the 1946 Congressional elections seemed to indicate the country was moving to the right and the conservative wing of the Southern Democrat[s] took heart, along with the Republicans[?]"[8] Why did he take the political risk of alienating the Southern Dixiecrats by sponsoring civil rights when his predecessor, a politically and electorally more popular figure, refused to take such a risk? Both Roosevelt and Truman needed the Southern bloc not only for electoral votes but also in order to pass their legislative agendas. By virtue of the one-party South and the seniority system, Southern Democrats enjoyed tremendous congressional power.[9] They had a large claim on federal patronage and the allocation of federal spending. Southern senators could filibuster legislative proposals and could retaliate against the president by using the strategy of obstruction, a strategy illustrative of their cohesive power.[10] Fear of retaliation, President Roosevelt claimed, is what prevented him from supporting antilynching legislation proposed in the 1930s. He could not risk congressional obstruction of other bills that had higher priority, such as those to remedy the recession at home and also the worsening situation in Europe.[11]

Truman's aggressive pursuit of race reform carried the potential of serious political damage to the maintenance of the majority coalition created in 1936. What was behind his willingness to pursue such a costly agenda? The domestic social and political pressures for racial reform were not strong enough incentives for the administration to risk the loss of congressional support for other programs that it valued more highly. Domestic pressures for racial reforms were not strong enough to jeopardize foreign aid programs, such as the Marshall Plan, and other defense and social legislation.

Truman's civil rights program occurred in the absence of substantive influence from African Americans. Some have argued that Truman's crusade was a political maneuver to capture black support in 1948.[12] But how significant was African American political power before 1948, when Truman ordered his Civil Rights Committee to investigate the status of the African American? How effective was African American political power in the face of traditional solid opposition of the Southern Democratic–Northern Republican coalition?

Because of the leadership position of Southern politicians in Congress, African Americans did not benefit much from their growing voting power in the North during the 1940s, and civil rights legislation continued to be suppressed in Congress. Putatively, for the African American voter in the South, the Supreme Court ruling in *Smith v. Allwright* in 1944 outlawed the white primary. In practice, though, Southern states adopted various measures to preserve the white primary and to circumvent the Court decision. Southern politicians passed amendments that added literacy and poll tax requirements, and "tests of good character and good citizenship."[13]

In sum, Southern congressmen and their state and local counterparts were able to stifle the voting power of African Americans throughout the 1940s. By the mid-1940s, 70 percent of the black population lived in the South. By 1950, non-whites made up only 20.1 percent of the potential voters in the South, 4.8 percent in the West, and 5.1 percent in the North.[14]

African American leaders liked to point out that the black vote was the balance of power in the 1944 and 1948 elections. But in both years, voter registration of blacks did not proceed according to the expectations of their leaders.[15] In 1947, the NAACP claimed that there were enough black voters to determine the outcome of a close presidential election in 1948. That claim was based on two assumptions: a close election and a highly unlikely scenario that the overwhelming majority of all potential voters would be registered, well organized, and unified behind one candidate.[16] African American political clout in the 1940s was not perceptible enough to pressure the Truman Administration to pursue civil rights reforms. Public opinion and political opposition in many Southern states, and complacency and indifference elsewhere, overshadowed the incipient progress that African Americans were making.[17]

problematic source
here —
Frazier 1957
from

In addition and as important, the syndrome of dejection, isolation, self-contempt, and other marks of oppression both in the
North and South left many African Americans politically apathetic.[18] The political influence of the black population evolved
slowly. "If blacks moved to the cities to solve their problems, they
soon discovered that their problems persisted, even increased."[19]
The African American migration to the North, the dilution of the
agricultural economy, the rise of industry and trade sectors, and the
growth of cities and urbanization in general were fundamental
trends that created favorable conditions for bringing about political change.[20] However, these conditions did not automatically convert the black voter into a power that would force the federal government to address civil rights reform in the mid-1940s.

Questions surrounding Truman's civil rights platform amidst
strong political opposition and without substantive black political
power will persist if scholars continue to adopt a purely domestic
view of the impetuses for civil rights reforms. Only an analysis of the
international context within which these reforms occurred can explain the timing and content of U.S. civil rights reform and the
incentives behind the government's actions. The traditional expla-

social
mvt.
theory

nation of the rise of social movements has generally focused on
changes in the domestic political and social environment. Such
approaches do not fully explain why Presidents Roosevelt and Truman acted differently over race issues or why certain figures in the
federal government pushed for civil rights reform when they did.
The "international setting, and particularly the way in which it
intrudes upon domestic politics, is a crucial . . ."[21] yet neglected
component of social movement theory. Current analyses of domestic political, social, and economic factors surrounding civil rights
politics provide insufficient theoretical or analytical leverage for
understanding the timing of the actions of the federal government
in the mid-1940s. The rich social movement scholarship and the
literature on the civil rights struggle tell only the domestic story.[22]
But even though, as I suggest throughout this work, the international context of the U.S. civil rights movement is extremely significant, it awaits comprehensive treatment. As Paul Gordon Lauren

perhaps last work that can make this claim

notes, "Unfortunately, the impact of [the Cold War] pressure has often been completely ignored in the study of the history of the U.S. civil rights movement."[23] This work, a part of a growing intellectual project concerned with internationalizing the study of race, civil rights, and international politics, attempts to fill the gap.[24]

The United States' efforts in the area of civil rights were the result of not only domestic pressures but also represented a calculated measure aimed at containing Communism. Anti-Communism and the uncertainty surrounding the outcome of the Cold War were the most salient issues of political concern. Cold War politics shaped U.S. foreign policy for several decades. It also had a significant influence over domestic politics.[25] The belief that "the civilization to which [the U.S.] belongs . . . confronts a critical danger indicated by the phrase 'Cold War'" became the principal element shaping American politics.[26]

The salience of Cold War thinking, especially the "Domino Theory" of Soviet containment, meant that U.S. policy makers perceived *any* loss of territory to the Soviets as a threat to national interests, whether that loss was in Mozambique, Laos, or anywhere else. The Cold War and its ensuing geopolitical and ideological competition between the two superpowers challenged U.S. efforts to shape the postwar era in its own image of democracy and the free enterprise system. The contradiction between this image and the government's racial practices at home, State Department officials realized, was an obstacle in the conduct of foreign relations with African, Asian, and Latin American countries. Consequently, the U.S. government's ability to preach democracy to Third World countries was seriously hampered by its domestic racism.[27] The Soviet Union's use of American racism to compete for influence in non-white nations was an effective weapon against the United States.[28] People all over the world were saying "if the U.S. wanted to appear as the champions of democracy throughout the world, [it] would do well to see first all [its] own colored population enjoys the benefits of democracy."[29] If ending institutionalized segregation and discrimination "could be achieved [this] would show the Africans and Asians whom the United States hoped to secure as allies in the conflict with the Soviet Union that steps were being taken to curb the American habit of humiliating people because of the color of their skins."[30]

I believe that the international context did far more to command specific components of the federal government's attention to civil rights than would have come from the government's own inclinations. While there were signs of a new open-mindedness among some government officials and Northern urban liberals toward the African American struggle, domestic pressures alone are not enough to explain the Executive branch's push for civil rights reforms in the mid-1940s. It was the international dimension of U.S. race policies that swung the pendulum. The decision by the Executive branch in general, and the Justice and State Departments and the U.S. diplomatic core in particular, to intervene on behalf of African American civil rights in the mid-1940s lies partly in the realization that world events had made the race problem "a global instead of a national or sectional issue to a greater extent than ever before in the history of the world."[31] While race relations were always considered a domestic issue, they ceased to be so as the United States ended its policy of relative isolation and assumed a leadership position in global political and economic affairs. It is within the Cold War context that the federal government decided to take drastic measures (by 1940s standards) to eliminate institutional racism, the number one domestic failure and the number one international handicap.[32]

The focus of this study is twofold. The first concern is how the international community pressured the American government to deal with the gap between its creed of democracy, equality, justice, and freedom and its practice of discrimination and segregation at home. The second concern is how African American leaders, to mobilize the international community[33] as well as new supporters at home, framed their struggle within the context of Cold War politics. The work's empirical mission is to incorporate the rich and untapped government documentation of international pressures and the American administration's response to these pressures with the prominent literature on U.S. civil rights. Records of the State Department, the U.S. mission to the United Nations, and the

United States Information Agency illustrate the important role international opinion and international pressures played in the shift in the federal government's position on race policy.

Of equal importance are the theoretical implications of the study. The work of social movement scholars – especially those who have studied movements in the U.S. and Western Europe – has been marked by an almost total lack of emphasis on the international roots of social movement emergence, development, and impacts. The nearly universal stress in social movement literature, in Europe and the United States, on the role of favorable conditions in shaping the emergence and development of collective action has betrayed a consistent domestic bias. That is, "movement scholars have, to date, grossly undervalued the impact of global political and economic processes in structuring the domestic possibilities for successful collective action."[34] In this book I argue that the pressure for shifts in the federal government race policy arose internationally; that international events provided leverage and new political opportunities that were successfully mobilized by civil rights advocates at home as well as utilized by foreign government and non-government entities to criticize the U.S. government.[35] While in the following chapters I substantiate, through empirical data, my arguments that international pressures played a prominent role in the federal government's decision to advocate civil rights reforms, I show in this introductory chapter how important it would be for social movement theory to take account of the international context of collective action.[36]

Social Movement Theory

The past two decades have witnessed a proliferation of studies of social movements. Movement scholars representing different theoretical approaches emphasize the importance of three broad sets of determinants in the emergence and development of collective action. First is the structure of political opportunities and constraints that confront the movement.[37] Second are the resources available for mobilization by members of the movement.[38] Lastly is the political and social framing process by which the movement hopes to enhance its support both within its own population but more importantly within the public at large for the purpose of attracting new allies.[39] While the first of the three approaches, that of political opportunity structure, is the most germane to my study, the other two approaches, those of resource mobilization and framing process, do pertain to the case of the American civil rights movement. Civil rights advocates, as I demonstrate in the next chapter, mobilized the support of the international community as well as framed their struggle in the context of America's national security and foreign policy interests and a necessary measure in the fight against Communism.

Political Opportunity Structure and Civil Rights

The attractiveness and utility of the concept of political opportunity structure lie in the concept's capacity to link institutionalized politics and social movements.[40] Scholars attempt to use changes in the internal structure or informal power relations of a given national political system to explain the emergence, development, and impacts of a particular social movement. The argument is straight-forward. Social movements emerge and develop in response to changes "not only among previously quiescent or conventionally oriented groups but also in the political system itself."[41] Some scholars point out the utility of political opportunity structure in explicating the variable of timing. The "when" of social and political change can be understood only by analyzing the political environment in which change occurs.[42]

Political opportunity structure has become a staple of social movement inquiry. Yet use of the concept has consistently betrayed a domestic bias. The vulnerabilities that allow movements to emerge and achieve gains are thought to develop internal to a given polity. But as William Gamson and David Meyer state, and as my empirical data indicates, "international politics intrudes upon domestic political opportunity structure . . . that national political opportunity structures are nested in a larger international environment that constrains or promotes particular kinds of opportunities. . . ."[43] It was the post–World War II international environment and America's new role in it that provided new opportunities for civil rights advocacy. The federal government's support for racial reform was "nested" in foreign policy interests and aspirations.

The current consensus among movement scholars, according to Doug McAdam, holds that political opportunity structure has four dimensions. First, the relative openness or closure of the institutionalized political system determines political opportunities. Second, political opportunities are intertwined with the stability or instability of that broad set of elite alignments that typically undergird a polity. In other words, political opportunities emerge when there are significant divisions among previously stable political elites. Third, political opportunities rise with the emergence of new allies within a previously unresponsive political system. Finally, the state's capacity and propensity for repression affect political opportunities.[44]

But each of these four dimensions is subject to influence by international factors. To illustrate this point and anticipate the argument I develop in the book, let me address each of the four dimensions as they pertain to my case study of the U.S. civil rights movement. By including the international context and the Cold War pressures that the U.S. government faced following World War II, I hope to develop a richer account of the emergence, development, success, and impact of the movement.

Relative Openness of the American Political System

In the pre–World War II years, there were definite hints of a new receptivity to civil rights policy changes on the part of some within the federal establishment. Supreme Court rulings in the 1930s and legislative proposals by Northern urban congressmen are two examples of the "winds of change" regarding America's black population. The gradual openness of political institutions that followed the 1930s New Deal reforms is well documented. The domestic factors contributing to this shift include the decline in the importance of King Cotton to the national economy, the decline of the flow of immigrants because of World War I, which resulted in a shortage of labor in the North and the luring of black labor from the South, and the great black migration to the North, which meant the increasing importance of African American voters and their entrance into competitive electoral politics. These factors contributed to the nationalization of the "Negro Problem" that initiated the federal government's intervention in an area previously perceived as a states' rights issue. In short, as the political leverage of African Americans increased, so did their access to the political establishment and their ability to push for reforms.

The number of Supreme Court rulings favorable to African American rights in the 1930s indicates the system's openness, especially following President Roosevelt's threat to "pack the court."[45] FDR's creation of the Federal Employment Practice Committee (FEPC) in 1941 was the first in a series of presidential executive orders by him and his successors in support of African Americans. Although the Legislative branch seemed to be immune from the pressures for change in racial policy until 1957, the number of pro–civil rights measures introduced in Congress rose. While there were only thirteen such measures during the 1937–8 session, the number multiplied after 1945. There were forty-one in the 1945–6 session, fifty-one in the 1947–8 session, and seventy-two in the 1949–50 session.[46]

In addition to the above "domestic" factors, I argue that the end of America's isolation during and following World War II meant a new opening of its institutions to the international community, especially the Executive branch. By 1948, the United States was a member of forty-six international organizations, many with binding charters.[47] As a democratic country and one that hoped to influence the policies of other nations, the United States found that its domestic policies were opened to inspection by other nations.[48] Race policies were no exception. As Brenda Gayle Plummer puts it, "The war had opened national frontiers to the race question in unprecedented fashion and linked domestic reform to vast changes in the world at large."[49] America's race problem, once viewed as a regional issue, became a matter of international concern. Thus I argue that it was a combination of domestic and international factors that rendered the American political establishment more open to the influence of civil rights advocates.

Divisions in Elite Alignments

Political and economic factors contributed to the end of the alignment of Southern and Northern elites, an alignment that had endured since the end of Reconstruction. The realignment in elite configurations was the result of diverging interests at two levels: between the representatives of the Southern and the Northern regions in Congress as well as between a Southern-dominated Congress and a chief executive who considered the international political and economic environment to be at least as important as the domestic environment.

Several factors caused elite cleavages in Congress in the 1930s and the years that followed. As mentioned above, the decline of King Cotton was crucial in undermining the economic and, indirectly, the political importance of the South. Southern cotton was no longer a cornerstone of the national economy. Accordingly, the political leverage that the South enjoyed and that enabled it to negotiate the end of Reconstruction with the North in 1876 was reduced significantly. Second, the great black migration to Northern urban centers meant the increasing importance of the African American vote. Northern politicians, especially those representing the seven states that absorbed eighty-seven percent of black immigrants,[50] could no longer afford to ignore the potential black vote in their political calculations. Third, the African American vote, which traditionally went to the Republicans, began shifting to the Democratic Party. By 1936, the black vote was part of the coalition of constituents that formed the basis for FDR's and the Democratic Party's strength. The shift of the black vote to the Democratic Party drove a wedge between the Northern Democrats who wanted to court the black vote and the Southern Democrats who sought to keep the African American in his or her place to preserve the "Southern way of life."

In addition to the domestic factors that eroded the alliance between the industrial North and the agricultural South, there were also international factors that contributed to the split between the Legislative and Executive branches. While members of Congress looked after their regional and state interests, Harry Truman, the first Cold War president, had to minimize the detrimental effects America's racism had on U.S. foreign policy interests and its international prestige. As Anthony Oberschall puts it, "A State has both a domestic and an international political environment."[51] In the context of the Cold War, the White House – with pressures from the Department of State – weighed the risks of inaction on civil rights issues against the country's foreign policy interests. The international environment took precedent over the domestic. The president had the duty of mediating domestic and international pressures. As Truman argued in 1947, America "can no longer afford the luxury of a leisurely attack upon prejudice and discrimination"; that the country could not wait for change "in the slowest state or the most backward community."[52] This was the same year that civil rights issues caused a split in the Democratic Party and the formation of the Dixiecrats as a third party.[53]

Truman's championing of civil rights constitutes no puzzle at all. On the contrary, it exemplifies a rational and coherent strategy of political expedience. Since the majority in Congress was not sensitive to the intersection between domestic race policies and America's fight against Communism, the Executive branch initiated change and led the nation.[54] In other words, "when controversy develop[ed], highly resourceful actors like [the] President . . . bec[a]me involved in policy arenas and thus removed decision-making from the community."[55] This is precisely what happened during World War II and in the years that followed. The Executive and Judicial branches advocated civil rights reforms while Congress did not pass a single civil rights bill until 1957. Thus, we may conclude that divisions among elites stemmed from domestic and international factors. These divisions provided opportunities and new pressure points for civil rights advocates to push for change.

New Allies

While President Roosevelt had offered, at best, lukewarm symbolic support to the civil rights struggle, he did signify the first real prospects for change in racial issues.[56] Even though the president recommended no civil rights legislation, he acknowledged that the status of African Americans was detrimental to convincing the world that the United States was at war for democratic rights[57] and that the allies were fighting for a "world in which all persons regardless of race, color, or creed may live in peace, honor, and dignity."[58]

First Lady Eleanor Roosevelt was a closer new ally to African Americans.[59] Mrs. Roosevelt "emerged as a conspicuous national voice calling for the end to racial discrimination and segregation. Although she was unable to persuade her husband to alter his political priorities, she did give weight and legitimacy to the growing sentiment among moderate to liberal whites in the [N]orthern states that racial segregation was wrong and must ultimately be ended."[60] She openly declared that the nation should not expect non-whites to feel that the United States is worth defending if the African American continues to be segregated and discriminated against.[61]

But it was Truman who would prove to be the African American's most dedicated ally. The president "within three years . . . establish[ed] himself as the strongest proponent of civil rights to occupy the White House up to this time."[62] He led the first and most aggressive campaign to end institutionalized racism.

Other administration officials were early supporters of civil rights reforms. Among them were members of the more liberal "new deal" Supreme Court, high-ranking officials in the Justice and State Departments, including members of the diplomatic corps, and Roosevelt's secretary of interior, Harold Ickes. We discuss these supporters in order.

While few pro–civil rights decisions in Supreme Court cases preceded President Roosevelt's 1937 threat to "pack" the Court with liberals, the trend of favorable Court decisions did accelerate following FDR's action. The Court itself became a new ally of the African American struggle for equal rights of citizenship and due process of the law.[63] One only needs to compare the Court's 1896 decision in *Plessy v. Ferguson,* establishing the constitutionality of the "separate-but-equal" doctrine, with that of *Gaines v. Canada* (1938), *Sipuel v. University of Oklahoma* (1948), *McLaurin v. Oklahoma* and *Sweatt v. Painter* (both 1950), and finally *Brown v. Board of Education* (1954), where the Court held that ". . . in the field of public education the doctrine of 'separate but equal' has no place. Separate educational facilities are inherently unequal." Further comparisons can be made to the Court's decision in *Love v. Wilson* of 1939, which nullified *Guinn v. United States* of 1915; or *Smith v. Allwright* of 1944, which outlawed white primaries, thus reversing *Grovey v. Townsend* of 1935. The Court ruled against segregated transportation as early as 1941 in *Mitchell v. United States, Morgan v. Virginia* in 1946, and *Henderson v. United States* in 1948. *Shelley v. Kraemer* in 1948 was the landmark case that initiated the end of institutionalized housing discrimination. Most of these cases were initiated and litigated by the NAACP, with the support of many organizations. In all the cases after 1946, however, either the Justice or the State Department, or both, submitted amicus briefs that identified racial segregation and discrimination as obstacles to U.S. foreign policy interests. Amicus brief participation brought federal resources and prestige to the aid of African Americans.

U.S. attorneys and solicitors general were valuable new allies of the African American struggle for equal rights. America's 1941 entry in World War II marked the beginning of an intensified effort by the Justice Department at prosecution and persuasion in civil rights. As John T. Elliff put it, "Wartime conditions offered unusual opportunities for the re-named Civil Rights Section [of the Justice Department] to expand its program. Since the United States was fighting against a German regime that tyrannized racial and religious minorities, protection of the rights of minorities at home became part of the war effort."[64]

In 1941, Attorney General Francis Biddle openly stated that civil rights violations were detrimental to "national morale and subversive to the democratic ideals which this nation seeks to defend . . ."[65] and that "a lynching has significance far beyond the community, or even the state, in which it occurs. It becomes a matter of national importance and thus properly a concern of the federal government."[66] As a result of the sympathetic attitude of the Justice Department, civil rights complaints rose from seven thousand in 1941 to over thirteen thousand in 1942, "although there was no significant increase in actual violations."[67] And the lack of congressional endorsement of antilynching legislation did not stop the Justice Department from investigating lynching and, on occasion, ordering the involvement of the FBI.

Attorney General Tom Clark, appointed in July 1945, was a strong advocate of federal prosecution of lynching cases and approved the filing of amicus briefs – both for the U.S. Supreme Court and in several state and lower federal court cases – in support of civil rights. In addition, he authorized an investigation of subversive organizations, with particular attention to anti–civil rights groups like the Ku Klux Klan.[68]

Solicitor General Philip Perlman also believed in the "new concept of governmental leadership in protecting civil rights." He urged the Supreme Court to abandon the "separate but equal" theory, arguing that it is wrong "as a matter of law, history, and policy," and that it is a deviation from the principle of equality under the law that is explicitly incorporated in the Constitution and its amendments.[69] One of Perlman's staff members, Philip Elman, was a valuable friend of African Americans. His tactics and legal strategies helped persuade Supreme Court justices to take far more reaching actions against the entrenched social practice of segregation. Because he knew the personalities and opinions of the justices he was serving more than anyone else did, he knew how to frame convincing advice.[70]

Herbert Brownell, President Dwight D. Eisenhower's attorney general, showed an eagerness to obtain adequate executive powers for combating segregation. He began his term by championing the desegregation of public facilities in Washington, D.C., stating that segregation in the nation's capital had been "a major subject of anti-American propaganda in the Kremlin."[71] Brownell also rejected demands that the federal civil rights program be trimmed to fit the states' rights doctrine.[72]

Secretary of Interior Harold Ickes, an early supporter of civil rights, was instrumental in the first housing desegregation case of *Shelley v. Kraemer* discussed in detail in Chapter Four. He publicly argued the links between anticolonialism movements sweeping Asia and Africa and equal rights advocacy at home. He expressed his concerns to Secretary of State John Foster Dulles that unless the United States addressed issues of colonialism at the 1945 United Nations' organizational meeting, "we will prejudice our moral and political leadership in the world and particularly with the millions of dependent peoples . . . who form an increasingly important segment of world opinion and power."[73] Under his administration, the Department of Interior was to be among the first executive departments to desegregate employee facilities and offices.[74]

Motivated by foreign policy concerns and being the major recipient of foreign criticism of American race policies, high-ranking officials of the State Department and members of the diplomatic corps became advocates for civil rights reforms. They played a crucial role in pressing aggressively for presidential leadership on the issue in the very early days of the Cold War. Since these officials were more susceptible and had the long-term vision to see the changing winds in global politics, they recognized the detrimental ramifications of American racism on their mission to sell the American way of life, especially to the former colonies in Asia, Africa, and the Middle East. State Department officials complained that "no American problem receives more wide-spread attention . . . than our treatment of racial minorities, particularly the Negro."[75] Fully aware that the East-West competition required the allegiance of these newly independent nations, officials ranging from secretaries of state to ambassadors and counsels all around the world pushed the administration to address race policy issues.[76] As Nigerian politicians put it, "Farsighted statesmen in the United States know very well that the emergence of Africa from colonial status to political independence will indirectly enhance the power and prestige of the American Negro."[77]

Illustrative of the new pro–civil rights orientation within the diplomatic core and ranks of the State Department was the remark by former Ambassador to India Chester Bowles. Said Bowles, "Our world responsibilities and the requirements of our national security no longer permit us the luxury of temporizing and evasion over civil rights here in America."[78] As we shall see, Bowles' statement exemplified the position of many foreign relations specialists.

In addition to new allies at home, African Americans found support and sympathy from the four corners of the world. Not only was international public opinion on their side but foreign government and non-government entities intervened on their behalf. African, Asian, Middle Eastern, and European nations criticized the U.S. government for the way it treated its black population. Activists in non-white nations supported the arguments African American advocates made that their conditions resembled the conditions of those living under Western colonialism. Western Europe, reeling from the loss of its imperial powers, was eager to align itself with the international call for democracy, equality, and antidiscrimination. Former colonists found an opportunity to get back at the United States for condemning colonialism. They denounced America's empty rhetoric of leadership of the free world while practicing the worst form of oppression against its own people.[79] The succeeding chapters demonstrate that the international community, as an ally of the African American, put significant pressure on the U.S. government.[80] In short, American racism "acquired a peculiarly new capacity to arouse righteous anger in these years of the rise of American world power."[81]

Repression of and Violence against African Americans

The fourth and last dimension of political opportunity theory is the capacity of the government for repressing social movements. Government coercion of insurgency limits the opportunities for collective action. One could argue that because of the decline of King Cotton and the consequent decline of the need for African American laborers in the South, violence against African Americans in the South was less necessary.[82] But evidence shows that this does not fully explain the decline of violence and repression, including the incidence of lynching, following World War II.[83]

One of the main reasons for the decline of violence toward African Americans, particularly in Southern states, was federal investigation and prosecution of criminal activities against African Americans.[84] Southern repression aggravated and activated criticism from Northern blacks, white liberals, and the media.[85] Southern repression also brought pressure and criticism from the international community. Especially the State Department heard the international outrage over violence and injustice toward African Americans loud and clear. A few examples would suffice.

Overwhelming international reaction followed cases such as the Charles Trudell and James Lewis 1946 case,[86] the Rosa Lee Ingram case in 1949,[87] the Willie McGee case in 1951,[88] and the Jimmy Wilson case of 1958,[89] in which Secretary of State Dulles had to contact Alabama Governor James Folsom directly to stop the miscarriage of justice. The Emmett Till murder of 1955 and the freeing of his two murderers ignited the African American community as well as the world.[90] According to Medgar Evers' wife, Myrlie, Till's murder was like no other. "It shook the foundations of both white and black . . . it somehow struck a spark of indignation that ignited protests around the world . . . it was the murder of this 14-year-old out of state visitor that touched off the world wide clamor and cast the glare of a world spot light on Mississippi racism."[91] A. Philip Randolph reminded Eisenhower that, "If the United States can send the armed forces 6000 miles across the sea to Korea to fight Korean [C]ommunists in the interests of world democracy, it would appear that the [f]ederal government should use its vast power to stop the lynching of a colored citizen by Mississippi racists in the interest of American democracy."[92]

In addition to Southern violence and injustice toward African Americans, there was also repression of insurgency by the federal government, especially in the context of the Cold War. Because of the Communist phobia that swept the country in the late 1940s and 1950s, the federal government was able to silence many of its critics.[93] With the rise of McCarthyism, the NAACP, for example, retreated from its earlier efforts to expose American racism to the world. It distanced itself from prominent figures such as W. E. B. DuBois and Paul Robeson who publicly denounced the gap between America's ideology and practice. DuBois and Robeson, who sought a wider audience among the international community, were tainted with leftist, Communist, and anti-American labels. As I show in the following chapter, both men, as well as many others, paid a high personal and professional price for their unconventional strategies. For instance, to prohibit them from contacting other groups abroad, the State Department imposed international travel restrictions on both between 1950 and 1958. But the federal government was heavily criticized for such measures. As Edwin P. Hoyt puts it, DuBois and Robeson's detention within the borders of the United States "was the single most costly act America might have taken in terms of propaganda to the colored peoples of the world."[94] Thus, I argue that the decline in state repression of African Americans was the result of domestic and international expression of outrage over such treatment. The combination of both is what pressured the federal government to intervene in the coercive methods of the states, specifically the Southern states.

In sum, the four dimensions of political opportunity stressed by social movement scholars are influenced by international as well as domestic factors. The civil rights struggle, development, and outcome benefited from new opportunities that arose as a result of international events. Therefore, works on collective action should consider and when applicable include "the critical role of international trends and events in shaping domestic institutions and alignments" and "the impact of global political and economic processes in structuring the domestic possibilities for successful collective action."[95] The battleground where challengers of a regime meet those who represent the regime may, on occasion, be the international arena and not just the domestic one.[96]

Mobilization, Framing, and U.S. Civil Rights

Besides political opportunities, two other ingredients are necessary for successful collective action: the mobilization of available and potential resources, and the process by which insurgents frame their grievances and define their situation.[97] Mobilization structures are defined as "those collective vehicles, informal as well as formal, through which people mobilize and engage in collective action."[98] As is the case with the political opportunity approach, the literature on the mobilization and organization efforts of civil rights activists on the local, state, and national level is rich. Well documented is the development of collective action through grassroots, local-community efforts, as well as through national political campaigns. Obviously, these domestic mobilization structures and organization were the backbone of the civil rights struggle without which America's longstanding racial divide could possibly still be standing. However, it is the part of the civil rights movement story that has been studied quite extensively.

In contrast, the mobilization efforts of civil rights activists within the broader international political environment to put pressure on the U.S. government have been the subject of little empirical and theoretical research in the disciplines of sociology and political science. Collective action scholars, as Dieter Rucht puts it, "have largely ignored the broader political environments in which social movement organizations are embedded."[99] The systemic analysis of how civil rights advocates used the rivalry between the U.S. and the Soviet Union to internationalize the black struggle is underdeveloped, as is the international community's response to this mobilization strategy.

In this section, I examine how America's new global leadership and its competition with the Soviet Union provided new mobilization venues and framing strategies for civil rights advocates. During the war and its aftermath, "Negroes thought in terms of bringing world opinion to bear on their plight . . . they were not unaware of the effect the emerging colored nations might have upon their own status"[100] and that "[i]t was not a matter of chance that the Negro movement caught fire in America at just that moment when the nations of Africa were [negotiating and] gaining their freedom."[101] Civil rights advocates framed their struggle in the international context of events: the emergence of Africa and Asia as independent nations and, more importantly as far as the U.S. government was concerned, as a necessary measure to combat Communism.[102]

Since the United States wished to be the preeminent player on the world stage, and not return to its isolationist position of the prewar years, the "colored people" of Africa and Asia, given their

new status in the postwar world order, took on a new importance.[103] The suspicions and resentment Africans and Asians expressed over the gap between the cherished American principles
and the nation's discriminatory racial practices were central themes
that African American leaders used. The process they engaged in
could be called frame extension; that is, they extended their grievances and need for redress to that of other groups who have or were
still suffering from discrimination.[104] Civil rights advocates successfully linked their fight at home with that of newly independent
colonies abroad. They stressed to government officials that attempts to secure the alliance of African and Asian nations require
reform measures at home. "It [was] this, precisely, that [had] given
American race problems their sharp international edge."[105]

The argument that "two-thirds of the world's population is non-
Caucasian . . . our position on the international round table is
greatly weakened when the charge of hypocrisy can be leveled
against us . . . We have no choice . . . but to narrow the gap between
America's professions and her practices,"[106] became a standard
line in the writings, speeches, and congressional testimonies of civil
rights advocates. Both state officials and the international community aided in the strategy of linking black civil rights to America's
influence in Africa and Asia. Truman's 1946 Civil Rights Commission concluded that, "Throughout the Pacific, Latin America, Africa and the Near, Middle, and Far East, the treatment which our
[N]egroes receive is taken as a reflection of our attitudes toward all
dark-skinned peoples."[107] President Truman himself announced
that "the top dog in a world which is over half colored ought to
clean his own house."[108] The State Department concurred that
Africans and Asians could not help but view the United States as
hypocritical because of its practices of racial discrimination at
home[109] and that lack of civil rights more than anything else
"causes more damage to U.S. prestige and the role of champion of
democracy and human rights"[110] it attempted to project, especially
among people of color.

It was not unusual for the international community to remind
the United States government that its racial practices were un-
becoming to a nation "which continually affirms to the world its

devotion to principles of liberty, equality, and equal opportunity for all citizens."[111] Indeed, a representative group of Africans confessed to State Department officials that they "will never cooperate with any country whose racial policy is short of equality and our emphasis is doubled in the event of treating [N]egroes on a standard short of human dignity."[112]

The East-West rivalry afforded civil rights advocates a second, yet interrelated, framing strategy to enhance their call for reform. They tactfully used the "Cold War politics" frame to enlarge their adherent base and gain the support of previously uncommitted bystanders. Arguing that race reforms were the best weapon against Communism transformed the issue into a salient one. Because of national security needs and foreign policy aspirations, civil rights leaders reasoned, Congress must pass civil rights legislation because "[it] will help us as a nation in the world struggle against [C]ommunism."[113] Black leaders argued that every lynching, every riot, every racial disturbance served to feed the Communist machine operating at home and abroad.[114] In the wake of Emmett Till's murder, the *Atlanta Constitution* announced that the "brutal murder assists the [C]ommunist propagandists. It delivers us into the hands of our enemies."[115] Senator Jacob Javits, a long-time civil rights advocate, told his colleagues that "[t]he greatest contest between freedom and [C]ommunism is over the approximately 1.2 billion largely [N]egro and oriental population . . . the greatest arguments used by the [C]ommunist conspirators against our leadership . . . [are that these colored people] will also be subjected to segregation . . . federal civil rights legislation is the best answer."[116]

Framing their case within the Cold War context granted African Americans new advocacy among the three branches of government. We will never know whether government officials would have pushed racial reforms on their own inclination or whether their anti-Communist beliefs were persuasive enough to drive them into action. The significant point here is that African Americans employed the strategy of frame bridging,[117] which proved effective in mobilizing support at home and among international entities who feared the spread of Communism. The Dutch, for example, worried that racial discrimination was detrimental to the U.S. "in her contest with the Soviet Union over the uncommitted areas of Asia, Africa and the Middle East . . . that weakening of America's moral leadership in the world indirectly hurts its allies. . . ."[118]

Mobilizing the international community went hand in hand with pressures at home. African Americans realized that World War II provided the opportunity "to persuade, embarrass, compel and shame our government and our nation . . . into a more enlightened attitude toward a tenth of its people."[119] By using multiple strategies and protest techniques, activists waged the African American struggle on the domestic and international fronts simultaneously.[120]

On the national level, organizations such as the NAACP and the Urban League focused on the courts and on lobbying members of Congress and officials in the administration. They skillfully used the fear of Communism to advance their fight for civil rights. They argued that reforms were also necessary to gain the alliance of Africans and Asians while undercutting the lure of Communism. On the other hand, changes in the global political configurations encouraged internationally acclaimed figures like Paul Robeson and W. E. B. DuBois to mobilize the international community. Both believed that "one important part of the solution to the Negro problem will be the pressure of other countries on America from the outside."[121]

In summary, the domestic bias in social movement theory prevents us from accurately explaining the different courses of action by Presidents Roosevelt and Truman over race issues or explaining the timing of the Executive branch's push for civil rights reform. Current analyses of political, social, and economic factors surrounding U.S. civil rights politics, though rich on the domestic story, do not adequately consider the international environment in which America's race policies were defined and reformed. My argument in this book recognizes the role international factors may play in three interrelated areas: shaping new political opportunities that confront social movements, affording new avenues or resources available for mobilization for collective action, and suggesting new international framings of domestic issues that attract new allies and widen the scope of support for social movements.

Research Questions

To understand the importance of the international context of the civil rights struggle and the role that international pressures played, three questions must be asked.[122] First, why, how, and to what degree of success were civil rights leaders able to mobilize and use international attention to pressure for U.S. racial reforms? These issues will be taken up in Chapter Two.

The second question concerns the pressures that foreign governments and non-government entities, foreign leaders, and foreign public opinion exerted on the U.S. government. How did foreign governments and international non-government agencies use political opportunities to criticize the United States and push for reform? How did Asian and African statesmen, in particular, take advantage of the East-West competition by using U.S. racism as leverage?[123] What types of foreign pressures? How intense were they? What specific areas of racial policy were targeted for criticism? How did incidents of discrimination at the domestic front experienced by both African Americans and foreign visitors fuel international outrage over U.S. racial discrimination and segregation?

The third and final question concerns the U.S. government's response to these outside pressures. Which government actions in civil rights matters could be linked to specific international pressures? What measures did the federal government take in anticipation of further foreign criticism? How was the Executive branch, including the Justice and State Departments, U.S. embassies and consulates, and the U.S. Information Agency (USIA) offices around the world, able to influence the course of civil rights reform by emphasizing the international ramifications of U.S. racism? What specific political opportunities for U.S. global leadership were obstructed by America's racial policies?

The second and third research questions will be addressed in Chapters Three and Four. Chapter Three begins with Truman's 1946 Committee on Civil Rights. It ends with the 1957 Civil Rights Commission that was created by the 1957 Civil Rights Act, the first civil rights legislation since 1875. I demonstrate, for example, the direct relationship between the formation of the United Nations in

1945 and the U.N. Subcommittee on the Treatment of Minorities in 1946 and the Truman Administration's initiative in 1946. I explore how U.S. government leaders increasingly used the international context of American racism to frame their arguments against segregation, to justify actions they took in matters relating to civil rights, and to build the congressional coalition that helped pass the 1957 Civil Rights Act.

In Chapter Four, I focus on outside pressures for U.S. racial desegregation and the government's response to the international community. Racial segregation is central to Chapter Four because State Department files at the National Archives identify it as the area that received the most international criticism. Historical documents suggest that the government primarily targeted segregation for policy reform in its early efforts, while eschewing a more aggressive policy toward other forms of discrimination such as lynching and obstacles to voting.[124] White House as well as State and Justice Department emphases on racial desegregation were characteristic of a domestic policy created for international consumption. The humiliating treatment that foreigners of color experienced while in the United States, especially in the nation's capital, was a primary impetus of the government's efforts to desegregate.[125] In landmark Supreme Court cases dealing with segregation, both the Truman and Eisenhower administrations intervened as "friends of the Court," thus further indicating the linkage between their own foreign policy goals and the pervasive racial discrimination and segregation at home. Although the *Brown v. Board of Education* decision is the most famous ruling for desegregation, it was preceded by several others in which the Justice and State Departments argued that racial segregation violated the United Nations Charter,[126] a binding agreement to which the United States was a party. These two agencies also emphasized to the Supreme Court the negative consequences segregation had on America's competition with the Soviet Union. An example is the government's brief in *Brown*, which argued that, "It is in the context of the present world struggle between freedom and tyranny that the problem of racial discrimination in the U.S. must be viewed."[127]

Southern resistance to school desegregation in the wake of the

Brown decision resulted in ugly confrontations. Two of these confrontations became international events that provoked outrage worldwide: the Autherine Lucy case of 1956, and the Little Rock crisis of 1957. I treat both crises in detail in Chapter Four.

Conclusion

I have argued that, in addition to domestic factors that energized the struggle for racial reforms, global developments during and after World War II pressured Truman's administration to become an advocate for racial equality. Truman sought three interrelated goals: to shape the postwar political configuration to the United States' advantage – that is, to maintain and expand Western-style capitalist democracy; to gain the alliance of newly independent colonies in Africa and Asia; and to contain Communism as much as possible. Ending legal segregation and institutionalized racism toward African Americans was not only a necessary step toward these three goals but the price of influence and the morally prestigious image in global leadership that the United States sought to have after the war.[128]

Second, I have argued that the political opportunities for race reforms created by postwar politics were unmatched in history. African Americans were able to appeal and widen the scope of America's race problems beyond the government's direct control. And as E. E. Schattschneider once wrote, the audience determines the outcome of the conflict.[129] In this case study, the audience in the international community became a factor in the government's calculations concerning race policy.

Finally, I have argued that the efforts of the American state to achieve its international goals by ameliorating its race problem at home are a crucial explanatory variable – a variable that has been either ignored or underdeveloped in much of the previous literature. The extent of foreign pressures on civil rights has remained largely unexplored despite the availability of rich and voluminous government documentation that attests to these pressures.[130] Extending social movement approaches to encompass international factors would address the question of timing of government activity in the 1940s. It would also explain the new forums and venues that opened up, and the new pressure points that advocates of change could utilize.

The connection between American racism and the peculiarly American phobia of "Communists," two of the most enduring and troublesome themes in American history, has until now received inadequate scholarly attention. United States government decisions taken in the interests of "national security" and "defeating Communism" have had an enormous impact on almost every aspect of American life, and U.S. race relations are no exception. These linkages form a hitherto underdeveloped chapter of the American civil rights movement history. It is to this exploration that I now turn.

Mobilizing and Utilizing International Pressure: A Strategy of U.S. Civil Rights Leaders

It is to induce the nations of the world to persuade this nation to be just to its own people, that we have prepared and now present to you this document.[1]

We in America criticize many nations. We know that international conscience has great influence. . . . One important part of the solution of the Negro problem here will be the pressure of other countries on America from the outside.[2]

How did African American leaders frame their struggle for equal treatment at home within the context of Cold War politics? I will argue, first, that while the civil rights struggle has always had an international dimension going back to the slavery era, the strategy of reaching out to the international community was only successful after World War II because of the changing dynamics of international relations. Black America's outreach to the international community, especially to people who had been oppressed by colonialism and discrimination, contributed to the international pressures exerted on the U.S. government to end legal segregation and discrimination. Second, civil rights advocates were able to mobilize the interest of the American political elite, previously either indifferent or hostile to change, by emphasizing the negative consequences of U.S. race policy on the fight against Communism. Third, the United Nations provided a forum for international debate. It provided African Americans with a weapon that they used to publicize their grievances and call for help. Lastly, the efforts of some internationally acclaimed African Americans such as Paul Robeson and W. E. B. DuBois contributed to the embarrassment of the U.S. government and drew mounting pressure on racist U.S. institutions.

The awkward position in which the United States found itself during and after World War II regarding the growing international concern for human and civil rights provided civil rights activists with a golden opportunity. Civil rights leaders launched a renewed publicity attack on institutionalized racial discrimination. They used the new global leadership role of the United States and the East-West competition over the emerging independent Asian and African nations to persuade U.S. government officials that racism in the United States had detrimental international ramifications on U.S. policy goals and national security. The success of civil rights in the 1950s and 1960s is partly the result of the dynamics and strategies activists used in framing America's race problem in an international context both at home and abroad.

Beginning with World War II, institutionalized American racism came under renewed pressure and attack by the international community. This was the result of three intertwined factors. First, World War II was in many respects a war against racism. Second, the emerging role of the United States as a world leader opened up its racial policies to the scrutiny of rest of the world. And, finally, the cost of American racism was escalating.

America's participation in World War II and the allies' victory in 1945 changed the social context within the United States. Victory symbolized equality and democracy and the defeat of racism. Victory constrained the subsequent social rhetoric of the victors. Allied powers "which incorporated racist dogma in their own legal codes and social structures, were impelled to proclaim their opposition to racism" in every form.[3] The horrific discrimination against the Jewish people in Nazi Germany put an end to previously accepted theories of scientific racism. Moreover, it paved the way for the African and Asian struggle against colonialism and for equality. African Americans were no exception. In particular, the United States' leadership in World War II, and its ideological emphasis on freedom and equality, forced the United States' own discriminatory practices under a microscope. This scrutiny only increased as the Cold War developed and as the subsequent East-West competition for allies intensified.[4]

The International Context of America's Race Problem:
A Historical Perspective

While this work focuses on civil rights leaders who solicited international support in the 1940s and 1950s, that period was not the first time the black struggle took on an international angle. Reaching out to the world had been a consistent strategy of U.S. civil rights activists since the beginning of the nation. This is clear in both the attempts of early civil rights activists to discuss their experience of racism on an international stage and in the attempts of W. E. B. DuBois to internationalize domestic debates about racism. American leaders were well aware of the international implications of the African American population's ill-treatment.[5] Yet, as the following examples demonstrate, conscious efforts to internationalize the discussion of racism did not meet with much success prior to the 1940s.

Briefly put, slavery had a major international dimension since the early nineteenth century. Since the 1800s, the institution of slavery was in rapid retreat throughout the Western Hemisphere. Except for Brazil, Cuba, and the United States, slavery was being outlawed. In the United Kingdom, for example, slavery was abolished in 1807. On the other hand, slavery in the United States was aggressive and expansionist until the Civil War. The perpetuation of slavery in the United States was a sensitive issue in its relations with other countries. British and French public opinion would not tolerate intervention in support of American slave owners. Lincoln was correct in his assessment of the European sentiment, as Karl Marx later confirmed. Marx wrote Lincoln in 1864 to congratulate him and praise America, "in which [there is] nothing to condemn or to lament it but the slavery and degradation of men guilty only of a coloured skin or an African parentage . . . and the Northern states to deliver the Union from this curse and shame."[6] U.S. race relations, then, have attracted international attention since at least the mid-1800s.

Moreover, blacks have had a consistent history of appealing to international sentiment for better treatment at home. There are many early accounts of runaway slaves and freemen who went abroad not only to secure their liberation, but also to gain freedom and equality for those left behind. They did so by publicizing and criticizing American racism. Frederick Douglass was among the most famous and eloquent.[7] His eighteen-month sojourn in England, which began in August 1845, served to publicize the African American abolitionist movement.[8]

However, it is important to note here that the world tides that were running against slavery in the United States did not extend to the civil and human rights of the African American. These tides against slavery were the same forces that subordinated non-whites around the world. Western imperialism was spreading into Africa and Asia beginning in the 1880s. In addition, theories of scientific racism and social Darwinism were widespread in the cultures of Western elites, including American elites, until around World War II. In other words, in spite of the abolition of slavery in Europe, the European governments continued the exploitation of colored races through colonialism.

Nevertheless, there were occasions when foreign governments criticized the United States for the treatment of African American soldiers overseas. During World War I,[9] and to the dismay of American military officials, black American troops were integrated with white French troops. This occurred in spite of U.S. instructions to the French on how black Americans must be treated and why. In a 1918 document issued by the United States Army authorities in Paris titled "Secret Information Concerning Black American Troops," the French were told that they had to respect the unanimous opinion of white Americans on the "Negro question" and that the friendly and tolerant attitude of the French toward the Negro would deeply offend the Americans and would symbolize an attack on their national beliefs and arouse their fear that blacks would believe in equality. American officials asked the French "not to spoil the Negroes." French officers were not to eat, shake hands, or seek to meet with blacks outside of the requirements of military service. The document added that, "White Americans become greatly incensed at any public expression of intimacy between white women and black men." To the embarrassment of the American government, the document was read in the French National Assembly in 1919, drawing widespread criticism. The French passed a resolution condemning the secret document and requiring everyone present on French territory to respect French law, which did not allow for discrimination based on religion, race, or class.[10]

A similar scenario took place in World War II when the segregation of blacks in the U.S. military drew criticism from Europe.[11] As Paul Robeson said in a 1944 interview with the *New York Times*, "There are 100,000 Negroes now in the army in the English theater of operations. Americans wanted their segregation, as at home. The English, however, insisted upon their being mixed . . . it shows the power of foreign opinion."[12]

The British were not the only ones concerned with the treatment of black soldiers at the hands of their white compatriots during World War II. Many French, Czechs, Poles, Norwegians, Dutch, Belgians, and others were surprised by the institutionalized color prejudice that they witnessed against African American troops.[13] However, the overarching point is that foreign criticism of segregation of blacks in the military forces had limited effects. It was rare and did not match the continuous efforts of civil rights leaders to mobilize international support for their plight and to convince the U.S. government of the negative implications American racism had on America's prestige and foreign relations. Moreover, it is clear that continuous efforts by civil rights leaders to effect change in U.S. race policies did not meet with success until the 1940s. In the next section, I turn to W. E. B. DuBois, who was a leading figure in the effort to internationalize the race problem of America and who exemplified this effort in both strategy and results.

W. E. B. DuBois: An Early Crusader

One of the most internationally acclaimed civil rights activists,[14] W. E. B. DuBois tirelessly exposed the contradictions of America's words and deeds until his death in 1963. It was DuBois who recognized the connection between the struggles of all colored people and that of the African American. In 1900, he established and headed the Pan-African Congress in London. He subsequently organized a series of conferences all over Europe: Paris (1919), Paris and Brussels (1921), London, Paris, and Lisbon (1923), New York (1927), and Manchester, England (1945).[15] DuBois was the NAACP's observer at the Paris Peace Conference of 1919. In addition to being one of the founders of the 1905 Niagara Movement, which resulted in the organization of the NAACP, DuBois is considered the father of Pan-Africanism.[16] The Pan-African movement encompassed African descendants from all over the world in the fight against colonialism and racism. The movement's importance cannot be overstated. It "expanded Afro-American consciousness by rescaling questions of racial justice to global dimensions. It thus created the space necessary to holistically assess U.S. behavior in the international arena."[17]

It is clear that DuBois was aware of the power of international pressure and foreign public opinion. He began to publicize the "Negro problem" both at home and in his travels and correspondence overseas. As if he could see into the future and predict the circumstances of the 1940s and 1950s, DuBois warned in 1907 that if the United States expected to take her place beside England and France,

she has got to find out how to live in peace and prosperity with her own black citizens. If she does not, she will always have in her contact with the rest of the world not only the absolute dislike and distrust of the darker two-thirds, but a tremendous moral handicap such as she met when she asked Russia to stop her atrocities and it was answered with perfect truth that they did not compare with the barbarities committed right here in the land of the free.[18]

Although President Woodrow Wilson headed the most racist administration since the Civil War,[19] DuBois saw an opportunity in the president's support for the League of Nations. He perceived that integration into international politics might force the U.S. government to grant African Americans their citizenship rights. On the eve of the president's trip to Europe to discuss the League, DuBois requested a meeting with him to discuss

a question of gravity and importance . . . that could embarrass the activity
of the American delegates . . . the world is wondering today how America is
going to avoid at least an indictment of inconsistency and perhaps a suspicion of insincerity . . . the international Peace Congress that is to decide
whether or not peoples shall have the right to dispose of themselves will
find in its midst delegates from nations which champion the principle of
the "consent of the governed" and "Government by representation." That
nation is our own and includes in itself more than twelve million souls
whose consent to be governed is never asked. They have no members in the
legislatures where they are in the majority and not a single representative
in the national congress. . . . Has this race not earned as much consideration as most of the smaller nations whose liberties and rights are to be
safeguarded by international convention? . . . The ideals of the Peace Congress have to do with the rights of distinctive peoples; a more distinctive
people than the American Negro would be difficult to imagine.[20]

President Wilson declined to meet DuBois.[21] Furthermore, Wilson's true colors showed when he joined Britain, Greece, and
Belgium in blocking Japan's effort to secure a racial equality clause
at the League of Nations. African Americans celebrated Japan's
victory over Russia in 1905. The significance of that victory was not
lost on racial equality advocates or its opponents. Here was a colored people whose industrial and military status was no less than
that of major powers and yet neither the United States nor Britain
would regard the Japanese as equals.[22] A British diplomat, present
at the Paris Peace Conference, observed that President Wilson
faced a grave situation. That racial equality of the yellow man with
the white man, in turn "might even imply the terrific theory of the
equality of the white man with the black."[23] Nevertheless, Japan's
contribution to the race issue should not be underestimated. By
raising the racial equality question at the Paris Peace Conference,
"the Japanese and their supporters served notice to the world that
they intended to make the discussion of race part of the politics and
diplomacy of the twentieth century."[24] Yet, it is clear here that
despite DuBois' efforts to internationalize the race policy of the
United States during the League of Nations' primary discussion,
official political interest was anemic at best.

Furthermore, as the Senate turned down membership in the

League of Nations and the United States returned to isolationism after World War I, African Americans became convinced that the internationalization of the race problem in the United States was the only solution. They believed that the "public opinion of the world must come to rule civilization by actual organization or by strong moral influence . . . because America is the one great nation which today recognizes least its international obligations."[25]

After World War I, the black intelligensia worked hard in their newspapers, pamphlets, public lectures, and congressional appearances at establishing their Americanism, only to be rebuffed by the nation's dominant ideologues.[26] In this atmosphere, separatist movements flourished.[27] The most prominent of the "Back to Africa" movements was led by Marcus Garvey and the Universal Negro Improvement Association (UNIA). Garvey called for the development of a powerful nation, located in Africa, to be the home of black Americans.[28] His newspaper, *Negro World,* influenced many of the future African nationalist leaders including Jomo Kenyatta of Kenya, Nnamdi Azikiwe of Nigeria, Kenneth Kaunda of Zambia, and Kwame Nkrumah of Ghana.[29] The UNIA had an international network of chapters. At its peak years (1918–23), estimates of its membership ranged from hundreds of thousands to a few million. Cedric Robinson writes that the scale of the Garvey movement makes it "by far the largest nationalist organization to emerge among [b]lacks in America."[30]

The point here is that black efforts to appeal to Schattsneider's "wider audience"[31] were consistent even before the advent of the Cold War. But as long as the United States was living in isolation, and as long as Asian and African peoples were under European colonial rule, black Americans were unable to effectively mobilize international public opinion for their support. Significantly, it was only the combination of Hitlerism and the Cold War that changed the dynamics of the African American civil rights struggle. One of the main purposes of this chapter is to demonstrate that the efforts of African Americans were successful only when the international environment and the United States' role in it changed. Therefore, explanations of civil rights reforms that focus exclusively on domestic factors are insufficient.

The War Years: The Beginning of U.S. Vulnerability

When the war broke out in 1939, many African Americans perceived it as a "white man's war." Columnist George Schuyler signified that perception when he wrote, "So far as the colored peoples of the earth are concerned, it is a toss-up between the 'democracies and the dictatorships' . . . what is there to choose between the rule of the British in Africa and the rule of the Germans in Austria?"[32] Journalist P. L. Prattis saw the war between whites as a blessing because they "would mow one another down" instead of "quietly murder[ing] hundreds of thousands of Africans, East Indians and Chinese. . . ."[33] The NAACP's *Crisis* expressed sympathy for the

brutality, blood, and death among the peoples of Europe, just as we were sorry for China and Ethiopia. But the hysterical cries of the preachers of democracy for Europe leave us cold. We want democracy in Alabama and Arkansas, in Mississippi and Michigan, in the District of Columbia – in the *Senate of the United States.*[34]

However, this perception of World War II as a white man's war changed as the war progressed. During the war, civil rights advocates seized the opportunity of America's integration into world politics and launched a renewed attack against their country's race policies. But because of the war, African American leaders called for a closing of the ranks until such time as an Allied victory was assured. The first successful use of an international strategy to shape the discourse on racism at home coincided rather neatly with the Allied war efforts. Here, instead of a direct international appeal, civil rights advocates launched a public attack on the U.S. government at home.

During the war, editorials in the black press hammered on the hypocrisy of American officials. Writings and full-page advertisements revealed the scandals of discrimination. The black press continued to denounce employment discrimination in factories and businesses with government defense contracts. In one instance, the NAACP ran an advertisement in several newspapers. It was entitled "Is This the Way of Life That Congress Has Voted 24 Billion Dollars to Defend? Could Hitler Be Worse?"[35]

Leading scholars, like Alain Locke of Howard University, wrote in 1942 that World War II was a challenge to the moral fitness of all democratic nations, and that calling attention to the immorality of the governments of Germany and Japan merely precipitated greater awareness of the inner contradictions of the American society. Locke concluded that the "Negro problem" could no longer be considered a domestic affair.[36]

Horace Cayton, a prominent African American scholar and journalist, was much more explicit in his writings. Cayton said the only difference between Hitler's plans for non-Aryans (were he to win the war) and the treatment of African Americans in the South was that Hitler was talking in future terms, while in the South the treatment was current practice.[37] He celebrated the fact that black Americans were identifying with non-white peoples throughout the world. Disillusioned and cynical about the possibilities of obtaining democratic rights by the process of education and goodwill, Cayton wrote that

the American Negro now hopes that forces outside of the country will act as a lever to give him greater measure of freedom within the country. . . . Articulate Negroes, and most certainly the Negro press, understand that the United Nations must make concessions . . . and are quick to point out that similar concessions will have to be made to the Negro in this country if the United Nations are to maintain any sort of ideological leadership and if democracy is to be used as the organizing force for the world.[38]

What Cayton expressed was a commonly held belief that, at worst, the white elites wanted to keep the Negro subordinate, and, at best, they had no moral conviction about how the Negro should be treated. Most civil rights leaders recognized that "there [was] a small corps of articulate and powerful whites who realize[d] the importance of greater participation for the Negro . . . to any stable world order which must follow."[39]

The *Crisis,* the NAACP's publication and the most influential black political journal of the time, featured many editorials and articles that drew similarities between the treatment of African Americans in the United States and that of the Jews in Nazi Germany. As early as 1938, African Americans were expressing their sympathy for the Jews because they experienced the same treatment in the South.[40] The *Crisis* printed the views of international figures on American democracy. For example, the journal told of Gandhi's response to an interviewer who was traveling to America to study in 1942. Gandhi suggested that his interlocutor "should unlearn a lot of American things when he returns to India; that he should try to experience some of the insults and humiliations and pin pricks that the American Negro lives with everyday . . . then write me how it feels to be a Negro in America."[41]

In general, the energy that African American leaders put in invoking the international implications of American racism on the Allied war effort reflected their conviction that racism and Nazism stemmed from common roots. They criticized U.S. hypocrisy in fighting Nazis in Germany and Fascists in Italy while practicing racial segregation and discrimination at home. They questioned U.S. officials on how the United States hoped to emerge as the leader of democracy and freedom while practicing discrimination within its own borders. Civil rights leaders framed their struggle with that of the Jews in Germany. They argued that U.S. racism would cost America its prestige, power, and security interests. Domestic appeals included public denouncements and warnings of trouble for the American government in dealing with the emerging African and Asian nations and in its leadership of the free world following the war. The first active threat civil rights leaders posed to the U.S. image abroad was the March on Washington Movement in 1941. The changes in the acceptable social rhetoric of nation states effected by the war enabled African Americans to reframe their own discourse about race relations in the United States. Moreover, the change in acceptable social discourse changed the bargaining position that African American citizens enjoyed at home vis-à-vis the United States government. In the following section, I discuss one pivotal moment when the bargaining position of African Americans was enhanced significantly.

A. *Philip Randolph and the March on Washington*

The war effort itself provided civil rights activists with further capacity (and justification) to protest. The fact that more than one hundred thousand black soldiers were fighting racism abroad constituted the perfect timing for civil rights leaders to call for change. A. Philip Randolph exploited this opportunity and threatened President Roosevelt with a march on Washington, one hundred thousand black people strong. The march on Washington was to protest the discrimination that was pervasive in war industries and the armed forces. Although the New Deal had aroused expectations of change among African Americans, Roosevelt had been reluctant to get involved in civil rights politics. The president increasingly relied on the support of Southern Democrats for his foreign policy agenda. Moreover, in the absence of the threat of Communism, and in the relative isolation of the United States before 1941, there were not enough political incentives for Roosevelt to disturb the traditional arrangement of home rule in the South. Roosevelt was not willing to risk the disintegration of the majority Democratic coalition he had brought together in 1932 and 1936.

Yet, Randolph's appeal "touched a sensitive nerve in the African American community at large . . ."[42] and precipitated a critical decision point for the president. "Across the country African Americans formed committees to coordinate support and began organizing transportation to Washington."[43] The threat of the march was convincing enough that after Eleanor Roosevelt and New York City Mayor Fiorello LaGuardia failed to persuade Randolph to cancel "this drastic move," President Roosevelt agreed to a conference with Randolph and other civil rights leaders. At the meeting, Walter White of the NAACP warned Roosevelt of the anachronism of an army presumably trained to fight against Hitler's theories of race while it practiced a similar philosophy in its own ranks.[44]

Some concessions had to be made because Roosevelt perceived a march on Washington to be detrimental both at home and to America's image abroad. The president acknowledged that the conditions of the African American were an obstacle in convincing the world that the country was fighting for democracy.[45] Five days before the scheduled march, Roosevelt issued Executive Order 8802, which established a Federal Employment Practices Committee (FEPC) to investigate employment discrimination in government defense industries. Before 1941, and despite many efforts to see Roosevelt, civil rights leaders were never able to meet with him.

According to Randolph, "the tables had turned . . . and the President of the United States was seeking a conference with Negro leaders . . . this was the largest meeting on the question of the American Negro."[46] This outcome illustrates that America's concerns about its image abroad began to change the dynamics of race policy at home.

Moreover, the conference with Roosevelt was the beginning of ongoing communications to persuade the president to introduce more reforms. Randolph, for one, continued to put direct pressure on President Roosevelt. He wrote Roosevelt that postponement of congressional hearings on the grievances of African Americans was undoing the Federal Employment Practices Committee's virtuous purpose. In addition, he argued that the United States was in a critical position in world affairs and any further delay in civil rights legislation would hurt its international leadership position. Randolph wrote that

the eyes of the colored peoples of this world, in North Africa, in India, in China, [are] turned toward America and toward you, Mr. President, asking for a sign; asking for renewal of their hope that this would be indeed the last great war . . . some issues cannot be compromised. Certain crucial conquests of your administration cannot be abandoned, lest the poison of totalitarianism corrupt us inwardly and the battle be lost at home – whilst our sons are fighting abroad on Arctic seas and in tropical jungles. . . . Mr. President, fate has made you the leader not merely of a party, nor even of a nation, but of an historic cause: the defense of the system of moral, ethical, and social values which we call civilization, and with which we oppose the vicious, lying dogma of totalitarian racism and all its cruel and cynical disciples and sycophants. It was in defense of this cause that you wrote Executive Order No. 8802 which today your enemies and ours, at home and abroad, deride as just another scrap of political paper . . . we submit with all due respect that you owe it both to your friends at home and to our allies abroad both to re-affirm without qualification the great principle stated in Executive Order 8802.[47]

Once this strategic opening occurred, civil rights advocates sought to maintain their improved bargaining position. In speeches at rallies, in editorials in the black press, and in letters to government officials, civil rights advocates focused on America's international standing. And now, with the prospect of embarrassing the U.S. government into change, came a new hope for racial reforms. Civil rights activists described America's democracy as miserable. They believed that, because of its treatment of blacks, America would have to "answer to the 1,700,000,000 colored peoples everywhere before the bar of world opinion," and that Gandhi and Nehru had rejected President Roosevelt's offer to mediate between India and Great Britain "because the Indian people [had] no faith in American democracy as it applie[d] to colored people."[48]

Increasingly, blacks focused on the international fates of African Americans at home and non-white peoples abroad to exploit strategic opportunities at home. A landmark event took place in 1943. The largest rally in black history to date took place in Madison Square Garden, where twenty thousand people gathered while several thousand more paraded outside. The significance of this civil rights rally was that it cemented the relationship between racism and colonialism, that the two stemmed from common roots. W. E. B. DuBois' famous statement that, "The problem of the twentieth century [will be] the problem of the color line,"[49] was filling the air.

Thus, the 1940s marked a significant change in the bargaining position of African Americans with the Roosevelt Administration. Civil rights groups understood that the new international climate had provided an avenue by which the U.S. government could be placed in a vulnerable position and attempted to exploit these new opportunities. In the early 1940s, the NAACP began paving the way to play an official role in the postwar arrangements and the wave of independence that would sweep Asia and Africa. The organization understood that racism was assuming "worldwide proportions and the American Negro is prepared to take his place in the world-wide struggle."[50] By aligning itself with the "non-white" struggle against colonialism and racism, the NAACP hoped to persuade American officials to grant African Americans their rights at home.

The NAACP offered its services as mediator to the British. Walter White advised the British ambassador to the United States that the only way to dissolve the tensions between Britain and its colonies was for the Allies, including the United States, to assure the colored people throughout the world that after the war they would be granted their civil rights. White suggested to Ambassador Lord Halifax that President Roosevelt appoint a committee that would include "a distinguished American Negro who is unmistakably Negro" to go to India immediately. Yet before the committee could leave for India, White argued, the United States had to prove its sincerity on the matter of color: "President Roosevelt should take a sweeping and unequivocal stand against discrimination on the basis of color in the United States." Such a step would help dissolve the skepticism that Nehru, Gandhi, and other Indian leaders felt toward the West.[51]

White's encounter with the British ambassador is indicative of his skill in situating the race issue in the United States within global affairs. He attempted to get the British to pressure President Roosevelt to adopt some measure of racial reform at home. As on many other occasions, civil rights activists argued that the liberation of black Americans was a condition for better relations among the Allies, the United States, and African and Asian colonies. How could the United States and its allies convince other colored people of their sincerity when African Americans were oppressed in their own land?

Lord Halifax himself expressed concern about the race issue in the United States. He told his home office that the United States must expect to "face a number of major internal problems after the war. . . . Prominent among them . . . will be the [N]egro problem, aggravated by the return of coloured men who will have served on terms of military equality with white members of the armed forces. . . ."[52] Clearly, African Americans were beginning to use their improved bargaining position vis-à-vis the United States government to cultivate international allies against U.S. racism.

After the War

Recall the question of how African American leaders successfully framed their struggle for equal treatment at home in the 1940s. By now, it should be clear that the conjunctural context of World War II and civil rights advocates' experience with internationalizing

U.S. racial policies provided an advantageous position for civil rights leaders. Thus, the opportunity structure clearly changed. But what is important in explaining the success of efforts to internationalize racial issues in the 1940s and the lack of success earlier is the strategic action of civil rights leaders in the post–World War II context and Cold War politics.

Once the war ended, civil rights leaders astutely exploited the launching of the United Nations and, later, the 1955 Bandung Conference as vehicles to both leverage their bargaining position vis-à-vis the United States government and to cultivate new allies in the U.S. government. Furthermore, they used international scrutiny not only to increase their bargaining position, but also to achieve real social and political reform at home.

Finally, no discussion of civil rights struggles in the 1940s and beyond would be complete without some attention to Paul Robeson. Robeson is important for this study because his efforts to discuss American racism on the international stage highlights both the actual moral ambivalence of the U.S. government to racial policies and the way in which international scrutiny forced the U.S. government to undertake actions that were not in accordance with its traditional moral ambivalence toward racism. Thus, in the remainder of this chapter, I discuss the strategic actions of civil rights leaders following World War II and end with an example of how international pressures forced the globally ambitious U.S. government to undertake some change in civil rights policies.

At the international level, African Americans for the duration of the war years were achieving modest success in placing the U.S. government's racial policies under international scrutiny. However, at the domestic level, the significant gains African Americans achieved during the war years were principally the result of increased production in war industries.[53] Once the war ended, "the wartime gains of Negro . . . workers [were] being lost through unchecked revival of discriminatory practices."[54] Between July 1945 and April 1947, for example, unemployment rose twice as much for non-white workers as for whites. As of 1950, the unemployment rate for African Americans was double that of whites.[55] Disproportionately high black unemployment persisted both in the private and public sectors. Studies conducted after the war found that income levels of whites were thirty to seventy-eight percent above those of African Americans.[56]

As for the Fair Employment Practices Committee (FEPC), Roosevelt's only substantive contribution to the African American struggle, it was more of a moral and symbolic victory for blacks than anything else.[57] According to Will Alexander, a long-time advisor to President Roosevelt and a member of the War Manpower Commission, the FEPC was effective as a propaganda agency on the race issue, but "as far as getting anybody employed in the war industries, I don't think it did. It was set up in such a way that it couldn't."[58] Another committee member commented that "all the armies of the world, both of the United Nations and the Axis, cannot force upon the South the abandonment of racial segregation."[59] A sure sign of the FEPC's impotency was that Congress did not authorize funding for it and it effectively died in 1946.

Therefore, the position of blacks worsened as the war ended. Government defense contracts were phased out and employment opportunities and pay scales for non-whites were suddenly worse than before the war. Segregation and discrimination continued in housing, education, and voting in the South. In addition, history repeated itself. Although the violence targeting African Americans and especially African American servicemen after the war was much less than what followed World War I, it was nevertheless still considerable.[60]

African Americans were in danger of losing the small gains made during the war. The efforts of many black leaders to close ranks during the war failed to secure just treatment after the war. In response to what they perceived to be a return to earlier traditional practices of institutionalized discrimination, civil rights advocates appealed to the world. The United Nations provided an important platform for this effort.

The United Nations was chartered and located in the United States. Not only did the international organization provide an international platform for protest for African Americans, it also brought foreign delegates to the United States to see for themselves the bleak conditions of discrimination under which African Americans were living.

The Emergence of the United Nations

The establishment of the United Nations and its location in New York allowed the outside world to examine and to experience institutionalized racism. Delegates from all nations and races sometimes witnessed the daily workings of segregation. To many of these people, Jim Crow laws came as a complete shock. Those who had heard of Jim Crow before coming to America often dismissed the stories as propaganda. They could no longer discount what they actually saw.[61]

The decision to locate the United Nations headquarters in the United States was a controversial one.[62] African American leaders and European critics protested the choice to locate the international organization in a country that enforced segregation laws.[63] DuBois actively opposed American cities, such as Philadelphia as well as the nation's capital, as possible sites because of their segregation practices. He warned that non-white U.N. delegates would be humiliated there.[64] The University of Maryland's offer to house the Food and Agriculture Organization (FOA) was rejected because it was segregated. FOA ended up in Rome.[65]

Stories of discrimination against U.N. diplomats and ambassadors mistaken for African Americans frequently appeared in American newspapers. Formal protests by foreign governments to the Department of State followed.[66] During congressional hearings, civil rights activists testified to the humiliation of visiting friends and dignitaries from Africa and Asia because of discriminatory barriers in Washington, D.C. They argued that these incidents attracted wide publicity abroad and were detrimental to U.S. foreign policy interests and to the reputation of the American people.[67]

Diplomats were not the only victims of ill treatment because of the color of their skin. African and other non-white university students reported that they faced discrimination both in the South and in the North.[68] In one survey, African students ranked "segregation and discrimination in the United States as the number one problem they encountered."[69] The fact that foreign students, who originally came to the United States to be trained and indoctrinated in the American way, were experiencing discrimination and segregation was alarming to State Department officials. Many of these students were being groomed for leadership in their countries.[70] Their experiences in America would certainly influence their opinions and future actions toward the United States. Thus, the creation of the United Nations and its placement in New York placed a penetrating and vivid spotlight on racial discrimination in the United States.

Petitions to the United Nations

The establishment of the United Nations, the U.N. Commission on Human Rights, and the Subcommission on the Prevention of Discrimination and Protection of Minorities provided the international platform African American leaders had long been waiting for.[71] Convinced that their government had to be pressured into change and that the emerging tensions between the United States and the Soviet Union might help bring their plight to the forefront, African American leaders made the ultimate call for help. They appealed to the United Nations.[72]

Three petitions presented to the United Nations by three different black organizations will be analyzed here. The National Negro Congress (NNC) presented the first petition in June 1946. The NAACP submitted the second petition in October 1947. Both were coauthored by W. E. B. DuBois. The Civil Rights Congress presented the third petition in December 1951. In the following section, I address the first two petitions. The third petition will be discussed, further on, as part of Paul Robeson's challenge to the U.S. government in general, and the Department of State in particular.[73]

The necessity to appeal to some sort of international forum was clear to the black leadership as early as 1941, when the NAACP Board of Directors authorized a committee to present the grievances of African Americans at the projected upcoming peace conference.[74] At a conference in 1945, A. Philip Randolph stated that African Americans "must work out strategy and techniques which would bring pressure on the American state." One of the techniques suggested was to embarrass the American delegation in San Francisco, where the first U.N. organizational meeting was to take place. Through public meetings, picket lines, and interracial delegations, civil rights leaders planned to expose the hypocrisy of the United States.[75]

As a result of the efforts of the NAACP, the State Department hired DuBois and Walter White to serve as official consultants to the American delegation at the 1945 United Nations organizational meeting in San Francisco.[76] At the meeting, both civil rights leaders were bombarded with questions from foreign correspondents and foreign delegates about the U.S. treatment of minority groups. DuBois and White were surprised at how much detail foreigners knew about U.S. race relations given the censorship on the press that was imposed during the war.[77]

In February 1946, the United Nations Commission on Human Rights was established. Four months later DuBois, hoping to seize the opportunity to place the cause of racial justice before the world, spearheaded an effort by the National Negro Congress to present a petition to the commission on behalf of African Americans, black Africans, and descendants of Africa in the West Indies seeking "relief from oppression."[78] The National Negro Congress sought five million signatures for its petition and was endorsed by an array of organizations, including the National Lawyers Guild, the CIO Public Workers of America, the National Maritime Union, and black veterans associations.

The National Negro Congress, emphasizing the African American, deplored poverty, poor schooling and housing, and high black mortality rates. It expressed

profound regret that we, a section of the Negro people, having failed to find relief from oppression through constitutional appeal, find ourselves forced to bring this vital issue, which we have sought for almost a century since emancipation to solve within the boundary of our country, to the attention of this historic body.[79]

The petition was sent to U.N. Secretary General Trygve Lie and to President Truman. The signatories of the National Negro Congress petition were a who's who of African Americans and African leaders. It included future African heads of states Jomo Kenyatta of Kenya, Kwame Nkrumah of Ghana, and Nnamdi Azikiwe of Nigeria.[80] While the type of European colonialism experienced in Africa did not exist in the same form in the United States, African American leaders nevertheless linked the oppression of blacks in the United States and the colonial oppression of the African people. They defined racial injustice in the United States as a test for the effectiveness of the newly formed United Nations as well as a potential threat to world peace.[81] Columnist Earl Conrad of the *Chicago Defender* commented on the NNC petition by writing, "We cannot allow this appeal to be sidetracked. . . . We cannot allow any United Nations committee to say that this is a 'local' matter. We cannot permit the United Nations body to take any reactionary 'states rights' position with regard to so great and numerous a people, and a problem linked so inextricably with the nation's and the world's problems."[82]

In less than a year, the NAACP followed in the footsteps of the National Negro Congress. Convinced that its battle for freedom must be fought on a worldwide front, the NAACP dedicated much of its financial and human resources in 1947 to filing a petition with the United Nations. Thanks to DuBois' international acclaim, the association received the endorsement of hundreds of black organizations, African and Caribbean groups, and overseas labor unions. The NAACP sought to achieve the widest possible publicity and circulation both in the United States and internationally. The NAACP's petition to the United Nations' Commission on Human Rights on behalf of the fourteen million blacks marked the second appeal in less than two years. As before, W. E. B. DuBois spearheaded the NAACP's effort.

In October 1947, the NAACP presented to the United Nations a 155-page petition entitled "An Appeal to the World: A Statement on the Denial of Human Rights to Minorities in the Case of Citizens of Negro Descent in the United States of America and an Appeal to the United States for Redress." In his address to the NAACP Annual

Conference, DuBois told his audience that the purpose behind the appeal was that "the whole world [would] eventually be able to read the grievances of American Negroes in printed and widely disseminated form."[83] In his statement to the U.N. Commission on Human Rights and the General Assembly, DuBois said that he spoke for the fourteen million citizens of the United States, "or twice as many people as there are in the Kingdom of Greece. . . . This protest, not designed for confidential concealment in your archives, is a frank and earnest appeal to all the world for elemental justice against the treatment which the United States visited upon us for three centuries. . . . We firmly believe that the situation pictured here is as much your concern as ours."[84]

It came as no surprise to the U.S. mission to the United Nations that the Soviet delegation championed the NAACP petition in the Subcommission on the Prevention of Discrimination and Protection of Minorities (SPDPM), which is under the U.N. Commission on Human Rights. The SPDPM was established on the initiative of the Soviet Union, and "there [was] every indication that that country and others [would] raise questions concerning [the treatment of black Americans]."[85] The Soviet delegate proposed a resolution that since the U.N. General Assembly had unanimously called for the end of "racial persecution and discrimination," and that governments should call on each other "to take the most prompt and energetic steps towards that end," the SPDPM should consider the petition presented twice to the United Nations by the "15 million Negroes residing in the United States of America, who are subjected to discrimination on racial grounds."[86]

The Soviet delegation accused the U.S. delegation of "stifling any measures to halt discrimination since discrimination continued to flourish in that country."[87] Members of the SPDPM refused to consider the NAACP's appeal because the Committee on Human Rights had not yet established procedures to handle petitions. To the dismay of the American delegation, none of the SPDPM members argued the dismissal on the grounds that the affairs of African Americans were a domestic issue that the United Nations had no business discussing. Jonathan Daniels, a consultant to the United

Nations, told SPDPM members that the Truman Administration was aware of the problem of African Americans in the United States and that President Truman himself had "authorized a comprehensive investigation of the Negro problem."[88]

It is important to note that the "comprehensive investigation" to which Daniels was referring was conducted by Truman's Committee on Civil Rights. It had become clear to American officials that other countries were using the United Nations and its divisions to pressure and embarrass the United States over its race problem. American racism was frequently injected in various debates and, therefore, U.S. representatives to the United Nations were always on the alert to avoid outbursts of criticism at U.N. meetings. For example, Mrs. Roosevelt, the U.S. representative on the Commission of Human Rights, refused to comply with the Truman Administration's advice to veto a clause in the proposed U.N. Human Rights Charter. The clause read, "Everyone shall have a right to take an effective part in his government directly or through his representatives; and to participate in elections, which shall be periodic, free and by secret ballot." Mrs. Roosevelt said she felt that omitting any reference to the right of political representation would provide opportunities for renewed attacks on U.S. race relations by other delegations and would be deleterious for U.S. foreign affairs.[89]

There is little doubt that Truman's Committee on Civil Rights was initiated partly in response to and in anticipation of further embarrassment caused by the international attention to racial issues in the United States.[90] The Commission was established in December 1946, a few months after the National Negro Congress petition was presented to the United Nations but before the NAACP's petition. President Truman realized that he must make some progress on the race issue and that he needed a damage-control devise. That a presidential committee was in place investigating the race problem and recommending reforms provided members of the U.S. delegation to the United Nations with a response to hostile delegates such as the Soviets. U.S. representatives were able to demonstrate that their government had embarked on a serious effort, under the orders of the president, to reform racial injustice and to bring the treatment of minorities at home to par with the ideals of equality and democracy the United States was preaching to others.

Although the Committee on Civil Rights report *To Secure These Rights* substantiated practically everything the NAACP petition claimed, the NAACP efforts to include their appeal in the agenda of the General Assembly failed. DuBois tried to convince the U.S. delegation of the merits of addressing the petition. He argued that

it would be a matter of fine and forward looking statesmanship if the U.S. would itself voluntarily bring this matter forward to be discussed before the nations, and attest that while our democracy is not perfect, we are perfectly willing to acknowledge our faults and to bring the matter before the world.[91]

State Department officials did not agree with DuBois' logic. They knew that the African American appeal could be explosive, especially to the Asian and African countries that were joining the United Nations as voting members. India, which gained its independence from Britain in 1947, had been especially critical of U.S. race relations. NAACP members were not surprised that the State Department was able to stifle the petition. They were well aware that all petitions had to be channeled through the Commission on Human Rights before going to the Social and Economic Council, and that the commission was not fulfilling its function. In an attempt to bypass the Human Rights Commission, DuBois asked the Indian delegation to present the NAACP petition to the General Assembly.[92]

In a letter to Vijaya Lakshmi Pandit, a member of the Indian delegation to the United Nations (and Prime Minister Nehru's sister),[93] DuBois said India should be aware that the real ambition of the United States leadership was to "succeed Great Britain as ruler of the colored world in Asia and Africa and to control their raw material and cheap labor." He warned Pandit that India might not be clearly informed about the caste system that was deeply ingrained in the American society. DuBois urged Pandit and her people to know and maintain contact with Negroes in this nation . . . The signers of this petition wish to lay before the assembly of the United Nations a case of injustice done by the United States of America against its own citizens. We are bringing this case to your attention and beg you to give it your earnest thought and discussion, not because we are enemies of this nation, but rather because we are citizens of this land and loyal to the freedom and democracy which it professes far and wide to observe. And in the face of this, the United States of America declares its practice of democracy before the world and sits in the United Nations.[94]

Efforts to bring the NAACP petition before the General Assembly of the United Nations in 1948 were blocked by opposition from the U.S. delegation. In particular, Eleanor Roosevelt, the most distinguished member of the delegation and a long-time advocate of civil rights, did not agree with the NAACP's strategy to involve the international community in their struggle.[95] DuBois pleaded with Mrs. Roosevelt that he

realized that no international action on our plight was probable nor, indeed, expected; but that I thought that the world ought to know just exactly what the situation was in the United States, so that they would not be depending upon vague references concerning our race problem, but would have factual statements before them.[96]

DuBois informed Mrs. Roosevelt that if the United States was unwilling to put the matter before the General Assembly, one or two nations were interested in doing so.[97] But Mrs. Roosevelt was not persuaded. She feared that the petition would be embarrassing and used by the Soviet Union to attack the United States. The situation might be so unpleasant, Mrs. Roosevelt said, that she would be compelled to resign.[98] In the end, the petition was successfully derailed.

African American leaders, especially after World War II, refuted the argument that their struggle was a domestic affair. Charles Hamilton Houston wrote that "a national policy of the U.S. which permits disfranchisement of colored people in the South is just as much an international issue as the question of free elections in Poland or the denial of domestic rights in Franco Spain."[99]

DuBois warned that the United Nations' international obligations would meet with failure if it refrained from helping minorities because it had "no business to interfere with internal policies of nations" as in the case of a "suppressed group like American Negroes [whose situation] resemble[s] in many respects the situation in the colonies."[100] He argued that the United Nations was in a position to act as a policeman over nations, including the most powerful nations:

[I]t means that the action of even the greatest nations which compose this organization must be amenable to the public will and to universal public opinion; that they cannot continue to feel themselves free to carry on a national program or any treatment even of their own citizens and affairs, which is, in the judgment of the world, a threat to world peace and world progress.[101]

According to DuBois, African Americans had a right to present their case before the United Nations and to say that

here in America where we profess democracy we have built a legal fascist caste system . . . and that for this reason the United Nations should take cognizance of this situation and at least make it known to the world in order that the world should publicly oppose this treatment of Negroes in the United States; and such international action should especially point out that this situation is a contradiction and direct nullification of the laws which this country itself has made for its own guidance.[102]

That the NAACP petition did not survive its uphill travels through the formal channels of the United Nations does not diminish its significance. Civil rights leaders used it to tell the world about the African American struggle and the grievances committed under their eyes and with the assistance of the U.S. federal, state, and local governments. In addition, U.N. foreign representatives used the petition to embarrass the U.S. delegation.

As a follow-up to its petition, the NAACP's Department of Special Research issued a report that discussed the legal dimension surrounding the mistreatment of the African American race to show that racism was not just a social condition, but also a legal process that was enforced by American institutions, especially "decisions of state courts and the United States Supreme Court restricting the rights of Negroes under state and federal constitutions. . . . Although this discrimination may be considered a domestic problem, its international implications remove its national limitations."[103] The report predicted the NAACP petition would have far-reaching implications for oppressed people everywhere; that

[t]he millions of oppressed people of the world, mostly and principally colored, are likely to be stimulated by this precedent-making petition to speak out for fair, humane, and just treatment. The objective of the protest, to obtain equality for American Negroes, should set a positive example of which even the United States government must sooner or later recognize the justice and act accordingly. The Boston speech of Attorney General Tom Clark on October 27, pointing out that he hopes Negroes will never again have to seek redress from other nations, is an immediate example of the good that should come from this official appeal.[104]

The NAACP petition had accomplished its mission. According to Walter White, it created an international sensation.[105] Requests for a copy of and permission to publish the petition came from everywhere – from national organizations and the news media to international organizations and the foreign press. Countries interested included Belgium, Czechoslovakia, Denmark, Egypt, Ethiopia, Haiti, India, Liberia, Mexico, Norway, Pakistan, Poland, Russia, South Africa, Greece, Italy, France, and China.[106]

The NAACP was "flooded with requests . . . particularly from nations which were critical of the United States . . . who were pleased to have documentary proof that the United States did not practice what it preached about freedom and democracy,"[107] and from U.N. delegates who "found a clear parallel with Nazi S.S. methods."[108] The petition was an explicit signal that since the U.S. government had failed to protect its citizens, African Americans would now reach out to the rest of the world for help.[109]

Although media coverage of the NAACP petition was somewhat limited, the few newspapers that commented on the document judged it as a successful strategy to mobilize international support and to place the race issue in the context of international human rights. For example, *PM* (a New York newspaper) said that U.S. Attorney General Tom Clark was "humiliated that there should be the slightest foundation for such a petition."[110] The *San Francisco Chronicle* reported that the NAACP knew in advance that the petition would be rejected but "their move [was] a good tactical stroke to publicize their cause."[111]

The Whole World Is Watching

Shortly after the defeat of Nazism and Fascism in World War II, anti-Communism became the center of American foreign policy as well as a domestic obsession. This atmosphere informed the strategies of civil rights activists.[112] Government officials often accused those who called for racial reforms of being Communists. African Americans and their organizations were accused of Communist infiltration at a disproportionate rate. Fearing that the anti-Communist rhetoric would tarnish their reputation and compromise their working relations with administration officials, conservative black organizations such as the NAACP revoked the idea of appealing directly to members of the United Nations and to the foreign press.[113]

Thus, NAACP leaders and other civil rights pioneers limited their appeal to the home front. Nevertheless, they focused their criticism of the U.S. government by packaging their fight in an international context. In articles and editorials, public speeches and conferences, and congressional hearings, and during meetings with administration officials, civil rights leaders emphasized the damage American racism caused U.S. foreign policy interests. They also warned that racial reform was the best weapon against the appeal of Communism domestically. The black press played an instrumental role in linking racial injustice to the anti-American sentiment abroad.[114]

African American leaders warned the government that it was an illusion to think that goodwill ambassadors, who the State Department was sending to Africa and Asia, could dismiss the image foreigners had of the pervasive discrimination in the United States. For example, Walter White of the NAACP told Senate members that when a well-known black minister was sent abroad to tell people, particularly those of color, that race prejudice in the United States was not as bad as the Soviets made it out to be, people asked him if it was not true that "you are freer here in Karachi than you would be in the capital city of your own country?"[115]

The *Crisis* criticized the distorted picture of U.S. race relations that some African Americans working for the State Department revealed to foreign audiences. The publication described Edith Sampson, a Chicago lawyer employed by the State Department to tour Europe in 1952, as living in "Cloud-Cuckoo Land." The *Crisis* reported that Sampson's false premise that blacks are "marching in a straight and unbroken line to the kingdom of full equality" was discredited by those in the audience who had the opportunity to visit the United States and see for themselves the horror of racism. In response to Sampson's claim that blacks were advancing, the *Crisis* concluded that "[a]s long as we cannot be served in a restaurant or be offered accommodation at a hotel because of skin color, we must not expect the world to be enthusiastic about the American Way."[116]

To convey the international support for the African American struggle, the *Crisis* reprinted stories that appeared in foreign newspapers about the struggle for equality. The German publication *Die Genenwart* had concluded that "the United States can no longer sell democracy abroad while it continues at home to refuse equality to Negroes. . . . Solution of the Negro problem may well determine America's rank in the history of humanity."[117] Other black publications also reported the impressions of foreign visitors. Stories like "Race Relations as Seen by Recent French Visitors"[118] and "Italian Press Views America's Racism"[119] were frequent.

The black press mocked U.S. government efforts to democratize other countries. An editorial entitled "Democratic Elections in Poland" expressed the bitter humor African Americans saw in President Truman's statement to the new Polish ambassador to the United States regarding elections in Poland. President Truman told the Polish ambassador that "it is a cause of deep concern to me and the American people that the Polish provisional government has failed to fulfill that pledge [of holding elections]." The *Crisis* editor asked President Truman and the American people why they did not object to the absence, by force, of black voters in the South.[120] Another editorial – "Democracy Defined at Moscow" – related how

African Americans were thrilled to read Secretary of State George Marshall's definition of democracy that he presented before the Moscow Council of Foreign Ministers. Marshall said that a country is not a democracy if certain rights like the right to work, life, liberty, and the pursuit of happiness are not granted to every citizen. The editorial illustrated, step by step, how the United States was not democratic and that "Messrs. Molotov and Vishinsky of the Soviet Union had difficulty hiding their smiles. . . . This is getting embarrassing."[121]

When the international community honored African American leaders for their work, the black press gave the U.S. government no credit for their distinction. For example, when in 1951 Ralph Bunche became the first African American to receive the Nobel prize, the press concluded that artificial race barriers prevented talented African Americans from rising to positions of statesmanship and that it "was the United Nations and not the United States that saw worth in this man."[122]

When the first World Assembly of Youth Conference met in New York, the black press used the opportunity to publicize the bad impression foreign delegates had of the United States. The workshop on discrimination "was by far the most popular, especially among foreign delegates. . . . This is only a slight indication of the tremendous importance which most young people of the world attach to discrimination and segregation, especially as it is practiced in the United States and South Africa." As in the case of locating the United Nations, African delegates to the World Assembly of Youth Conference expressed reservations about holding the assembly in the United States, because of segregation laws.[123]

Although the atmosphere of anti-Communism constrained civil rights advocates from appealing to United Nations members directly, these advocates developed successful strategies for communicating international support for and attention on civil rights issues at home. United Nations members who were sympathetic to the plight of African Americans were instrumental to these efforts, and through their own means created a synergistic and reinforcing condemnation of U.S. racial policies.

Segregation and Military Service

Significantly, African American leaders used the improved bargaining position that these efforts conferred upon them to achieve real social and political gains at home. At the same time that a comprehensive antidiscrimination campaign was being launched, civil rights leaders focused on the desegregation of the U.S. military service.

To the African American leadership, the contradiction between preaching and practicing of democracy was nowhere more evident than segregation in the military. Black Americans were rigidly segregated with minimal role assignments. They could not enlist in the Navy except in the all-Negro messman's branch. They were excluded from the Marines and the Air Force. In the Army, black Americans enlisted only in the four all-Negro units.[124]

To close ranks during the war, African American leaders such as Walter White struck deals with President Roosevelt that they would not pursue desegregation in the armed forces and not resist the segregated draft for the duration of the war. After the war, these deals were called off and civil rights leaders renewed the attack on the segregated military.[125]

A. Philip Randolph spearheaded the Committee against Jim Crow in Military Service, which held its own hearings. The findings and testimonies of the committee were well publicized and its proceedings were published and widely disseminated. Among those who testified in front of the committee were American war correspondents who recalled their embarrassment when asked about American hypocrisies. William Walton of *Time* and *Life* asked, "what can we say in reply to this? We can always be accused of hypocrisy because we are hypocritical . . . the few Germans with whom we could talk would merely say to us 'we have our Jewish problem, you have your Negro problem. We handled it our way. You handle it almost the same way.' "[126]

Randolph simultaneously led a campaign threatening open resistance if the country adopted a segregated peacetime military draft. He called for the inclusion of racial integration amendments in pending legislation for universal military training. He threatened a Gandhian-type civil disobedience. Randolph also recruited internationally acclaimed African Americans like boxer Joe Louis to promote his campaign and attract international attention.[127]

During public hearings before the Senate Armed Services Committee in 1948, Randolph expressed the general sentiment of black Americans: "I reported to President Truman that Negroes are in no mood to shoulder a gun for democracy abroad as long as they are denied democracy here at home." While Randolph was not directly threatening the administration, his prediction of what to come was unmistakably clear. He told the committee that Congress, and the American people, had to know that passage of a Jim Crow draft would result in a mass civil disobedience movement similar to the "magnificent struggles of the people of India against British imperialism" and that "the conscience of the world would be shaken as by nothing else when thousands and thousands of us second-class Americans choose imprisonment in preference to permanent military slavery."[128]

Randolph promised the committee members that he would personally "advise Negroes to refuse to fight as slaves for a democracy that they cannot possess and enjoy" and that "the government now has time to change its policy . . . in the interests of the very democracy it is fighting for." He added that African Americans would win the fight for freedom, if not by "appealing to human decency" then by their civil disobedience and that he was prepared "to oppose a Jim Crow army till I rot in jail." Taking an anti-Communist approach to enhance his appeal, Randolph stressed the need to counterattack anti-American propaganda. He said that "the myth has been carefully cultivated that Soviet Russia has ended all discrimination and intolerance, while here at home the American [C]ommunists have skillfully posed as champions of minority groups."[129]

Civil rights activist Pauline Myers, director of the Provisional National Committee to Abolish Segregation from Universal Training Programs, told Senate members that "there is revolutionary dynamite inherent in a Jim Crow army. . . . United minorities of all colors . . . are not only America's best but America's only real defense." Myers argued that a Jim Crow military service was detrimental to U.S. prestige and U.S. foreign policy objectives:

[S]uch a practice cannot help but adversely affect delicate international negotiations. . . . It is not overstating the case to say that the granting of equal rights and privileges to Negroes . . . is one of the crucial issues at one of the critical points of history. . . . This country now stands at a turning point in its relations to its friends among the nations of the world. Either it must finish the task of making democracy work in race relations or it must reconcile itself to seeing the entire world of color move in directions which are consistent neither with their own traditions nor with those of this country.[130]

Aware of the importance of America's image abroad, Randolph frequently met with Truman Administration officials to convey impressions foreigners, especially labor groups, had of the United States as a result of the mistreatment of African Americans. Randolph told Truman that Burmese trade union leaders, as people of color, did not know where they stood with the Americans and that Indonesian officials were of the opinion that U.S. racism led to the loss of precious opportunities to gain the confidence and respect of the people of Asia.[131] Under these pressures, and because it was an election year, President Truman issued Executive Order 9981 in July 1948. It prohibited discrimination in the armed forces and created a committee to supervise the implementation of the order.[132]

The Cold War and its attendant pressures on the United States government to find allies against the Soviet Union improved the initial bargaining position of civil rights advocates in the United States. These advocates acted strategically to maintain that position and to achieve real social and political gains. It is the context and the strategic actions that explain the success that civil rights advocates enjoyed in the 1940s.

What should be clear here is that the United States government was not pushing for racial reforms because of moral reasons.[133] Indeed, the government was ambivalent to civil rights issues on moral grounds. Nowhere is this more obvious than in the way the United States government greeted Paul Robeson's activities. In general, Randolph and many other civil rights leaders confined their protests to the mainstream channels of protest. The high personal and professional cost to African Americans who challenged the American establishment, especially during the McCarthy years, prevented them from criticizing the U.S. government to the outside world. Nevertheless, international pressure was instrumental in keeping U.S. racism an issue at the forefront of international concerns. Paul Robeson was one of the few who dared to challenge Congress and the State Department during the Red Scare and paid a heavy price for his approach.

The Paul Robeson Challenge

While Randolph's threat of a civil disobedience campaign focused attention on America's hypocrisy in protecting democracy abroad yet denying African Americans their rights at home, Paul Robeson's theme was more threatening to the American government, so much so that in 1949 he was branded "enemy No. 1" by the government.[134] Robeson campaigned extensively to attract international attention and embarrass the government. His activities ranged from making speeches at home and abroad to organizing meetings and writing.

Robeson's direct attack on the U.S. government did not start until after the war. In 1946, he met with President Truman to discuss antilynching legislation. He argued that the federal government's position toward lynching was inconsistent with its preaching to the world. Robeson expressed the irony that the United States championed the Nuremberg trials when it was "so far behind in respect to justice to Negroes in this country." Truman's response was that African Americans should not tie domestic matters to international events.[135] Robeson warned the president that if the federal government did not stop lynching, African Americans themselves would.[136]

On the same day that he met with Truman, Robeson delivered a speech over the Mutual Broadcasting System directed to the Berlin German Democratic Republic. It was entitled "I Stand Here Ashamed." He denounced the "horrible contradiction that renders hollow our highest aspirations of freedom. I speak of the wave of lynch terror, and mob assault against Negro Americans. . . . People of America, we appeal to you to help . . . as we have appealed to the President and the Attorney General of the United States."[137]

The Department of State revoked Robeson's passport in 1950, saying that his frequent criticism of the mistreatment of African Americans in the United States during his travels was detrimental to the interests of the U.S. government.[138] In spite of travel restrictions, some believed that "Robeson was being heard all over the world."[139] His deep involvement in the civil rights struggle and the persecution he faced at the hands of congressional committee members and State Department officials served to enhance his growing international prestige.

Despite passport restrictions, invitations from people and organizations around the world continued to pour in, urging Robeson to visit, to speak, and to sing. He could not go. In 1952, he held a concert at the Canadian border between the State of Washington and the Province of British Columbia for thirty thousand people assembled on the Canadian side of the border. These invitations from abroad were a

form of pressure on the government for they demonstrated an international interest in the racial situation in the United States at the time. Consequently the State Department heads during both the Truman and Eisenhower administrations proposed that Robeson could get his passport back if he would sign an affidavit agreeing that he would sing but not speak abroad. Robeson rejected the offer.[140]

By 1958, the international call to reinstate Robeson's passport had become overwhelming. Ordinary citizens, leaders, and prominent politicians in Africa, India, China, and the Soviet Union were persistent in their lobbying. One of the groups protesting the State Department's passport policies, which it called "America's Paper Curtain," comprised thirty-four of the world's leading scientists headed by Albert Einstein.[141] On the home front, Robeson fought the State Department through the courts. In *Rockwell Kent v. John Foster Dulles*,[142] the U.S. Supreme Court ruled in favor of Robeson. He received his passport in June 1958 and a month later left for

Europe, where he lived for five years. Some argue that the detention of Paul Robeson and other internationally acclaimed African Americans caused further damage to America's prestige, especially among the colored peoples of the world.[143]

Why did Robeson spell danger to the U.S. government? There are two obvious reasons. First, Robeson, like DuBois, was well known internationally. His personal acquaintances included many of the newly emerging leaders of Africa and Asia.[144] Robeson used his fame while in the spotlight to pressure the American government. He was the symbol of the African American struggle.[145] Robeson's persecution at the hands of U.S. officials in the late 1940s and 1950s pushed him further into the spotlight as the preeminent African American figure in the world, with international attention focused on what he did and what was done to him. For instance, when Robeson planned appearances in the South, the press described him as explosive as a stick of dynamite. One reporter wrote that

because of the powder keg propensities of the American Negro question in world politics, Robeson's position and personal safety have become of vital concern and the U.S. State Department would want no part of explaining to an exultant Russia, and other Iron Curtain countries, how come Robeson was suspended from a tree "Deep in the Heart of Texas." . . . He might single-handedly force the harassed White House or Congress the long demanded civil rights for Negroes.[146]

Moreover, Robeson refused to find shelter in anti-Communist rhetoric. The Red Scare did not scare him. On the contrary, at the peak of McCarthyism, Robeson talked of the positive aspects of the Eastern Bloc, most notably the just treatment of minorities. Robeson used Communism as a vehicle to deliver relief from Jim Crow. By exposing American racism to the world, Robeson was pushing for reforms.[147] He compromised his career and material benefits to dedicate his efforts to the African American struggle. In 1949, while touring Norway, Robeson announced his retirement. "From now on," he said, "I will make speeches. . . . I will give my life for the colored people's right to live."[148] That same year, he addressed the World Congress of Partisans of Peace in Paris and gave perhaps his most radical speech. He denounced the treatment of blacks in America and said that they would not go to war with the Soviet Union or carry arms on behalf of people who kick them around in their own home.[149] He added that "we colonial peoples have contributed to the building of the United States Government which is similar to that of Hitler and Goebbels."[150]

Although what Robeson said in 1949 was not much different than what A. Philip Randolph told Senate members in 1948, Robeson's speech marked the end of his career as well as of his civil liberties.[151] One reason for the different outcomes is that Robeson took his message to a foreign audience while Randolph funneled his threat through conventional means and confined his comments to a group of the American establishment.[152] Randolph also framed his arguments within the "Cold War politics" discussed in the previous chapter.

In 1951, at a time when Congress was immersed in the Un-American Activities hearings, Robeson and William Patterson, a noted civil rights lawyer, presented a petition to the United Nations in the name of the Civil Rights Congress. DuBois, who had authored the 1946 and 1947 petitions, was one of the ninety-four signers of the third petition. The original plan was for Robeson to present the petition in Paris. Without a passport, though, Robeson had to be content with a presentation at the U.N. headquarters in New York, while Patterson simultaneously presented the petition in Paris.[153] The State Department tried to stop Patterson through its embassy in Paris. Embassy officials ordered Patterson to the embassy. Patterson refused.[154] Upon his return to the United States, Patterson joined DuBois and Robeson in their "house arrest."

What encouraged the Civil Rights Congress to present its petition was the adoption by U.N. members of the Convention on the Prevention and Punishment of the Crime of Genocide in December 1948. The third petition on behalf of African Americans was entitled "We Charge Genocide." The 240-page document charged the United States government with the crime of genocide against African Americans and urged international intervention.[155] It also protested the cases of the Trenton Six and the Martinsville Seven.[156] The Civil Rights Congress hoped and we fervently believe that it was the hope and aspiration of every black American whose voice was silenced forever through premature death at the hands of racist-minded hooligans or Klan terrorists, that the truth recorded here will be made known to the world; that it will speak with a tongue of fire loosing an unquenchable moral crusade, the universal response to which will sound the death knell of all racist theories.[157]

The petition pointed out the detrimental consequences of U.S. racism on world peace:

This genocide of which your petitioners complain serves now, as it has in previous forms in the past, specific political and economic aims. Once its goal was the subjugation of American Negroes for the profits of chattel slavery. Now its aim is the splitting and emasculation of mass movements for peace and democracy, so that a reaction may perpetuate its control and continue receiving the highest profits in the entire history of man. That purpose menaces the peace of the world as well as the life and welfare of the Negro people.[158]

The petition was a magnificent embarrassment to the United States. At a time when President Truman and State Department officials were charging the Soviet Union and its allies with human rights violations, African Americans of international acclaim were accusing their country of precisely the same. The lengthy petition included the documentation of 153 killings, 344 crimes of violence against black citizens, and many other human rights abuses occurring between 1945 and 1951. According to the Civil Rights Congress, the purpose of filing the petition with an international organization was that "history has shown that the racist theory of government of the U.S.A. is not the private affair of Americans, but the concern of mankind everywhere." The Civil Rights Congress believed that "the test of the basic goals of foreign policy is inherent in the manner in which a government treats its own nationals and is not to be found in the lofty platitudes that pervade so many treaties or constitutions. The essence lies not in the form but rather, in the substance."[159]

As in the case of the two previous petitions, "We Charge Genocide" did not go far within the channels of the United Nations.

The U.S. delegation to the United Nations was able to quash the document. Nevertheless, the arguments of the petition reached an international audience and were often cited. During heated exchanges between the United States and other countries, especially with the Soviet Union over the admission of China to the United Nations, the "Russians [were] able to wash our face with the race question while the Afro-Asians suppress[ed] sardonic smiles." On one occasion, the Soviet ambassador to the United Nations told the American delegation "that if the way citizens of a country are treated is the basis for membership in the U.N., then the United States should be voted out of that body because of her treatment of Negroes."[160]

Robeson was perceived as dangerous to the conduct of U.S. foreign affairs because of his interest in American foreign policy, especially toward Africa and Asia. His analogy between the plight of his people and those of the Third World alarmed the government. In 1955, he reasoned that the State Department denied him the constitutional right to travel because he interfered in U.S. foreign affairs: "I did speak up for the African people when I was abroad. I spoke up for my people here in America, the descendants of African people. And I'll speak again."[161] Robeson posed such a threat that the U.S. government used illegal and unconstitutional tactics to silence him. In 1977, the NAACP revealed that the State Department made diplomatic threats to discourage other governments from inviting and honoring Robeson as a humanitarian and activist for human rights.[162]

Robeson's insertion into American Cold War politics demonstrates that civil rights reform was not catalyzed by changes in the moral leanings of the State Department. Rather, as his own exclusion and subsequent inclusion illustrate, civil rights reforms were made because they were expedient measures at a moment of intense competition by the United States for international allies against the Soviet Union. In the final section of this chapter, I discuss how African American leaders used the Bandung Conference to continue their successful framing of racial policies at home within an international context and to maintain their bargaining position vis-à-vis the government on civil rights issues.

The Bandung Conference: The Historical Emergence of 1.4 Billion People of Color

In April 1955, twenty-nine Asian and African nations attended a historical conference in Bandung, Indonesia, to discuss racism and colonialism. The decade preceding this event witnessed radical political change as millions of people broke away from colonialism. India, Burma, Indonesia, Egypt, and China – among other nations – all achieved independence through popular struggles. The Bandung Conference represented 1.4 billion people. Its organizers believed that they could inject the voice of reason into world affairs and end racism and colonialism by mobilizing more than half the human race.[163] Bandung also symbolized Africa and Asia's apprehension about atomic diplomacy.

Neither the United States nor the Soviet Union were invited to Bandung since both were regarded as part of the problem of Western domination and discrimination. Protests from the West for being excluded prompted one writer to respond that, "for centuries Asian and African nations had watched in helpless silence while white powers had gathered, discussed, and disposed of the destinies of Asian and African peoples – gatherings in which no Asian or African had ever had any say."[164] The contrast in the reaction to the conference between the West and the East was stark. The West reacted with silence or direct opposition. John Foster Dulles condemned Third World neutrality as "an obsolete . . . immoral and short-sighted conception."[165] The Soviets, on the other hand, congratulated, praised, and hailed the conference as a beacon of light in the struggle of African and Asian people against Western imperialism. This prompted the *Times of India* to report that,

Russia with one foot in Europe and another in Asia has been more quick to appreciate the significance and implications of Bandung than the West. While Washington and London fumble feebly, obsessed by visions of colored hordes clouding a lily-white horizon like locusts swooping on pastures new, Moscow, Moses-like, beckons the dispossessed hosts onwards to the Promised Land.[166]

Many prominent African American personalities such as writer Richard Wright, Louis Lantier of *Ebony,* Carl Rowan of the *Minneapolis Tribune,* and New York Congressman Adam Clayton Powell did attend. Robeson and DuBois could not go because of travel restrictions. Robeson sent a message to this momentous "first international conference of colored peoples in the history of mankind." His message was "itself cited by the State Department as still another reason why [he] should not be permitted to travel." In his message, Robeson expressed optimism that the Bandung Conference would have a positive impact on the U.S. treatment of African Americans.[167] He hailed the conference as a sign of "the power and the determination of the peoples of [Africa and Asia] to decide their own destiny."[168]

Coverage of the conference in the American press was limited and negative in tone. *Newsweek* magazine characterized the conference as "an Afro-Asian combination turned by [C]ommunists against the West."[169] The *Christian Science Monitor* stated that, "The West is excluded. Emphasis is on the colored nations of the world. . . . Colonialism is out. Hands off is the word. . . . This is perhaps the great historic event of our century."[170] The black media covered the conference in celebration. It was described as "without question, the most important international enclave to be held in the history of mankind," and that "one can't begin to calculate the broad implications of such a meeting." Bandung was "a call for freedom and human dignity." Adam Clayton Powell predicted a different world in the post-conference era.[171]

The Bandung Conference provided an unparalleled, newfound sense of "belonging" and a "spirit" of solidarity among the people of Africa and Asia. Its saliency was reflected in discussions of the United Nation's General Assembly. In October 1955, for example, by a vote of twenty-eight to twenty-seven, the question of Algeria's freedom from France was forced on the agenda by many of the Bandung Conference's members. James L. Hicks of the *Baltimore Afro-American* wrote that these Afro-Asian countries "had turned the United States and the colonial powers around in the first major test of strength in the U.N. since the dark races held their own conference at Bandung,"[172] and that "[t]he white people of the Western world laughed last spring when the dark nations sat down together for [the] conference . . . but the darker nations . . . are now having the last laugh."[173]

Bandung's nonalignment ideology created an alternative to viewing world politics as a bipolar, East-West competition. It also crystallized the condemnation of racism by millions of non-whites who understood the vast and irreconcilable difference between the high moral preaching of America and other Western societies and their treatment and policies toward people of color. The Bandung Conference brought this discrepancy forward in all its clarity. Congressman Powell relayed to the U.S. Senate the impact of the conference on U.S. foreign policy goals, especially in the context of the Cold War.

Powell, who was advised by the State Department not to attend the Bandung Conference as a member of Congress, went to Indonesia as a private citizen. Upon his return to the United States, Powell testified in front of the Senate Committee on Foreign Affairs. He warned the Senate that the second Asian-African meeting would take place in Cairo twelve months hence and that "if in the next twelve months we do not positively and specifically do some of the things that [the 29 countries participating in Bandung] ask for in their final communique . . . the United States will not be able to stand up and fight for the cause of democracy and the cause of the U.S." Powell said he perceived that what the people of the Asian-African conference were saying to the United States was that they would fight Communism in Asia and Africa, if the United States would fight racism and colonialism. "I think that is the sum of it," Powell concluded.[174]

Powell conveyed to the Senate Foreign Affairs Committee that black South African leaders at Bandung expressed regret that the U.S. military had stationed its aircraft carrier in Cape Town, where African American sailors were segregated the same way South African blacks were. This, according to Powell, was perceived as indicative of the government's approval of racial segregation. "It was a tremendous psychological blow to the prestige of the U.S. among the natives and the colored people in Africa," Powell concluded.[175]

Adam Clayton Powell used the Senate inquiry into the Bandung

Conference as an opportunity to push for racial reforms at home. He told the Senate that African Americans like himself could help the State Department accomplish its foreign policy agenda. Powell advised the Senate that America should tell the people of Asia and Africa that it has 20 million colored people because "[i]t is a good selling point."[176]

As far as the U.S. government was concerned, the most important and immediate consequence of the Bandung Conference was that it changed the political configuration of the United Nations. Third World nations would now use the United Nations to promote their solidarity as a voting bloc rather than align themselves with one of the two superpowers.[177] Increasing every year in number and importance at the General Assembly, African and Asian nations were wielding an important influence on matters of international concern. As early as 1950, the developing countries of Africa, Asia, and Latin America constituted over fifty percent of the total U.N. vote.[178] Aware that the U.S. needed the alliance of non-white nations and that the Soviet Union was sparing no effort to influence the African and Asian leadership, civil rights leaders continued their strategy of framing the struggle for racial justice in an international context both at home and abroad.

Conclusion

In this chapter, I have illustrated the African American leadership's awareness of the nexus between U.S. racial policies and the government's ability to sell democracy abroad, especially in Africa and Asia. The strategy of reaching out to the international community for support remained fruitless until World War II. The prevalence of European colonialism, the absence of the threat of Communist infiltration in Africa and Asia, and the state of relative isolation the United States lived in before the war were factors that contributed to containing the civil rights struggle, at least in the perception of government officials, within the confines of domestic politics. The establishment of the United Nations in 1945 gave much hope to African Americans. The international organization was the first in history to include the principle of human rights in its legal charter document.

Throughout this chapter, I have shown how civil rights leaders mobilized foreign public opinion to bring about political and social change. On the one hand, there were direct appeals in the form of petitions to the United Nations, and in the speeches and writings of internationally acclaimed African Americans such as Paul Robeson and W. E. B. DuBois. On the other hand, there was a continuous campaign of presenting the need for change and for civil rights legislation as part of America's national security and geopolitical fight against Communism. Organizations such as the NAACP and the Civil Rights Congress, and individuals such as W. E. B. DuBois, Paul Robeson, A. Philip Randolph, and Walter White played a vital role in pushing civil rights onto the world stage. The black press played a substantial role in enlightening African Americans, raising their expectations and reminding the nation of its contradictions and injustice. As Plummer puts it, "The ideological readiness of Afro-Americans in 1945 owed a substantial debt to the work of the black press. . . . In many respects, this was black journalism's golden age."[179] And although the U.S. government succeeded in tabling the three petitions to the United Nations, African American activists succeeded in bringing their grievances to world attention and internationalizing the problem of race discrimination in America.

Political accounts of the civil rights movement have tended to overlook the importance of the interplay of domestic politics and international developments. Because of the focus on state-society levels of analysis, the extent to which the international political environment contributed to the successful outcome of the U.S. civil rights struggle has traditionally been underdeveloped if not overlooked. The influence of international political tensions throughout this period was, indeed, considerable. In the wake of World War II, international events provided new and unique opportunities that civil rights activists could seize upon both to publicize their grievances and to solicit pressure on the U.S. government. As Paul Robeson put it, "speaking the truth abroad has been of great value to the American Negro struggle."[180]

Civil Rights Commissions: A Vehicle of Government Response to International Pressure

The foreign policy of any nation depends necessarily for much of its effectiveness on the moral influence which that nation exerts throughout the world. There is no question that the moral influence of the United States is weakened to the extent that civil rights proclaimed by our constitution are not fully observed in practice.[1]

The position of the United States in the world today makes it especially urgent that we adopt measures to secure for all our people their essential rights.[2]

Under what circumstances did the U.S. government begin to assess its responsibility toward and recognize its concrete interest in the civil rights of African Americans? Briefly put, domestic and international factors formed a network of pressure that forced the Truman Administration to undertake reforms. For the first time, America's foreign policy interests and quest for global leadership prompted the administration to undertake an active interest in civil rights progress. Although other countries had been concerned about U.S. racism earlier in this century, what was new after 1945 was the way in which world opinion regarding the United States held new importance, challenges, and implications for the administration. The end of colonialism and the ensuing competition between the United States and the Soviet Union for African and Asian allies motivated certain political actors in the United States to heed international

criticism of its racial policies. Moreover, one important consequence of the administration's increased sensitivity over racial policies was that civil rights leaders wrapped their struggle in the moral
authority of the United Nations' Charter. These leaders explicitly
linked their efforts to achieve racial reforms with the desired triumph of the democratic world order that so consumed the United
States during the Cold War.

In this chapter, I argue first that the timing of Truman's civil
rights reforms can be explained only by the particular combination
of U.S. global ambitions during the Cold War, and the opportunities afforded the United States by the wave of independence that
swept over Asia and Africa following the Second World War. I argue
secondly that the machinations surrounding the creation of the
United Nations put the United States civil rights policies under the
microscope and afforded international critics and civil rights advocates very powerful opportunities to pursue civil rights reforms.

Truman responded most directly to international pressure by
forming his 1947 civil rights commission. The civil rights commissions of this era served as a filter for subsequent executive orders,
Supreme Court rulings, and congressional actions. These commissions were used by State Department officials and the U.S. delegation to the United Nations to respond to foreign criticism of U.S.
racial policies. Here, I examine two civil rights commissions that
collaborated with the State Department to establish the interrelation between domestic race policy and international relations: Truman's Civil Rights Committee of 1947 and the first Civil Rights
Commission enacted by the 1957 Civil Rights Act. These commissions are the foundations upon which racial policy reforms were
based in the postwar years, and in the 1960s and beyond.

The 1947 Civil Rights Committee

As is often said, timing is everything in politics. The timing of the
first U.S. civil rights commission is no exception. The issue here is,
why did Truman first form a civil rights committee in 1947 and not
in some other year? While accounts of the domestic environment

have captured the political and social pressures by African Americans as well as white liberals, the international context is the variable that has the greatest explanatory weight in understanding the timing of Truman's efforts. The changing world order that resulted from the formation of the United Nations, the emerging Cold War, the end of colonialism, and the gradual independence of African and Asian countries are evolutions in world politics that influenced U.S. domestic affairs, including race relations. As Richard Dalfiume argues, there could be no doubt that the Cold War was behind Truman's civil rights crusade; that "if you read Truman's speeches – just about every speech . . . he made on the civil rights issue – he always brings up this point: The rest of the world is watching us. We must put our own home in order. So there is no doubt about it. You can trace this right on through."[3]

The period following World War II witnessed growing apprehension among America's allies and increasing attention among its foes regarding the racial situation in the United States. World War II itself had been waged against a vicious form of racism; Americans, in their more sublime moments, had denounced the racism of the Nazis and racism in general. Yet at the wake of the war, "with the exception of South Africa, perhaps no country in the world . . . possessed such widespread notoriety for its domestic racial policies as the United States."[4] Simultaneously, by the end of the war, the peoples of Asia and Africa would offer additional painful reminders of the centrality of the race issue in world politics, and by virtue of the new bipolar competition for allies, would focus attention on U.S. race policy.

The United Nations provided an important focal point for international criticism of U.S. race policy. As early as its inception, the United Nations made some white Americans feel uncomfortable, for it was an organization of equal and sovereign nations that had no tolerance for the policies to which the United States, their host country, subscribed in dealing with African Americans. The United States was successful in inserting the term "domestic jurisdiction" in the U.N. Charter that prohibited any interference by the international organization in domestic affairs. Yet the "spirit and purpose" of the Charter imposed important obligations: that nations could no longer claim exclusive right to treat their citizens as individual nations might have wished. Now, other countries were watching. As we shall see, the United States was not excluded from such scrutiny.

One of the important consequences of the scrutiny U.S. civil rights policy received as a result of the creation of the United Nations was that African American leaders now had an important vehicle to link their efforts to muster international and domestic support for civil rights reform with direct pressure on the United States government. African American leaders pointed out that if the United States' goal was a world community of peaceful nations, it must not exempt itself from the requirements it imposed on others. At a time when the United States hoped to reshape the postwar world in its own image and into a capitalist free-market economy, the international attention given to racial segregation and discrimination was an obstacle and an embarrassment to the U.S. government. African American leaders knew this and exploited the opportunities implied by this embarrassment.

Truman's desegregation efforts cannot be explained solely by his need to court African American voters. In fact, Truman took significant domestic political risks in the pursuit of desegregation. Thus, Truman's desegregation efforts are not adequately explained by domestic factors alone as many scholars have argued;[5] foreign policy goals were fundamental in forcing the president's hand.

An examination of the momentous 1947 Civil Rights Committee's report *To Secure These Rights* illustrates how international events played a significant role in motivating Truman's decision to give priority to racial reforms. It was not politically feasible for the Truman Administration to dismiss accusations of being "a hypocrite in international affairs" for demanding democratic measures elsewhere while denying the same to its black citizens at home. *To Secure These Rights* was a blueprint for the Truman Administration's civil rights reforms.[6] The report preceded Truman's executive orders in the area of civil rights, and Supreme Court rulings in favor of desegregation in housing, transportation, and educational institutions. In addition, this document came before rulings that outlawed Jim Crow laws in the South and the series of Civil Rights Acts from

1957 to 1965 guaranteeing full citizenship and protection of the law to African Americans. *To Secure These Rights* is therefore a pivotal document that elucidates the motivations and timing of civil rights reform in the postwar United States.

The 1947 recommendations of *To Secure These Rights* outlined "virtually every major proposal that would appear in Congress for the next decade,"[7] including every section of the Civil Rights Act of 1957, the first civil rights legislation since 1875. It "galvanized civil rights movements into action, in efforts to gain implementation of its recommendations. It also gave President Truman and other members of the administration a blueprint to follow."[8] The report confirmed the grievances of and the crimes committed against African Americans while endorsing the efforts of the African American leadership to secure legislative outcomes. Among its recommendations, the committee called for stronger criminal statutes, antilynching legislation, abolition of the poll tax, protection of black voters in federal and primary elections, and the prohibition of discrimination in interstate transportation, public education, and federal employment.

President Truman realized the implications of domestic racial policies on the new family of nations that consisted of all kinds of people. He concluded that the government of the United States had to play a crucial role in creating and promoting a social order that was worthy of the leading nation in the free world.

The years following the end of the war constituted a continuing revolution in world affairs, punctuated by the early Cold War period of 1947–9, the conquest of China by the Communists beginning in 1946, the Soviet acquisition of the atomic bomb in 1949, the independence of India, Pakistan, and Burma in 1947–8, the ongoing negotiations between France, Britain, and their African and Asian colonies concerning the colonies' upcoming independence and emergence into the international community, and the Korean War from 1950–3. In addition to the ongoing changes in postwar global affairs, the formation of the United Nations paved the way for debates over preventing discrimination and upholding international human rights. These debates left the United States in an awkward position that became even more so as the nations of India, Pakistan, Afghanistan, Indonesia, and Burma joined the United Nations.[9]

Another factor contributing to America's vulnerability was the spread of Communism. By 1948, the European states of Yugoslavia, Albania, Rumania, Hungary, Bulgaria, and Poland were Communist states; Czechoslovakia, a favorite of U.S. foreign policymakers, became Communist by virtue of a coup d'etat. The United States also had to contend with the "loss" of China to Communism in 1949. This was a particularly difficult geopolitical change because it frustrated America's foreign policy strategies. The Roosevelt Administration portrayed China as filling the power gap in the Far East after Japan's defeat. Originally, Roosevelt had hoped that the Chinese would be instrumental to broader U.S. policy interests in Asia. The loss of China to Communism heightened the awareness of the State Department to the potential dangers of the Communist doctrine among the newly independent nations. The global situation that the United States government encountered between 1945–9 was gloomy: The Soviets had claimed strategically important allies in Europe and Asia. This left Africa and other parts of Asia open to competition between the bipolar giants.

In the wake of this competition, U.S. race policy became the focus of attacks by the Soviet press, other foreign critics, and African American leaders. While the U.S. government was accusing the Soviet Union and its allies of human rights violations, the absence of free elections, and the repression of dissidents, African Americans and foreign critics of the United States were accusing the U.S. government of the same treatment toward its minorities.[10] In addition, the Soviet press launched a massive attack on U.S. race policies in 1946. *Trud* and *Pravda* provided accurate and gruesome details on recent lynching of blacks. The Soviet press listed the states that outlawed desegregated schools, public facilities, and mixed marriages.[11] As Lauren puts it,

Just as the Nazi experience had turned a mirror toward domestic racial discrimination, so now the Soviet campaign effectively held up a magnifying glass and invited the rest of the world to look through it and see the

United States at its worst. Policymakers in Washington found this to be not only a supreme embarrassment but also "extremely dangerous" in global competition. . . . This assessment weighed heavily upon Truman's decision to create the special President's Committee on Civil Rights. . . .[12]

It was under these circumstances that President Truman issued Executive Order 9008 on December 5, 1946, establishing the Civil Rights Committee. He authorized the committee, composed of fifteen distinguished white and African Americans,[13]"to inquire into and determine whether and in what respect current law-enforcement measures and the authority and means possessed by federal, state, and local governments may be strengthened and improved to safeguard the civil rights of the people."[14]

It is clear that the committee viewed its portfolio as part of U.S. foreign policy. The committee worked closely with the Department of State in preparing its report to the president. Robert Carr, executive secretary of the committee, wrote Secretary of State George Marshall that the committee had spent much time and attention on the international implications of the civil rights problem in the United States. He added that the committee was disturbed by the pervasive belief that America's record in the field of race relations was being used against the nation overseas. Carr challenged Marshall to state whether he believed that the formulation and conduct of a sound and desirable foreign policy was handicapped by "our bad domestic record in civil rights and if so, [did] this mean that American security [was] in fact endangered by this condition?"[15]

To respond to the committee's inquiry, State Department officials met with members of the U.S. delegation to the United Nations to discuss the international implications of the country's race relations on its foreign policy interests. State Department officials and the U.S. delegates reached "a unanimous agreement that the conduct of our foreign policy is handicapped by our record in the field of civil rights and racial discrimination."[16] The group further advised the civil rights committee to refrain from publicizing examples of the country's civil rights record "lest it further serve the interests of Communist propaganda."[17]

Based on the conclusions reached by the State Department officials and the U.S. delegation to the United Nations, Secretary of State Marshall wrote the Committee that

> [t]he failure to secure the full and equal enjoyment of these civil rights has affected the conduct of our foreign relations in two ways. On the one hand, isolated incidents have occurred which involved directly the nationals of other states. Perhaps even more damaging, however, have been the violations practiced against groups of our own citizens. These practices have been alluded to frequently in the foreign press. . . . Since it is a major objective of the foreign policy of the United States to promote world-wide respect for and observance of civil rights, our failure to maintain the highest standards of performance in this field creates embarrassment out of proportion to the actual instances of violation.[18]

The committee's stand on the international implications of the American civil rights record was unequivocal. Committee members were convinced that "the way to bring an end to foreign criticism of our civil rights record is to take steps to improve that record rather than to argue with our critics about their motives or honesty of their reporting." Moreover, committee members believed that if the United States could demonstrate that dark-skinned U.S. citizens were truly the equals of whites, this would create a reservoir of sympathy for America among people of color throughout the world. Carr hoped that the committee's report would lead to

> a genuine improvement in our civil rights practices at home and . . . strengthen our international position. . . . Every act adds to the picture of a strong united America and creates and wins friends for us among the foreign "relatives" of our own racial, religious and national minorities.[19]

The committee report, *To Secure These Rights*, explains the timing of this initiative and conveys the growing alarm that international pressures placed on the United States. In it, the committee argued that there were three justifications for redressing civil rights abuses in the U.S.: moral, economic, and international. With respect to the international arena, the report noted that the United States' position and security in the highly interdependent postwar world were inevitably tied to the security and well being of other countries. While American foreign policy was designed to inspire peace and progress and positive influence throughout the world, the domestic civil rights situation had impeded the fulfillment of the nation's foreign policy goals. Furthermore, the report concluded that the treatment of "our Negroes" was perceived as a reflection of America's attitude toward all the dark-skinned people of Africa, Asia, the Middle East, Latin America, and the Pacific, among others:

We cannot escape the fact that our civil rights record has been an issue in world politics. The world's press and radio are full of it. This committee has seen a multitude of samples. We and our friends have been, and are, stressing our achievements. Those with competing philosophies have stressed our shortcomings. They have not only tried to create hostility towards us among specific nations, races, and religious groups. They have tried to prove our democracy an empty fraud, and our nation a consistent oppressor of underprivileged people. This may seem ludicrous to Americans, but it is sufficiently important to worry our friends. . . .[20]

Further, *To Secure These Rights* argued that the Soviets were beyond convincing because their political purposes were best served by constantly accusing the United States of civil rights violations. Nevertheless, the American government had an obligation to deprive the Soviets of such ammunition. It would be necessary to convince "the peoples of the world" who bear goodwill toward the United States. The report argued that, therefore, achievements in race relations and racial justice needed to be substantive. The report concluded with a stern warning: *"The United States is not so strong, the final triumph of the democratic ideal is not so inevitable that we can ignore what the world thinks of us or our record."*[21] In support of this stance, the committee quoted from a letter from Acting Secretary of State Dean Acheson to the Fair Employment Practices Committee in May 1946. Acheson stated:

The existence of discrimination against minority groups in this country has an adverse effect upon our relations with other countries. We are reminded over and over by some foreign newspapers and spokesmen that our treatment of various minorities leaves much to be desired. While sometimes these pronouncements are exaggerated and unjustified, they all too frequently point with accuracy to some form of discrimination because of race, creed, color, or national origin. Frequently we find it next to impossible to formulate a satisfactory answer to our critics in other countries; the gap between the things we stand for in principle and the facts of a particular situation may be too wide to be bridged. An atmosphere of suspicion and resentment in a country over the way a minority is being treated in the United States is a formidable obstacle to the development of mutual understanding and trust between the two countries. We will have better international relations when these reasons for suspicion and resentment are removed. I think it is obvious . . . that the existence of discrimination against minority groups in the United States is a handicap in our relations with other countries. The Department of State, therefore, has good reason to hope for the continued and increased effectiveness of public and private efforts to do away with these discriminations.[22]

As a result of these findings, Truman undertook a serious confrontation with allies in Congress. The president sent a special civil rights message, based on the findings of *To Secure These Rights*, to Congress on February 2, 1948. It was the first such message that any president had ever submitted to Congress. Truman recommended that Congress enact legislation because the "serious gap between our ideals and some of our practices . . . must be closed." He asked Congress to adopt the recommendations of the Civil Rights Committee. At the end of his message, Truman suggested that the country's foreign policy goals necessitated congressional action on civil rights:

If we wish to inspire the peoples of the world whose freedom is in jeopardy, if we wish to restore hope to those who have already lost their civil liberties, if we wish to fulfill the promise that is ours, we must correct the remaining imperfections in our practice of democracy. We know the way. We need only the will.[23]

Immediately after Truman's message was read in Congress, the Voice of America broadcast it as the story of the day. This signaled the emergence of the U.S. civil rights movement as a factor in Cold War diplomacy.[24] The Truman Administration, the civil rights leadership, and foreign critics of U.S. race relations had all linked the country's treatment of African Americans to America's new role in global politics and its fight against Communism.

As Richard Neustadt has noted, Truman could not have ignored the committee's report.[25] Certainly, Truman's decision to appoint the committee and heed its recommendations arose from the growing importance of the African American vote, the outcry of civil rights activists over the violent campaign launched against returning African American servicemen in the South, and the overall changing domestic political environment. However, the Cold War provided critics with leverage for dealing with African American grievances. The inescapable "winds of change" persuaded U.S. officials that civil rights change was necessary. Simply put, if the United States were to pursue global leadership and lure African and Asian countries away from Communism, the government had to show that African Americans had equal rights in their own country. In sum, the beginning of Truman's assault on race policy in the United States had its origins in concerns about the United States' ability to cultivate useful allies in the political and ideological competition with the Soviet Union.

I now turn to a consideration of whether explanations that focus on domestic factors adequately explain the timing of Truman's initiatives. If one wants to consider the individual preferences of Truman, one has to confront the fact that on racial matters, Truman was still a Southerner. As David McCullough writes, "old biases, old habits of speech continued, surfacing occasionally off-stage, as some of his aides and Secret Service agents would later attest." Truman still used the epithet "niggers," as a commonplace referent for African Americans. McCullough quotes Truman's sister as saying, "Harry is no more for nigger equality than any of us."[26]

But despite personal proclivities, Truman, as president, knew he could no longer turn away from the glaring racial injustices. Truman realized that the differential treatment afforded millions of African American citizens would more than indirectly affect the outcome of the power struggle between the United States and the Soviet Union. As U.N. delegates debated issues of international human rights, crimes of genocide, and the right of colonized peoples to independence, the Soviet Union and its allies attempted to discredit U.S. claims that "all men are created equal." For example, a Polish delegate to the United Nations described the United States as undeserving to lead the world since it had "almost exterminated the Indians, and they put them in zoos, which they call reservations," and that with regard to their black population, "they are violating their Constitution every day."[27] Thus the evidence demonstrates that whatever his own inclinations, Truman was at the very least sensitive to the fact that race policy at home was hindering geopolitical aspirations.

If we consider other possible explanations for Truman's early civil rights efforts, we find that he was moving against the current elite political opinion. For example, the same month that the U.N. General Assembly adopted the Declaration on Human Rights, Texas Attorney General Price Daniel ruled that white students could not attend Texas State University for Negroes because the Texas Constitution required segregation. Furthermore, although the Democratic Party, with Truman as its presidential candidate, endorsed a civil rights plan as part of its platform in 1948, the issue of civil rights divided the Democratic Party and enabled the anti–civil rights Dixiecrats to challenge Truman. Because of their political power, dominance, and seniority rule in Congress, especially in the Senate, Southern Democrats were able to stifle civil rights legislation. Note that the actions of these Southern politicians were not contrary to the public sentiment of indifference, if not hostility, toward African Americans.[28] Finally, as detailed in Chapter One, African American electoral power could not have been the primary factor behind Truman's championship of civil rights reform.

In fact, Truman's efforts to reform civil rights policy were so discordant with the domestic political tides of the day that Truman had to find vehicles other than Congress to effect policy reform. Realizing he could not get Congress to act, Truman in July 1948 issued Executive Order 9980 prohibiting discrimination in federal employment and Executive Order 9981 desegregating the armed services. Moreover, in December 1948, the president ordered the desegregation of eating facilities at the Washington National Airport. That airport was a point of entry for many visiting foreign dignitaries.

To Secure These Rights was significant because it set the tone for civil rights reform in postwar America and because it increased the aspirations of both African American and white civil rights advocates. In the series of briefs submitted to the Supreme Court regarding subsequent desegregation cases, the Justice and State Departments repeatedly cited *To Secure These Rights*.[29] But it was a slow beginning. During the next ten years, Congress not only failed to adopt any of the Civil Rights Committee's recommendations, but it also did not pass a single civil rights bill. Exclusively the Executive branch and the Supreme Court made progress during these years. As is evident throughout this work, the Department of State, which was the target of international pressure in most cases, played a particularly important role in civil rights politics. I argue that the Executive and Judicial branches were at the forefront of civil rights change because the administration was under enormous international pressure to clean its own house. It undertook this task well before other significant domestic political forces swung behind civil rights reforms.

Congressional Hearings and the International Implications of Racism

Recall the need to explain the timing of civil rights reforms as they unfolded in the two decades following World War II. By now, it should be clear that Truman initiated civil rights reforms in 1947. Truman's efforts were the blueprint for civil rights reforms in the United States in two senses: first, the methods that the Truman Administration used to effect civil rights reforms, including executive orders, amicus briefs, and Justice Department investigations of civil rights violations, became standard operating procedure for civil rights changes; second, Truman's efforts placed the Executive branch in the vanguard of civil rights reform. It is this latter pattern that I discuss in the remaining sections of this chapter.

Although hearings on proposed civil rights legislation after 1946 consistently referred to the negative consequences of segregationist policies and the difficulties they posed for the State Department in dealing with other nations, Truman was unable to push his civil rights program through Congress. Moreover, even though public officials as well as private citizens linked domestic racial policies and foreign policy interests, reform was not forthcoming from Congress. Among those who frequently testified before Congress were Walter White, Clarence Mitchell, and Roy Wilkins of the NAACP, A. Philip Randolph of the Brotherhood of Sleeping Car Porters, Maurice Sheehy of the National Citizens Council on Civil Rights, Benjamin Epstein of the Anti-Defamation League of B'nai B'rith, Roger Baldwin of the American Civil Liberties Union, Senators Jacob Javits, Joseph Clark, and Hubert Humphrey, and Congressmen Adam Clayton Powell and William Dawson, the only two African Americans in the U.S. Congress.[30] These civil rights advocates used the argument that U.S. race relations were harming national interest and national security at a time when the United States and the Soviet Union were engaged in a Cold War and competing for the "hearts and minds" of African and Asian peoples.[31]

Because of the Cold War and the government's anti-Communist foreign policy, civil rights advocates were able to argue that civil rights legislation was a necessary bulwark against Communism and that it was a component of U.S. national security. Proponents of civil rights attempted to transcend partisan issues that in the past had stifled civil rights reform. Winning the Cold War, curtailing Communism, and spreading the economic, political, and ideological influence of the United States all over the world were seen as bipartisan efforts; racial reforms became essential to meet these goals.

During Senate hearings held by the Subcommittee of the Committee on the Judiciary, civil rights proponents linked national security and compliance with the United Nations Charter to the passage of civil rights legislation. They undoubtedly saw the political opportunity in invoking the belief that

not only does America's internal strength, but her influence abroad, rest in large measure upon the vitality of our free institutions. The forces affecting the world today, to which these free institutions are inevitably linked, do not allow us the luxury of a laissez-faire approach to civil rights.[32]

Civil rights leaders argued that charges of hypocrisy greatly weakened America's position in the international community and that as more people inhabiting Africa and Asia won their freedom, this problem would become increasingly acute. In addition, civil rights leaders viewed the propaganda emphasizing America's weaknesses in civil rights as helping to make the difference between new nations aligning themselves with the Soviet system or the American way of life.[33] Only the passage of civil rights legislation, they argued, could counter anti-American Cold War propaganda.

Moreover, civil rights activists pointed out that no one could predict which of the emerging nations might develop into new world powers. Therefore, the United States had no choice but to establish the friendliest possible relations with developing nations. Civil rights advocates claimed that every lynching, every riot, every racial or religious disturbance was broadcast to the world and served to feed the Communist machine operating in this country and abroad.[34]

To protect itself against accusations of Communist infiltration, the NAACP used anti-Communist rhetoric to call for racial reforms. Roy Wilkins testified before Congress that it was no secret that the United States was in a contest to persuade the peoples of the world that they should follow the American democratic way of life rather than the Communist path held out to them. He stated that the federal government had thrust upon itself the leadership of the postwar world order and that "with the constantly emerging evidence of totalitarian terrorism within our own state . . . why should any people choose democracy as a way of life?"[35] Wilkins flatly told Congress that,

Two-thirds of the world's population is non-Caucasian. We make military and political agreements with these people; we do business with them. Our position on the international round table is greatly weakened when the charge of hypocrisy can be leveled against us. Propaganda emphasizing American weakness in civil rights may help to spell the difference on some occasions between new nations aligning themselves with the Soviet system or the American way of life. We have no choice . . . but to narrow the gap between America's professions and her practices. . . . We can rob the [C]ommunists of their own best weapon by taking action on human rights ourselves.[36]

New York Representative Adam Clayton Powell exploited the government's perception that Indochina "was slipping away from the free world" to advise the House Committee on Interstate and

Foreign Commerce that "nothing would be a greater blow to [C]ommunism than the passage by the United States Congress of a civil rights bill."[37]

While progress in civil rights had been through the courts and executive orders, civil rights leaders called on Congress to do its share. They told Congress that

no less important than the substantive effects of this congressional failure are its symbolic implications. In our government scheme, Congress is the most popular, the most representative branch of government. It is regarded as being closest to the people. But surely it would not serve America's interest abroad to have the world believe that in the field of civil rights Congress is a truer barometer of the hopes and aspirations, the fears and prejudices of the American people than the Supreme Court and the White House. . . . For the last decade our country has been struggling to win the support of the hearts and minds of the peoples of the world for the democratic cause. We have been vulnerable on the score of prejudice and discrimination against darker-skinned Americans, especially vulnerable among those two-thirds of the world's inhabitants who are themselves colored.[38]

Pushing for antilynching legislation, civil rights activists testified that people all over the world looked to the United States as a model form of government. Therefore, the United States could not afford to see "its authority flouted by the lawless mob; that the prestige of this nation, its form of government, and its advocacy of equal justice under the law" was at issue with respect to the antilynching legislation. The establishment of criminal and civil procedures against mob violence directed at individuals and groups by reason of race, creed, or color, they argued, would serve to restore and enhance the prestige of this nation.[39] Unlike the lynchers and their supporters who did not care about the implications of their actions on America's foreign policy interests, civil rights supporters argued that enactment of civil rights legislation would help the country's struggle against Communism, that

One of the best criteria for predicting how a nation will behave in its international relations is its record of achievement among its own people. We judge the Soviets in this manner and part of our skepticism about their sincerity on world issues is grounded in our awareness of how brutally the Kremlin has conducted its domestic policies, how little regard it has had for human rights. We should consider our own behavior from the same perspective. . . .[40]

They drew comparisons between the eras of the Civil War and the Cold War, reminding Congress that Lincoln decided upon eman-cipation of the slaves not only as an "act of justice" but also as a "military necessity." They argued that the times were similar and civil rights legislation was needed, again, on both grounds; national security dictates such measure.

Civil rights advocates warned,

You can rest assured that the Kremlin will not permit even these hearings to go unnoticed, and will gleefully exploit any failure on our part to truly exemplify the democracy we preach to the rest of the world. You can rest assured the eyes of millions of uncommitted peoples throughout the world – people who may sway the balance between a world of freedom and a world of totalitarian oppression – are upon this issue in the United States, and upon what we do about it – upon what we do about it at this very hearing, and in this very Congress. [C]ommunism and the atom have only heightened our age-old dilemma of good and evil, and raised the stakes of moral choice.[41]

Civil rights activists were not the only ones to use the strategy of linking America's racist policies to its international standing to lobby for civil rights legislation. Some members of Congress also used the opportunities provided by America's new position in inter-national affairs to influence their colleagues in the Senate and in the House. Senator Joseph Clark of Pennsylvania argued that the failure of the U.S. government to protect the basic civil rights of all American citizens, without regard to race or color, was "presently crippling the efforts of our government to create that atmosphere of mutual respect and confidence throughout the free world on which our national security and our defense against international [C]ommunism both depend."[42]

Senator Jacob Javits of New York criticized Congress for its weak position on civil rights given the country's struggle to maintain international peace. Referring to his experience as a member of the

Committee on Foreign Affairs and his personal contact with U.S. foreign affairs problems, he said,

I saw this very clearly in November and December last year in Pakistan, India, [S]outh and [S]outheast Asia where I traveled. The great contest between freedom and [C]ommunism is over the approximately 1.2 billion largely Negro and Oriental population who occupy the underdeveloped areas of the Far East, the Middle East, and Africa.

The senator reminded his colleagues that the most powerful argument the "Communist conspirators" use against "our leadership of the free world" is to tell the dark-skinned people of Africa and Asia that following America's leadership will subject them to nothing less than the segregation and discrimination that Americans are perceived as tolerating "within certain areas of the United States." Javits concluded with a recommendation: "federal civil rights legislation is the best answer."[43]

Because racial discrimination was pervasive in Washington, D.C., and non-white foreigners were not spared incidents of discrimination and segregation, civil rights leaders did not hesitate to publicize institutionalized discrimination in the nation's capital. The director of the Washington Fellowship told the Senate that stories of segregated buses in the nation's capital were covered by the media in places as far away as Bangkok. He related that such stories were

played up . . . in the scores of countries in which live people with darker skin. . . . Washington is the capital of the world not in only the political sense, but even more in the sense of moral and spiritual leadership which we can give; we have got to earn that right and that privilege.[44]

Hammering on the negative publicity that South Africa's Apartheid policies were receiving all over the world, Elmer Henderson, the director of the American Council on Human Rights, testified to Congress that "the world knows, and we cannot hide the fact that Washington is the only national capital, except that of South Africa, which practices legally enforced segregation."[45] The NAACP spokesman, Reverend Stephen Gill Spottswood, asked Congress how it expected Asian and African peoples "to accept democracy over [C]ommunism when we fail to abolish segregation in every form in the nation's capital . . . and to fire a new shot of liberty that will be heard around the world."[46]

Supporters of civil rights legislation cited incidents of racist encounters that foreign dignitaries, as well as foreign students, had suffered.[47] While segregation of African Americans may have been acceptable to certain members of Congress, segregation of foreign dignitaries would certainly not be. In one incident, a barber in Cincinnati refused a high-level government official from Ceylon who was touring the United States on official business. Following his U.S. trip, the official made anti-American statements in London "that were heard all over the world." Walter White testified that "this kind of experience completely negates all the fine speeches or splendid radio broadcasts that we make on the Voice of America to tell the world how much we believe in democracy." White concluded to the Senate that during his overseas travels,

It was depressing to talk to leaders . . . in many countries who believed that the United States was perfecting the atom bomb mainly as an instrument to strengthen white supremacy and continue colonial rule. Their fears were to some extent based on the fact that we had used the bomb in Japan but not used it in Europe . . . the continued practice of racial discrimination sends warning signals to the darker people of the world that the atomic bomb is a threat to their freedom.[48]

Even though international pressures had enhanced the significance of U.S. civil rights, Congress was slow to act. Opponents used the Cold War to argue against civil rights legislation. They frequently depicted proposed civil rights legislation as Communist-inspired. Senator Strom Thurmond of South Carolina[49] stated that "propagandists have tried to sell the American people on the idea that the defeat of these bills would provide Russia with new arguments against us. That is not a valid reason in favor of the bills. If we permit Russia to control our domestic policy by deferring to what she might say about us, then we shall have bowed to the dictates of [C]ommunism."[50] He advised Congress to stick to the mandate given to it by the people of the United States in ordaining the

Constitution as the basic law of the land, instead of minding what the Russians were saying.[51]

Congressman John Dowdy of Texas went further in his criticism of the Justice and State Departments. He stated that proposed civil rights legislation "would set up a despot in the Attorney General's Office with a large corps of enforcers under him; and his will and his oppressive action would be brought to bear upon American citizens, just as Hitler's minions coerced and subjugated the German people. I would say this – I believe this would be agreed to by most people: that, if we had a Hitler in the United States, the first thing he would want would be a bill of this nature."[52]

The congressional coalition of Southern Democrats and Northern Republicans working against civil rights reforms was resilient. It successfully withstood domestic and international pressures as the efforts of civil rights advocates, black and white, public officials and private citizens, failed to produce legislative measures. Thus, Congress remained alone and steadfast in resisting the civil rights changes that were in progress.

As these examples demonstrate, without direct executive action, civil rights advocates were not able to achieve policy reforms. Thus, civil rights reforms cannot be explained without reference to the international vulnerabilities of the Executive branch. Nowhere is this relationship between the actions of the Executive branch, international pressure, and actual policy reform more evident than in the activities of the 1957 Civil Rights Commission. As we shall see, the 1957 Civil Rights Commission was preoccupied with the negative consequences of U.S. race policy on U.S. global ambitions. The Civil Rights Act of 1957, the first civil rights legislative measure since 1875, established the Civil Rights Commission,[53] partly in response to changes in the dynamics of the geopolitical order.

Simultaneously world affairs were becoming increasingly more complex. The Cold War was in full swing. More African and Asian countries were negotiating their independence. The Soviet Union was readily offering economic, military, and political assistance to Africa and Asia. In 1955, as discussed earlier, leaders of twenty-nine African and Asian countries participating in the Bandung Conference formed the nonaligned voting bloc at the United Nations.

Thus, the United States found itself competing for power and leadership in a world where the West could no longer dictate policy. The need for African and Asian allies further pressured the United States into resolving its own domestic problems. Furthermore, international criticism of the United States increased to a fever pitch following a series of highly publicized events such as the Charles Trudell and James Lewis case of 1946, the Rosa Lee Ingram trial of 1949, the Willie McGee sentence in 1951, the Emmett Till murder in 1955, the Autherine Lucy school desegregation case in 1956, and the Little Rock crisis of 1957–8. Southern defiance to the *Brown v. Board of Education* decision crystallized to the whole nation and to the whole world that the federal government could not leave racial policy to the ebb and flow of partisan politics. By 1957, even President Eisenhower, a staunch advocate of states' rights and an opponent of federal intervention in civil rights, was ready to support civil rights legislation.[54]

The 1957 Civil Rights Commission

The 1957 Civil Rights Commission, enacted into law by the civil rights act of the same year,[55] became the de facto liaison between the State Department and Congress on all matters pertaining to domestic racial policies.[56] In 1958, commission members told Under Secretary of State Christian Herter, as did Truman's committee over a decade earlier, that any report that failed to take into account the interrelationship between domestic and foreign policy in the field of civil rights would be deficient.[57]

Thus, the commission requested a report from the Department of State about the impact that treatment of minorities in the United States had on U.S. foreign relations and the extent to which such treatment was a factor in the country's dealings with other governments. In addition, the commission wanted an appraisal of how Communist-bloc countries utilized incidents of racial strife in their propaganda against the United States.[58] The Department of State submitted a full report to the commission consisting of two parts: a review of the impact of racism on U.S. foreign policy and an area study by continent of the media coverage and international interest in U.S. race relations.[59]

First, the State Department reported that the treatment of African Americans in the United States was of world interest and a continuing factor in shaping attitudes toward the United States. Thus, America's domestic racial policies influenced its relations with other countries. The report argued that sensitivity to racial discrimination was understandably keenest in Africa and Asia, "where a sense of self identification is involved, and where racial discrimination in the U.S. is inevitably linked with the presence or recent memory of white colonialism and domination."[60] State Department officials announced to members of the Civil Rights Commission that they were very disturbed that the source of international criticism and pressure over U.S. racial discrimination was not confined to Africa, Asia, and Eastern Europe.[61] The implications of American racism "affect the atmosphere in which we conduct relations with [Western European] countries."[62]

The report further noted that racial discrimination and segregation raised and reinforced doubts about the sincerity and strength of America's concern for the welfare of others, particularly the nonwhite world. Moreover, the report continued, racial discrimination not only provided a target for anti-American propaganda, but it also spilled over to other issues of international importance.[63]

As to the effect of U.S. racial policies on negotiations with other governments, the report stated that "there is no doubt that nonwhite government leaders have strong feelings on this issue, which in some cases [were] intensified by their personal experiences with discrimination in this country."[64] The report used the 1958 Accra Conference of Independent African States, during which resolutions were passed that condemned racial discrimination and segregation in the United States, as evidence to show the intense concern of the nations of Africa and Asia with U.S. racial policies.[65] An impressive African American delegation was invited to the Accra Conference. It included Claude Barnett and Etta Moten Barnett of the *Associated Negro Press,* Horace Mann Bond, former president of Lincoln University, journalist Marguerite Cartwright, John A. David of the American Society of African Culture, U.S. Representative

Charles Diggs, James Lawson of the Universal African National Movement, Frank Montero and Homer Jack of the American Committee on Africa, and Maida Springer of the AFL-CIO. In addition, Paul and Eslanda Robeson and Shirley Graham DuBois were also there. W. E. B. DuBois was too ill to attend.[66]

The State Department report continued by noting how America's racial policies provided an opportunity of a different nature for the white rule in South Africa. White South African politicians used racial friction in the United States to defend their own discriminatory practices. The ruling Nationalist Party pointed to racial discrimination in the United States to justify Apartheid and to question America's standing to criticize other countries' racial policies. South Africa's leaders argued that the U.S. government's failure to end segregationist policies in the United States disqualified it from judging South Africa's racial policies, such as when the United States supported a U.N. resolution condemning Apartheid in 1958.[67]

As far as the Communists' exploitation of the race problem in the United States was concerned, the report stated that Moscow's criticism was very effective because it quoted from non-Communist publications and sources. Therefore, the Soviets were more credible. The report added, "Soviet propaganda attacks on U.S. racism were geared into every political maneuver to 'expose' the 'American way of life.'"[68] The Little Rock crisis of 1957–8, for example, enabled Moscow to challenge the United States at U.N. debates over Hungary in 1957. The Soviets attempted to discredit the moral position of the United States on Hungary by pointing to the "unbelievable crimes and violations of the most elementary human rights taking place in the [S]outhern United States."[69] The Soviets hit the United States repeatedly, not only for permitting the "racists" to abuse its own citizens, but also for daring to reproach others while "its own hands were dirty."[70] The Soviets, the report said, advised United Nations delegates from Asian and African nations that in the country in which the United Nations was meeting, "people of their color are being persecuted."[71]

The State Department believed that the effects of civil rights abuses on foreign policy were so detrimental that it supplemented the information the Civil Rights Commission requested with a lengthy report of its own. The department disclosed "essential information that would help [the commission] assess the damage U.S. race relations were causing and the potential of further damage if Congress fails to adopt more aggressive civil rights measures."[72]

The State Department report to the Civil Rights Commission went on to argue that in Africa, awareness of what was happening in the United States was not widespread, but was confined to a small group of people in each territory who were sufficiently educated to be interested in the outside world.[73]

The important thing is that this group is in a position to react, since in the present conditions of African development, it plays an increasingly important role in business and labor unions, education and the professions, and, in the independent states and those soon to be independent in government and politics.[74]

Of those Africans who were able to obtain firsthand impressions of American life, the most numerous were students, many of whom represented a rising generation of African leaders and specialists whose influence and importance in their own countries were assured by the very scarcity of the skills that they were acquiring in the United States. The report noted that "some of these students obtain their knowledge of American racial practices the hard way – as victims of some form of [U.S.] discrimination."[75] The report predicted that African curiosity about such American racial problems was likely to increase; the multiplication of independent states in tropical Africa was likely to lead to an increase in direct contacts with the United States; the number of African students in the United States would probably grow; and education, literacy, and the development of communications media were likely to open the world to an increasing number of Africans.[76] Using Liberia as an example of the increasingly negative impact of discrimination on visiting students, the report said,

Reaction to U.S. racial discrimination has increased as many Liberian students come to the U.S. for education and go back to their country with unpleasant experiences of discrimination. They have become more critical toward the United States than the older generation of Liberian leaders. These returning students will play an increasingly important role . . . a growth of racial feeling will have an adverse impact on the close international cooperation between Liberia and the United States, and on the United States trade and investment in Liberia, which has so far been the prime mover in the country's economic development.[77]

State Department officials warned the commission that as Africans gained control of their own affairs, they would be able to react more directly to events throughout the world. As African leaders began to take stands and make decisions, the United States' racial problems left it at a disadvantage in its dealings with these emerging leaders.[78]

The State Department perceived that an additional problem for the United States in Africa was that the unflattering image of its race relations increased receptivity to anti-American propaganda on other themes.[79] The growing attractiveness of Pan-African ideas and emphasis placed by such African leaders as Ghana's President Kwame Nkrumah on development of the "African personality" suggested that Africans might become increasingly sensitive to problems of racial discrimination abroad and that they would link it to other situations they faced.[80]

The State Department provided the commission with two examples in which African leaders used the racial situation in the United States to rally political support in their countries, as well as on the continent: Ghana's President Nkrumah and Kenya's political and labor leader, Tom Mboya. Nkrumah announced that his country would be a haven for persecuted blacks everywhere, including African Americans. Mboya told U.S. Representative Charles Diggs that U.S. racial problems were hindering good relations between the United States and Africa.[81] The State Department stressed the importance of President Nkrumah to its foreign policy goals in Africa as Ghana had achieved great prestige and influence in African affairs.[82] Yet, as in most newly independent African and Asian countries, Ghana's political elite had "not escaped an underlying tendency to interpret the world in terms of racial conflicts and problems. . . ."[83]

The State Department listed in its supplementary report some of the embarrassing incidents of discrimination in the United States against Ghanaians who would later become leaders in their own country. Nkrumah, who had studied in the United States, recorded in his autobiography his firsthand experiences with American racism:

> . . . when I compared [U.S.] racial segregation with the modernity and advancement of the country it made my heart sink. I well remember my first experience of active racialism below the Mason-Dixon line. I was traveling by bus on one of my lecture tours from Philadelphia to Washington and the bus stopped en route at Baltimore for the passengers to refresh themselves. I was parched from thirst and I entered the refreshment room at the terminal and asked the white American waiter if I could have a drink of water. He frowned and looked down his nose at me as if I was something unclean. "The place for you, my man, is the spittoon outside," he declared, as he dismissed me from his sight. I was so shocked that I could not move. I just stood there and stared at him for I could not bring myself to believe that anyone could refuse a man a drink of water because his skin happened to be a different color.[84]

Another incident involved Ghana's Finance Minister K. A. Gbedemah, who was in the United States on official business in 1957. A Howard Johnson's restaurant in Dover, Delaware, refused him service even after he had identified himself to the manager. Gbedemah's story made headlines in Africa. The Ghanaian press reminded the American people that Ghana had given Vice President Richard M. Nixon[85] and Senator Adlai Stevenson a warm reception six months earlier, prompting them to ask, "is this what we get in return?"[86]

Other similar incidents had happened to A. K. Adjei, minister of labor and cooperatives and leader of Ghana's delegation to the United Nations; Daniel Chapman, former cabinet secretary and the Ghanaian ambassador to Washington in the early 1960s; and Robert Gardiner, head of Ghana's civil service.[87] The State Department concluded its assessment of Ghana's impressions of the United States by reminding the commission that school integration incidents had had a particularly strong impact on Ghanaians.[88]

To avoid further such incidents against foreign dignitaries of color, the State Department began sending representatives to accompany them wherever they went in the United States.[89] Nevertheless, the White House and the State Department continued to find themselves in critical situations. Such incidents of discrimination against Africans traveling in the United States compounded the suspicions such travelers felt toward the country, the State Department report said. Furthermore,

. . . where such individuals are officials of the government or otherwise prominent in local affairs, American interests are adversely affected in a number of indirect ways – day-to-day operations are made difficult by unfriendliness or lack of cooperation.[90]

It is important to note that Nigeria, like Liberia and Ethiopia, was considerably more conservative and less militant than newly independent Ghana, Guinea, and Mali. The Pan-Africanist leadership of militant nations like Ghana mobilized its people by exposing them to information concerning American racial discrimination. It was a sign of power and independence to be able to criticize the most powerful nation in the world by using race to rally sentiments. The competition between the Soviet Union and its allies against the United States gave leverage to African leaders to manipulate, criticize, and, sometimes, challenge the United States at international gatherings. The U.S. government could not easily disregard the actions and opinions of African leaders. Ghana's vote in the U.N. General Assembly was equal to Sweden's, and Guinea's vote to Britain's. The State Department acknowledged this, for it believed that the United States' race problems provided African leaders with political opportunities that created a "potentially dangerous climate in which government and political leaders could, if they so wished, stir up public opinion against the United States for almost any reason whatsoever."[91]

In the Middle East, the report continued, the American race problem had become fodder for anti-American expression. In Iraq, street demonstrators protesting unpopular United States policies, such as its support of Israel and the Baghdad Pact, used the Little Rock crisis to vent their anger.[92] A government official in Egypt, referring to the Autherine Lucy case, described public sentiment to embassy personnel, saying "people read about this girl and said 'so that's American democracy! They can have it.' "[93]

The State Department's report added that despite U.S. anti-colonial efforts, the U.S. had found itself being classified by Indians with the United Kingdom, France, the Netherlands, Portugal, and other colonial powers. Periodic news stories of racial discrimination in the United States helped enforce India's belief that the United States was fundamentally committed to "white supremacy" and that it was more concerned with collaborating with other white nations to maintain its hegemony than it was in aiding the peoples of Asia and Africa. The report said that as far as responsible Indians were concerned, the country's treatment of African Americans under-mined its claims to leadership of the non-Communist world and tarnished its image as a democratic country.[94]

The State Department noted that because of high illiteracy rates in Indonesia, the few thousand members of the governing elite were the most critical of race relations in the United States and were particularly sensitive to such issues.[95] In Japan, people reacted to news of racial discrimination in America with cynicism since the United States, during its postwar occupation of Japan, claimed the role of Japan's mentor in the name of democracy.[96] The report concluded that demonstrations in Caracas against the Little Rock crisis during Vice President Nixon's visit in 1958 were a clear example of exploitation of the U.S. race policy in Latin America.[97]

As far as Europe was concerned, the report listed some examples of Western European outrage over racial incidents in the United States. In France, Little Rock had become a household name, while the Willie McGee and the Emmett Till affairs drew greater head-lines than they did in the United States.[98] The report stressed that coverage of civil rights violations in the press was "by no means limited to left journals."[99]

In Finland and Scandinavia, the treatment of African Americans "continues to attract general interest and arouses more criticism of the United States than any other matter."[100] Illustrative of the general sentiment in Italy was the position of the Vatican's publication *Osservatore Romano* during the Little Rock crisis. *Osservatore Romano* stated that "whoever professes racist principles, whoever defends them should not be allowed to exercise political rights, nor be eligible for any public office, just as in the case of most serious criminals."[101] This was not the first time the Vatican drew attention to racial discrimination in the United States. In 1950, the Vatican issued a report in which Pope Pius expressed friendship, affection, and sympathy for African Americans, and called upon American Catholics to redress the injustices bestowed on African Americans.[102] Such strong condemnation of racial policies in the United States had an impact far beyond the country's own shores because the Catholic Church in the United States had always been an influential actor in global affairs.

Discriminatory treatment of African Americans in the United States adversely affected the relations between the United States and the United Kingdom, Canada, and the West Indies. According to United States Information Agency reports, race problems in the United States cast a shadow on its moral position in the ideological struggle with the Soviet bloc, raising doubts about the U.S.'s ability to rally to its cause the increasingly important and politically active non-white segment of the world's population. State Department officials emphasized the poor position of the United States in dealing with British Commonwealth countries since the Commonwealth united nations of various races. The effect of American racism was very pronounced in the West Indies, "where the Negro race is politically dominant."[103] In addition, Spain and Portugal "entertain[ed] considerable misgivings with regard to the value and depth of American culture, and challenge[d] any apparent American claim to moral ascendancy."[104] In sum, the report concluded, the racial question kept the United States in a vulnerable position with regard to many of its allies worldwide.[105] As far as the impressions of Soviet citizens were concerned, the report said that, "Americans have been struck by the sophisticated understanding of the racial problem displayed by some of the more educated Soviet citizens."[106]

The State Department first channeled its report to the Civil Rights Commission, then to the White House,[107] and subsequently to Congress on September 9, 1959. Focusing on the three most

crucial areas of discrimination (voting, public education, and housing), the report warned Congress that "high vision, serious purpose, and imaginative leadership, in all branches of government
[are] the only solution to this problem that threatens to divide
America into two societies."[108] The commission emphasized, "the
pace of progress during the 96 years since emancipation has been
remarkable. But this is an age of revolutionary change. The colored
peoples of Asia and Africa, constituting a majority of the human
race, are swiftly coming into their own. . . . The future peace of the
world is at stake."[109]

The commission's report aptly demonstrates that executive action on civil rights reform was stimulated first and foremost by
international pressure at the moment that the United States was
competing fiercely with the Soviet Union for new strategic allies.
Certainly, Eisenhower had to react to the domestic situation caused
by Southern defiance to Court rulings on desegregation. Yet, as the
commission report illustrates, the administration placed primary
emphasis on the relationship between civil rights policy at home
and its global aspirations.

Conclusion

In this chapter, I have argued that international events following
World War II explain the timing of the Executive branch's active
role in addressing U.S. racial policies. International critics made it
clear that traditional and institutional discrimination against African Americans contradicted the democratic principles that the government professed in opposing Communism. The fear that Communism might sweep Africa and Asia and thus the United States
might not maintain its global leadership of the free world helped
pressure the U.S. government into cleaning its own house. The two
civil rights commissions discussed in this chapter equipped the
Truman and Eisenhower Administrations with a blueprint for racial
policy reforms. They also served as a response to growing international criticism. The commissions, especially the 1957 commission
with its congressional backing, were the first weapons against institutionalized racism in the United States.

Abroad, friends and foes alike were linking the mistreatment of African Americans to the country's inability to address issues of justice and democracy elsewhere. Both civil rights commissions stressed the interrelation of U.S. domestic policies and U.S. foreign policy goals. This linkage moved the debate on civil rights to the level of national interest, national security, and prerequisites of international relations and the fight against Communism. International politics took priority over states' rights, which for decades had helped to deter civil rights reforms. As Hubert Humphrey put it at the Democratic National Convention of 1948,

There are those who say to you – we are pushing this issue of civil rights. I say we are a hundred and seventy-two years late. . . . The time has arrived . . . to get out of the shadow of states' rights and walk forthrightly into the bright sunshine of human rights.[110]

Truman's 1947 committee and the 1957 Civil Rights Commission were pivotal in the battle against discrimination and segregation. Because these bipartisan independent agencies were able to demonstrate through original investigations, reports, and recommendations that Congress must act more promptly and more energetically, the two commissions should get significant credit for the civil rights legislation that followed. It is clear from State Department and USIA records that international pressures for race reforms in the United States were a force behind the commissions' reports and recommendations. The implications of the civil rights battle for America's foreign policy were too detrimental for any commission to overlook. The State Department made sure that the commissions did not underestimate the repercussions of continued racial injustice.

CHAPTER FOUR

International Pressure and the State's Response to Racial Segregation

School segregation has been singled out for hostile foreign comment in the United Nations and elsewhere.[1]

I fully realize that the attitude of President Eisenhower in mobilizing the North American Army towards Little Rock for the purpose of giving protection to nine Negro students is in large part determined by the convenience of international politics. The non-white peoples inhabiting the planet are many and very great. The persecution of Negroes is of no advantage to the international policies of the United States.[2]

It would be difficult to exaggerate the harm being done to the prestige and influence, and indeed to the safety of our nation and the world. Our enemies are gloating over this incident and using it everywhere to misrepresent our whole nation.[3]

The United States aspires for world leadership. She is anxious to introduce democracy in China, in Western Europe, in Japan, and in Southern Korea. It is time the "teachers" of democracy first applied the lessons of democracy at home before exporting it abroad.[4]

According to Justice Department memoranda prepared during the years of World War II, there were "safe" and "unsafe" areas for federal intervention in race matters. At the top of the list of "unsafe" areas was regulating "the intimate relations with the Negro," and "unsafe intervention" covered segregation practices that "should be reserved to the states and local alleviation."[5] The puzzle that emerges then is, why would first the Truman and later the Eisenhower Administration undertake civil rights reforms aimed specifically at desegregation, especially when it was widely recognized that such actions had high political cost? The Justice Department memoranda explicitly stated that, "So long as the South feels the federal government means to regulate its intimate relations with the Negro, the South will fight any federal intervention. This flame can easily be fanned into a terrifying conflagration."[6] In other words, desegregation is the wrong starting point for civil rights reforms. Why, then, was desegregation the focus of both the Truman and Eisenhower Administrations?[7] There were many facets to racial oppression in the United States. Lynching, job and housing discrimination, and the absence of due process and protection of the law are just a few examples. However, if one were to identify the area of U.S. race relations that received the most international criticism based on available State Department files, it would unquestionably be racial segregation of African Americans and of non-white foreign dignitaries and visiting students. Therefore, during and after the war years, segregation received a considerable share of the State and Justice Departments' attention to civil rights.

I argue that because segregation received the bulk of international attention, the Executive branch pursued desegregation specifically because of its saliency in the eyes of the world. Here I discuss first, litigative actions of the Justice and State Departments that promoted desegregation during the Truman years, and second, the litigative efforts of the State Department in *Brown v. Board of Education* and Eisenhower's decision to send federal troops to intervene in the Little Rock crisis. These litigative actions, along with Eisenhower's decision to use federal troops to enforce desegregation, exemplify the substance of civil rights reforms under the two administrations. International criticism of U.S. race policy was motivated first by several celebrated desegregation cases, and second, by the treatment non-white foreign diplomats, students, and business visitors received in the United States. I discuss each of these motivations in turn.

Two episodes of Southern resistance to school desegregation, used here as case studies, illustrate the interaction among federal and state governments and the international community: the Autherine Lucy case of 1956[8] and the Little Rock crisis of 1957–8.[9] In the Little Rock crisis, federal intervention, as President Eisenhower told the nation, was partly due to the crisis becoming an international event that enjoyed full display in the print media through radiophotos, newsreels, and television.

The fact that the Autherine Lucy case and the Little Rock crisis occurred at a time of American vulnerability abroad contributed to the government's resolve to address civil rights concerns. By the 1950s, the United States had launched comprehensive international economic development programs. As part of this effort, the country sponsored thousands of students from Asia and Africa to come to America. However, the Soviet Union was following the same strategy of economic, political, cultural, and military support of the newly independent countries. In fact, the Soviets provided more capital to Asian, African, and Middle Eastern nations than did the United States. Because the United States focused its foreign aid on rebuilding Europe, the Soviet Union was able to claim alliance with colonized peoples, while the United States became the ally of the colonial powers.[10] As Arthur M. Schlesinger, Jr. put it, "In Asia, in Africa, in Latin America, in industrial growth, in space, [C]ommunism was on the offensive."[11] The Soviets strategically attacked the U.S. government's decisions of how and where it spent money. A Soviet U.N. delegate reminded all in the General Assembly that while the United States

finds it possible to spend billions of dollars for the armaments race, for the maintenance of military bases and for financing aggressive military blocs with a view to obtaining world control and subjecting the peoples of other countries to the interests of American monopolists, hundreds of thousands or even millions of Americans of colored race are suffering because of lack of opportunity and lack of food and shelter because of racial discrimination.[12]

Revolutionary events kept the U.S. government on the alert and intensified its efforts to nullify its critics: a follow-up conference to Bandung in Cairo, Egypt of thirty-nine Asian and African countries where Western racism was denounced; the Hungarian crisis of 1956; the Berlin crisis throughout the 1950s; U.S. intervention in Lebanon in 1958; and the U.S. government's refusal to take a firm stand against the Union of South Africa's Apartheid policy and the French colonial policy in Algeria. To complicate matters further, America's support for Israel alienated the Arab nations. All of these international events conspired to place the United States on the defensive.

The technological advances the Soviets demonstrated in October and November 1957 by launching Sputnik I and II, thereby ending America's scientific "superiority," did not enhance America's international standing. At the same time, more and more Asian and African countries were gaining their independence, becoming voting members of the United Nations, and joining the nonaligned voting bloc initiated at the 1955 Bandung Conference. Asian and African countries were also beginning to exploit the competition between the United States and the Soviet Union successfully.

On the home front, the civil rights movement persevered. The lynching of fourteen-year-old Emmett Till, the 1955–6 Montgomery bus boycott, unjust court sentences in the South that the international community perceived as racially discriminatory, Southern defiance to school desegregation, and the 1958 death sentence of Jimmy Wilson in Alabama were examples of events that received international publicity and captured world attention. As international pressure mounted, so did the U.S. government's need for more intervention and for a solution to racial segregation. The Red Scare in the early 1950s intimidated some civil rights activists as well as government officials who pursued a progressive role in the struggle. However, the second half of the 1950s was marked by an intensified call, both at home and abroad, for U.S. civil rights reform.

The government's response to crises such as the Autherine Lucy case and the Little Rock crisis must be placed in a wider context. It should be contextualized within the international environment surrounding U.S. geopolitical goals and military competition with the

Soviet Union. The boundaries and implications of both cases were not solely domestic. These incidents attracted international attention and explicit international pressure, causing the Eisenhower Administration, particularly the State Department, to perceive these events as having crucial international significance for the United States as a world power.

International condemnation of U.S. racial policies was compounded by other realities. Non-white foreign dignitaries and students visiting the United States were not spared de jure segregation in the South and de facto segregation in the North. I include in this chapter some incidents of racial discrimination against foreign dignitaries and the outrage that these incidents produced. Responses to such incidents ranged from personal complaints to the Department of State, to ambassadors officially protesting to the Secretary of State. Racial incidents involving foreigners made headline news and provided renewed pressure points on U.S. officials both at home and abroad.

The Eisenhower Administration moved reluctantly in its first term. However, the course of events in the second term left Eisenhower with no choice but to confront the legion of influential domestic and international advocates of civil rights reform. The civil rights movement, largely invisible throughout Eisenhower's first term, was well established by the second. This is the background and these are the circumstances in which the Eisenhower Administration decided to intervene on behalf of African Americans.

Segregation, Foreign Policy, and the Supreme Court: 1948–53

Because of the need for concrete progress in changing the country's racial policies, the Truman Administration was creative in circumventing the legislative bog and congressional inaction. It used an avenue that had not been used before.[13] On October 30, 1947, one day after the Civil Rights Committee delivered *To Secure These Rights* to the president, Attorney General Tom Clark announced at a press conference that the Justice Department would participate in *Shelley v. Kraemer,* a case that challenged the constitutionality of legal enforcement of restrictive housing covenants.[14]

Shelley v. Kraemer was the first in a series of Supreme Court cases in which the Executive branch filed amicus curiae briefs in support of desegregation. By stressing to the court the international implications of U.S. race discrimination and focusing on the damage that segregation had caused in U.S. foreign relations, the Executive branch added a novel dimension to U.S. race politics. The government, in essence, legitimized the arguments of critics both abroad and at home that the country's racial friction posed difficulties for a country of superpower status and one that preaches democracy – that U.S. race policy was an international liability.

The State Department assisted in preparing the brief in *Shelley v. Kraemer.*[15] The brief stated that "the United States has been embarrassed in the conduct of foreign relations by acts of discrimination taking place in this country."[16] During oral arguments, the Justice Department made good use of President Truman's Civil Rights Committee report, *To Secure These Rights.* Solicitor General Philip Perlman said that the Court's enforcement of restrictive covenants would hamper the United States in its conduct of foreign affairs.[17]

In the amicus brief in *Shelley v. Kraemer,* the government reminded the Supreme Court that international agreements and resolutions signed by the United States prohibited racial segregation. The brief cited the United Nations Charter[18] by which the United States redefined its public policy with reference to racial equality:

Article 55 of the United Nations Charter states that the U.N. shall promote . . . uniform respect for, and observance of human rights and fundamental freedoms for all without distinction as to race. . . . Article 56 of the Charter states that all members of that organization pledge themselves to take joint and separate action in cooperation with the organization for the achievement of the purpose set forth in Article 55.[19]

In 1948, the Court agreed with the State and Justice Departments and ruled that restrictive covenants were not enforceable in court. Court enforcement of anti-Negro housing covenants among white private property owners was a violation of the Fourteenth Amendment.[20] Civil rights supporters celebrated the *Shelley* decision at home and overseas. Indian newspapers hailed the Court decision as "another victory in the battle for civil rights that is going on in America."[21]

Two years later, the administration took another step in its efforts against segregation. The issue at hand was the validity of railroad dining car segregation under the Interstate Commerce Act. Most interesting about *Henderson v. United States* was that the United States government intervened on the plaintiff's side against the Interstate Commerce Commission, another part of the government. In its amicus brief, the government included "recent remarks of representatives of foreign powers" in U.N. debates and subcommittee meetings that "typify the manner in which racial discrimination in this country is turned against us in the international field."[22]

The brief footnoted a U.N. Soviet representative arguing that "[g]uided by the principles of the United Nations Charter, the General Assembly must condemn the policy and practice of racial discrimination in the United States and any other countries of the American continent where such a policy was being exercised."[23] Another Soviet representative was quoted as asserting that "[in] the Southern states, the policy of racial discrimination was actually confirmed by law and most strictly observed in trains, restaurants, cinemas, and elsewhere."[24] A Polish U.N. representative was also quoted as saying he "did not believe that the United States Government had the least intention to conform to the recommendations which would be made by the United Nations with regard to the improvement of living conditions of the coloured population of that country."[25]

The government brief quoted from the Soviet newspaper *The Bolshevik* that,

The theory and practice of racial discrimination against the Negroes in America is known to the whole world. The poison of racial hatred has become so strong in post-war America that matters go to unbelievable lengths; for example a Negress injured in a road accident could not be taken to a neighbouring hospital since this hospital was only for "whites."[26]

The brief also included an editorial in the *Soviet Literary Gazette*, entitled "The Tragedy of Coloured America," which said that the United States was a country within a country. Coloured America is not allowed to mix with the other white America, it exists within it like the yolk in the white of an egg. Or, to be more exact, like a gigantic ghetto. The walls of this ghetto are invisible but they are nonetheless indestructible. They are placed within cities where the Negroes live in special quarters, in buses where the Negroes are assigned only the back seats, in hairdressers where they have special chairs.[27]

As in *Shelley,* the Supreme Court in *Henderson* ruled against segregation in railroad dining cars. The U.S. delegation to the United Nations used the *Henderson* ruling to "illustrate to delegations of the United Nations the progress being made in the United States through democratic procedure."[28] The government briefs in *Shelley* and *Henderson* explicitly linked racial segregation and U.S. efforts in fighting Communism. As long as Communism posed a threat to U.S. foreign policy goals and national security, the White House, the Justice and State Departments, and the Supreme Court had to take part in fighting racial segregation and discrimination at home.

The Supreme Court had a busy year in 1950 reviewing several segregation cases. Justifying its interest as amicus curiae in *McLaurin v. Oklahoma State Regents for Higher Education*[29] and in *Sweatt v. Painter,*[30] the Justice Department perceived the cases to "have great importance . . . because they test the vitality and strength of the democratic ideals to which the United States is dedicated"[31] and that "racial segregation is itself a manifestation of inequality and discrimination."[32]

The Truman Administration warned that racial discrimination and segregation created serious foreign policy repercussions and that the highest court of the land

is here asked to place the seal of constitutional approval upon an undisguised species of racial discrimination. If the imprimatur of constitutionality should be put on such a denial of equality, one would expect the foes of democracy to exploit such an action for their own purposes. The ideals embodied in our Bill of Rights would be ridiculed as empty words, devoid of any real substance. The lag between what Americans profess and what we practice would be used to support the charges of hypocrisy and the decadence of democratic society.[33]

To remind the court of the global "winds of change," the administration concluded its brief with an explicit description of the intersection of domestic policies and international politics. It argued that

> it is in the context of a world in which freedom and equality must become living realities, if the democratic way of life is to survive, that the issues in these cases should be viewed. In these times, when even the foundations of our free institutions are not altogether secure, it is especially important that it again be unequivocally affirmed that the Constitution of the United States, like the Declaration of Independence and the other great state papers in American history, places no limitations, express or implied, on the principle of the equality of all men before the law.[34]

As in *Shelley* and *Henderson*, the Supreme Court ruled in favor of *McLaurin* and *Sweatt*. However, the constitutionality of the doctrine of "separate but equal" that was established by *Plessy v. Ferguson* in 1896 remained intact until the *Brown* case four years later.

Thus is the nature of civil rights reform under the Truman Administration. These reforms focused all but exclusively on desegregation.[35] As we shall see, this focus remained exactly the same under the Eisenhower Administration. The two most celebrated civil rights initiatives that occurred during Eisenhower's term in office were the *Brown v. Board of Education* case and Eisenhower's decision to send federal troops into Little Rock. In each of these cases, the Executive branch focused specifically on ending segregation.

Brown v. Board of Education, 1954

It has been said that Eisenhower's principal contribution to U.S. civil rights was his appointment of Earl Warren as chief justice. Warren replaced Fred M. Vinson, who died of a heart attack in September 1953, and his appointment was confirmed by the Senate only two months before the May 1954 *Brown* decision. Not only did the new chief justice push forward the *Brown* case but he labored hard to get a united Court with a single unanimous opinion. The

Court decision in *Brown v. Board of Education* sealed the Eisenhower Administration's efforts to resolve the problem of school segregation. In its brief, the government argued that,

The United States is trying to prove to the people of the world, of every nationality, race, and color, that a free democracy is the most civilized and most secure form of government. . . . We must set an example for others. . . . The existence of discrimination against minority groups in the United States has an adverse effect upon our relations with other countries. Racial discrimination furnishes grist for the [C]ommunist propaganda mills, and it raises doubts even among friendly nations as to the intensity of our devotion to the democratic faith.[36]

The brief quoted Secretary of State Dean Acheson's letter to the attorney general. Acheson wrote,

During the past six years, the damage to our foreign relations attributable to [race discrimination] has become progressively greater. The United States is under constant attack in the foreign press, over the foreign radio, and in such international bodies as the United Nations because of various practices of discrimination against minority groups in this country. As might be expected, Soviet spokesmen regularly exploit this situation in propaganda against the United States, both within the United Nations and through radio broadcasts and the press, which reaches all corners of the world. Some of these attacks against us are based on falsehood or distortion; but the undeniable existence of racial discrimination gives unfriendly governments the most effective kind of ammunition for their propaganda warfare.[37]

Explaining the State Department's interest in *Brown,* Acheson said,

The hostile reaction among normally friendly peoples, many of whom are particularly sensitive in regard to the status of non-European races, is growing in alarming proportions. In such countries the view is expressed more and more vocally that the United States is hypocritical in claiming to be the champion of democracy while permitting practices of racial discrimination here in this country. . . . Other peoples cannot understand how [school segregation] can exist in a country which professes to be a staunch supporter of freedom, justice, and democracy. The sincerity of the United States in this respect will be judged by its deeds as well as by its words.[38]

Concluding his letter, the secretary of state repeated that "racial discrimination in the United States remains a source of constant embarrassment to this government in the day-to-day conduct of its foreign relations . . . it jeopardizes the effective maintenance of our moral leadership of the free and democratic nations of the world."[39]

Because segregation was rampant in the District of Columbia, where foreign dignitaries and diplomats lived and visited, the government, in its *Brown* brief, singled out the nation's capital:

This city is the window through which the world looks into our house. The embassies, legations, and representatives of all nations are here, at the seat of the [f]ederal [g]overnment. Foreign officials and visitors naturally judge this country and our people by their experiences and observations in the nation's capital. . . . The shamefulness and absurdity of Washington's treatment of Negro Americans is highlighted by the presence of many dark-skinned foreign visitors. Capital custom not only humiliates colored citizens, but is a source of considerable embarrassment to these visitors. Foreign officials are often mistaken for American Negroes and refused food, lodging and entertainment.[40]

It is important to note that not only was Washington, D.C., singled out in the government's brief, but the brief also highlighted racism against non-white foreigners. It is obvious from the above quote that if foreigners had been spared the indignation of racial segregation, the intensity of the government interest, as a concerned party, would not have been the same, at least not at that particular time. The government briefs in all the above cases express deep concern about segregation and global perception of American racism at the inception of the Cold War.

The State Department used the *Brown* decision to convince its critics of the progress in race relations. Within an hour of the Supreme Court's decision, the Voice of America broadcast the news all over the world in thirty-five different languages.[41] Carl Rowan, an African American journalist frequently sent by the government on speaking tours to Asia and Africa, wrote that U.S. embassy officials in India told him to expect less criticism over U.S. racial discrimination because "the United States Information Service, the Voice of America and other agencies had done a thorough job of publicizing" the Supreme Court decision.[42]

Officials in Brazil viewed *Brown* as "establishing the just equality of the races, which is essential to universal harmony and peace."[43] The press in French West Africa celebrated the decision, although some skepticism was expressed over its implementation. In Dakar, the American consul general informed the State Department that

while it is, of course too soon to speculate on the long-range effects of the decision in this area, it is well to remember that school segregation more than any other single factor has lowered the prestige of the United States among Africans here and the over-all results, therefore, can hardly fail to be beneficial.[44]

Brown v. Board of Education helped improve America's image abroad but only for a short time. With growing Southern defiance of the Supreme Court ruling, *Brown* became a double-edged sword. International critics used it as proof that the country was not sincere in granting African Americans their rights of full citizenship and protection of the law. Southern white defiance became a test for the federal government as well as the effectiveness of the judicial system.

Southern Defiance

The Autherine Lucy Case

In the arena of school segregation, the 1956 Autherine Lucy case was the first episode to become an international event. An opinion survey conducted by the United States Information Agency of Western Europe indicated that "the Autherine Lucy case qualifies as not less than an international *cause celebre* with from a quarter to a third in Western Europe alluding more or less specifically to the incident as a basis of recent unfavorable impressions of the treatment of Negroes in the U.S. . . ." The USIA report concluded that the positive impact of the *Brown v. Board of Education* decision was losing ground; more importantly, the country's prestige in other areas besides race relations was suffering because of the Autherine Lucy case and similar incidents. Of importance to the State Department was that "the opinions of the more influential elite were no less adverse than the opinions of the rest of the population in every country surveyed."[45]

International University Student Youth, an organization representing students from five continents, protested the "color bar" in American education. They sent to the United States delegation to the United Nations a petition expressing deep concern over the "spirit of racial intolerance and inveterate hatred against members of another race that have become evident in one of the most important countries and strongholds of the free world." The petitioners expected that justice would be served to Lucy "on the lines of the historic ruling of the U.S. Supreme Court."[46]

The University of Copenhagen offered Lucy a full fellowship "since the students [at] Alabama University prevented her from completing her studies." Officials at the University of Copenhagen sent a copy of their offer to the President of the University of Alabama.[47] Respected Danish academics and rectors of Danish universities sent Lucy sympathetic messages and warm wishes for her "continued fight for democracy and human rights." Newspaper editorials expressed "distress that such things happen in the so-called 'free America!'"[48] The strongest blast was in the Danish independent newspaper *Information*, which castigated the "apartheid policy" of the Southern states when it stated, "In old Europe one can smell the smoke of witches' fires and of Nazism. . . . In other continents, people of a different color clench their fists."[49]

U.S. embassy officials in Copenhagen informed the State Department that preoccupation with America's racial problems remained constantly at an abnormally high level:

. . . the Danes react with an emotion seemingly out of character with their usual easy-going manner . . . living themselves in a closely knit, all white, uni-racial, economically homogenous society, the Danes lack comprehension of the depth and complexity of the problem and thus see it only in black and white.[50]

However, the embassy warned that irritation over the excessive Danish preoccupation with the beam in other fellow's eye should not obscure the real and continuing damage to American prestige from such tragedies as the Emmett Till case and the unfortunate riots attending Miss Lucy's efforts . . . so long as southern defiance of the Supreme Court's decision continues and incidents take place, the Danes can be expected to continue their avid interest and frequently to misread or exaggerate various incidents to the detriment of U.S. prestige and reputation.[51]

In Sweden, the Autherine Lucy affair renewed criticism of the United States' treatment of African Americans. The Swedish press covered the Lucy case so extensively that "it is not too much to say that today she is one of the best known Americans in Sweden."[52] Swedish newspapers portrayed the U.S. racial situation as bad and seriously worsening, and this "has unquestionably resulted in damage to America's prestige." According to U.S. embassy officials in Sweden, the Swedes regarded most American attempts to achieve racial harmony as hypocritical. They were of the opinion that no matter what the Supreme Court did, the die-hard Southerners would always come up with something like interposition. The Swedish people were indignant over the Lucy case and the memory of previous "injustices" such as the Till murder of 1955. To make matters worse, U.S. officials in Sweden added that, "the powerful entertainment personality of Josephine Baker" told the Swedish people from "first hand experience" about how "terrible the United States was to its Negroes." At one event where she was the main speaker to five thousand people, Baker's speech, delivered in English, was translated into Swedish and sold as the main program, thus giving her views even greater circulation in Sweden.[53]

In France, U.S. consulates received several protest letters.[54] In The Hague, front-page newspaper headlines "deplored" the "disgraceful," "humiliating affair," and "scandalous incident" of Autherine Lucy. The influential independent newspaper *Labor Het Parool* in The Hague quoted the U.S. Declaration of Independence, commenting that "many friends of us who continue to see that big republic as a bulwark of freedom can only hope that growing realization of enormous harm which this detestable discrimination causes to the good reputation of America will help put an end to such disgraceful scenes." The liberal *Algemeen Handelsblad* concluded that repeated efforts of the Deep South to obstruct Supreme Court rulings are causing serious harm to U.S. interests abroad.[55]

The State Department ignored Autherine Lucy's sudden fame in the international press. However, the department expressed concern over Lucy's response to the Polish people. In a letter published in Polish newspapers, Lucy thanked the Poles, who were "cruelly persecuted for the sole reason of being Poles, and would easily understand my situation."[56]

In Nigeria, the *Daily Service,* one of the largest and most influential newspapers, published a cartoon entitled, "Alabama University doesn't care that Abe Lincoln said that all men are created equal: but maybe it don't apply to girls."[57] The paper asserted that Paul Robeson had been labeled a Communist just because of his race and that Robeson found democracy in "New Moscow" rather than New Mexico. U.S. officials in Lagos assured the State Department that the writer of the article was not a Communist.[58] Lucy also made front-page news in India. Particularly disturbing to the State Department was that the Lucy incident overshadowed the *Brown v. Board of Education* decision and the overall progress in U.S. race relations.

The Indian press warned that despite the commitment of the federal government to promote desegregation, "the sorry spectacle in the South is detracting not a little from the prestige of American democracy and all it stands for."[59] The daily *Lokasevak* charged that race relations in the United States appeared to be "even worse than [in] the Union of South Africa." To the Indians, the fact that African Americans decided to launch a Gandhian-type movement "clearly demonstrates how acute racial discrimination still is in the United States."[60] A United States Information Agency official confirmed that the agency's attempts to publicize progress in the arena of U.S. civil rights, such as the *Brown v. Board of Education* decision, were being overshadowed by racial incidents and that "if it were not for our racial problems, we would be way ahead of the game by now. As it is, it seems we are just able to hold our own."[61]

Following the 1956 Autherine Lucy affair,[62] international outrage over school segregation in the United States subsided, but did not disappear. The State Department continued to receive discouraging news from U.S. consulates and embassies about the damage to the country's prestige. U.S. officials in Turkey said that "in the Embassy's opinion, no other subject causes more damage to U.S. prestige and [the] role of champion of democracy and human rights ineluctably thrust upon it." Turkish leaders believed America's image would suffer throughout the democratic world, and that "color discrimination in the United States is serious because it further injures Western prestige already suffering under the 'colonialist' label."[63]

In Canada, America's race problems continued to make headlines. *La Patrie*, with the largest circulation of any French-Canadian newspaper, concluded that the color problem in the United States was proof that slavery officially and legally existed under one form or another.[64] But it was not until the Little Rock crisis of September 1957 that another full-scale international outburst over U.S. racial conditions broke out.

The Little Rock Crisis

Five days following the outbreak of the Little Rock crisis on September 4, 1957, Congress passed the first civil rights legislation since Reconstruction.[65] But the positive impact of the 1957 Civil Rights Act was lost on the international community because the world was watching events unfold in Little Rock. Governor Faubus dispatched the Arkansas National Guard to prevent nine courageous African American students from entering Little Rock Central High.[66] The whole world watched the most dramatic clash between federal and state authorities since the Civil War. They saw pictures of armed soldiers and screaming whites bearing down on a black girl with books in her arms and incomparable courage, dignity, and perseverance trying to pass by the troops and simply enter the school.

The Little Rock crisis occurred at a time when the U.S. government could least afford another black eye internationally. President Eisenhower's decision to intervene twenty days into the crisis by sending the 101st Airborne to Arkansas was not totally voluntary.[67] Eisenhower opposed desegregation of the armed forces in 1948, resisted federal intervention in racial issues since 1953, refused to endorse the 1954 *Brown* decision,[68] and in 1956 declared that achieving equality should be handled at the local and state levels because racial issues were "matters of the heart not of legislation." Not only had the civil rights struggle reached its peak at home, but also, as argued earlier, America's position in global affairs was increasingly vulnerable at the time. On September 24, the president was forced by threats of violence to mobilize federal troops to restore order in Little Rock and to escort and protect the nine African American students who were to attend Little Rock High. The troops remained in the school for the entire school year. While major constitutional issues such as states' rights were involved in the dispatch of troops to Little Rock, Eisenhower explained his action to the nation by stressing the international ramifications of the crisis. His secretary of state and the great majority of the nation's press followed suit.[69]

The Little Rock crisis provided more evidence to U.S. critics all over the world. Most criticism came from Europe and Africa, but Asia,[70] the Middle East,[71] South America,[72] Canada, and Australia[73] contributed their share. Critics included elite groups, university students, labor unions, and professional syndicates as well as average citizens whose sentiments were revealed in public opinion surveys. The volume and intensity of international criticism and the expressed concerns of U.S. officials over the implications of Little Rock were tremendous.

Little Rock captured the attention of "the very large majority of the population in major world capitals, invoking worldwide reaction."[74] Not only was international opinion about the treatment of African Americans in the United States "highly adverse, but more often than not the predominant feeling [was] that Negro-white relations have been worsening rather than improving over the past few years."[75] The strongly prevailing feeling in cities across the world was that the current developments lowered America's standing and prestige in the world.[76] The United States Information

Agency estimated that the "losses" to the United States were "of such a magnitude as to outweigh the effects of any recent factors which have contributed to increases in U.S. standing."[77]

The U.S. diplomatic mission in Denmark was "embarrassed over Danish reaction to Little Rock." The Danish people were appalled by the violence. The embassy asked the State Department for help in responding to the public protest.[78] Because of Little Rock, derogatory news coverage of the United States filled the Swedish media. The liberal *Svenska Morgonbladet* strongly condemned "the United States, which went to war to fight Nazism and its racial persecutions." The semiofficial publication *Morgan Tidningen* expressed concern over the damage to U.S. prestige abroad.[79]

Swiss editorial and news coverage of Little Rock exceeded any previous publicity given to the United States "with photographs appearing in newspapers and newsreels."[80] The entire crisis was described as "inflicting grave damage on the moral position of the [W]estern world at a precise time when the U.N. General Assembly [is] debating the Hungarian tragedy."[81] U.S. embassy officials concluded that the events would "undoubtedly adversely affect American position and prestige in the mind of the average Swiss" and that the general reaction was "one of sober dismay over display of such violence" and resulted in "incalculable harm" done to the Western position throughout the non-European world.[82]

According to the American consul general in Amsterdam, even the reserved Dutch, who usually did not publicize their feelings, spoke with fervency about what was happening to African American children in Little Rock. The Dutch viewed discreetly the actions of public officials, such as state governors, forcibly denying African American children the right to a good education. Dutch citizens viewed Little Rock "as un[be]coming of a nation which continually affirms to the world its devotion to principles of liberty, equality, and equal opportunity for all citizens." In addition, the consul general reported that the Dutch worried

lest what is happening in Arkansas weaken America, in her contest with Soviet [C]ommunism over the uncommitted areas of Asia, Africa and the Middle East – areas where there is a real sensitivity to color discrimination.

They believe that a weakening of America's moral leadership in the world indirectly hurts America's allies. . . . *Papers urge President Eisenhower to use his great office to resolve the issue as soon as possible. De Waarheid* used the Little Rock incident saying "Washington wishes to impose its will on the World but in Arkansas Eisenhower is powerless. Neither President Eisenhower nor Adlai Stevenson are endeavoring to halt American colonialism – the 6th Fleet's operations against Syria and the actions of the Arkansas militia against the Negro are but different sides of the same policy."[83]

In Amsterdam, U.S. officials were told that there was very little difference between "Hitlerian methods and the activities of American racists" and "that hurts America in the eyes of the world." A news editorial entitled "Just the same as the actions of the little bastards of the Hitler Jugend . . . Shame on America" asked if there was "no one in the U.S.A. who can tell these boys full of hate that some 150 years ago their ancestors fetched Negroes as slaves from Africa, making big money on those cargoes of human flesh. These people do great harm to American friendship. What dirty minds."[84]

The Irish accused the Southern states of "put[ting] a new heart into Negro-baiting KKK" and of giving Communist propagandists "considerable material for innumerable sermons to colored people everywhere."[85] The news media in Luxembourg concurred with the Irish that Little Rock did more harm to "America's moral voice, especially among colored people of the world, than is befitting for the leader of the free world"[86] and that Little Rock was "a happy find for the [C]ommunists as a means of overshadowing the condemnation of the Hungarian massacre and the new anti-[S]emitism in the Soviet Union."[87] Arkansas Governor Faubus was mocked for comparing the occupation of Little Rock by federal troops to the German occupation of Paris and the Soviet attack on Budapest.[88] *Luxemburger Wort,* the official mouthpiece of Luxembourg, declared that Little Rock had made a very bad international impression, that the United States had been wasting dollars and weapons to stop the Russian offensive in the Middle East and elsewhere among colored peoples, and that "Little Rock was like a cold shower."[89]

The British expressed cynicism that Americans should lecture them about having "an empire in India" and "a colony in Africa" while they had Little Rock. A British correspondent told American journalist Mike Wallace that "respectable people in Britain are saying they do not want to hear of Rev. Billy Graham coming to preach another crusade. He'd better stay home and christianize the Americans. We have been preached at enough."[90]

In Belgium, Little Rock drew greater interest than any other American domestic issue. Newspapers sharply questioned the sincerity of the high moral attitude adopted by the United States in international affairs. According to the American embassy in Brussels, the Belgian media seemed more concerned about the effects of the Arkansas events on American prestige in Asia and Africa than about their effects on Belgium.[91]

Letters and petitions from Europe were also directed at U.S. officials. Student bodies in Austria sent open letters to Arkansas Governor Faubus comparing his actions and attitude with those of "Hitler . . . whose regime persecuted men only because of their race." The letters stated that African American soldiers fought against Fascism in World War II and yet the governor was denying their rights. The letter concluded that "events in Arkansas have most seriously shaken the belief of the world in the freedom mission of the U.S. . . ."[92] The International Federation of the Union of Education, "in the name of seven and a half million teachers," expressed its indignation to President Eisenhower over the events at Little Rock and demanded "respect for the rights of Negro children and the banning of all educational segregation."[93]

Of course the Soviets had a field day with Little Rock. To them, the "racial terror" in Arkansas was "not just instances but the custom in America"; that "white-faced but black-souled gentlemen commit their dark deeds . . . then these thugs put on white gloves and mount the rostrum in the U.N. General Assembly, and hold forth about freedom and democracy"; and that the U.S. government was "more concerned about the 'international repercussions' than the violations of human rights."[94]

Reaction to Little Rock was restrained in some European countries. In Germany, for example, the people's awareness of their own vulnerability on the question of persecution of racial minorities did not permit them to blame Americans or report with indignation the events in Arkansas. In addition, German political parties were competing for U.S. support. Nevertheless, editorials stressed that the United States must guard its "world-wide reputation as benefactor and guardian of democracy" and not provide "grist for Soviet propaganda."[95]

In Africa, Little Rock provided an avenue for attacking U.S. foreign policy and for criticizing the leadership the United States was seeking in Africa and "the cause of liberty of the individual throughout the world."[96] With the competition between the United States and the Soviet Union for an African sphere of influence at its height, Little Rock provided opportunities for political maneuvering not lost on many of the African nations. In Kenya, Little Rock received more attention than developments in Ghana, Malayan independence, or the United Nations debates on Hungary. The Asian community, a minority in Kenya, expressed sympathy for African Americans, given that they themselves "would perhaps become victims of discrimination at the hands of Africans" when Kenya gained its independence. In editorials, the vital interest of Asians was revealed in statements such as, "the African leadership must be made to feel that this colony can become self-governing without instilling fear and suspicion in the minds of non-Africans."[97]

Political parties in Uganda used Little Rock to compete for "the title of sole Uganda champions of American Negro rights" in order to draw voters and to increase their political clout.[98] The Uganda National Congress, one of the leading African political parties, sent Eisenhower a letter questioning, in light of Little Rock, the sincerity of his declared aims. The letter suggested that:

Before America can tackle any international problem, she should first and foremost show a clean record at home and we believe this is a prerequisite to American success abroad. . . . We are aware of the American policy of establishing influence in the emergence of African countries but we would like to inform you and the people of America that such attempts are incompatible with the present events in your country. Mr. President, your Congress has been scandalized and the American prestige and respect are at stake . . . [we] will never cooperate with any country whose racial policy is short of equality and our emphasis is doubled in the event of treating [N]egroes on a standard short of human dignity.[99]

The United Congress, the second leading party in Uganda, also sent a letter to Eisenhower expressing "great shock" that the Little Rock crisis could take place in a country that Uganda perceived as a leader of human rights and stated that such "obstruction of justice" was damaging to the prestige of America in Africa. The American Consulate in Kampala asked the State Department to respond to both political parties in Uganda.[100]

Governor Faubus was the target of Nigerian attack "for giving the U.S. one more black-eye in the eyes of the world."[101] Asian and African U.N. delegates, one editorial observed, would be in jail if they happened to be in Little Rock. The editorial asked "what moral right have Americans to condemn apartheid in South Africa while still maintaining it by law?"[102] The Nigerian news media concluded that the United States could not be champion "of the colonial peoples while championing inequality in its backyard."[103] Despite this harsh criticism, embassy officials characterized the Nigerian attack as tolerant and warned that "this tolerance will [not] continue in the presence of any future racial disturbances" in the United States.[104]

In Mozambique, Little Rock became a symbol of black-white relations in the United States at a time when America was trying "to condemn colonialism or racial segregation elsewhere in the world." Embassy personnel warned the State Department that "there seems to be no question but that our moral standing has been very considerably damaged" and that "any pretension of an American to advise any European government on African affairs at this point would be hypocrisy."[105] The French in West Africa exploited Little Rock to tell the world that, when it came to race, they did a better job in Africa and France. The French regarded Little Rock as a political opportunity to blackmail the United States. They hoped Little Rock "would make the U.S. a little more sympathetic to France's problem in Algeria, especially at the [up]coming U.N. session."[106]

Although news coverage of Little Rock in South Africa was overshadowed by coverage of the Soviet Sputnik and Muttnik, the episode was "one of the worst [U.S. officials] have had to cope with."[107] Influential Afrikaners who supported Apartheid used Little Rock as proof that integration would not work and that those forces against integration were gaining ground in the United States.[108]

There were those who described federal intervention in Little Rock as a continuation of America's role in protecting human rights, a role it carried during World War II in Europe.[109] Eisenhower was viewed as merely completing the work begun by President Lincoln.[110]African politicians in French West Africa told U.S. officials that until Eisenhower actually sent the troops to Little Rock, African opinion was that the president "would not dare use federal troops to enforce desegregation."[111] However, the international community perceived its own activism as a contributing factor to Eisenhower's decision to intervene.[112]

Celebrating the U.S. government action in Little Rock, officials in Rio de Janeiro praised the freedom of the U.S. press in reporting racial incidents, compared to the "concealment of crimes by Russia."[113] Others appealed to the United Nations for measures that would force Americans to respect the law. Violations such as those that occurred in Little Rock, they argued, should never be allowed to happen again. They further argued that "democratic people everywhere are disturbed and ashamed at the continued racist discrimination against and [the] oppression of the Negro people in the United States."[114] Eisenhower's tardy intervention received mostly positive international response,[115] with some accusing him of procrastination "which leaves a bitter aftertaste"[116] and for failing to take a stronger stand on civil rights legislation.[117] The Swedish press reminded Eisenhower that the Western world would be watching with concern and that federal authorities that were unsuccessful in implementing the law would be a serious threat to the position of the United States in the free world.[118]

Federal intervention in Little Rock helped improve the United States' image abroad. Nevertheless, federal action could not stop the long-term negative impact the event had on U.S. prestige, international public opinion, and the United States' geopolitical objectives. In 1958, USIA surveys revealed that "irritation at the United States is very widespread" and that Little Rock was one of the leading causes of anti-American sentiment. While international opinions of race relations in the United States were already negative, "Little Rock confirmed previously held views of racial discrimination."[119] There was a dramatic decline in foreign confidence that "what America says" equaled "what America does." USIA officials rationalized the unchanged impressions of some countries over the Little Rock crisis by "the fact that America's standing in the area of race relations [in these countries] was already in a very depressed state prior to the Arkansas desegregation incidents, and hence not readily susceptible to further decrease."[120]

Americans who traveled overseas brought home bleak assessments of the Little Rock aftermath. For example, after a five-month world tour, Dr. Maurice Eisendrafth, the president of the Union of Hebrew Congregations, told the *New York Post* that the country's failure to address race relations, magnified by Little Rock, had alienated millions of Asians and Africans and stated that "the reservoir of goodwill toward America is being dried out." Dr. Eisendrafth suggested that Eisenhower should impress on state governors the dynamics among America's foreign policy interests, its national security, and its race policies at home.[121]

The detrimental implications Little Rock had on the U.S. image abroad was summed up in a 1958 State Department report. The effect of the incident

is definitely adverse to our interests. . . . It clearly results to some extent in the weakening of our moral position as the champion of freedom and democracy, and in the raising or reinforcing of doubts as to the sincerity of our professions of concern for the welfare of others particularly in the non-white world. Moreover, it provides a solid target for anti-American propaganda.[122]

how so?

In the aftermath of Little Rock, the federal government became more active in enforcing public school desegregation. The passage of the 1957 Civil Rights Act was the beginning of the end for state and local government hegemony in the field of civil rights.[123]

As noted earlier, ugly racial incidents that foreign officials and foreign students experienced in the United States heightened the Truman and Eisenhower Administrations' concerns, especially the

State Department's, over institutionalized and legalized racial seg-regation. The following section illustrates how such incidents added to the pressures on the U.S. government and left the Tru-man and Eisenhower Administrations in a vulnerable position.

a not much of a narrative here...

Diplomatic Embarrassments: Segregation "Fiascoes" Involving Foreign Dignitaries and Foreign Students

As noted previously, locating the United Nations in New York meant that hundreds of influential non-white diplomats came to the United States for the first time and found themselves face to face with American prejudice and segregation. Many found their skin color a barrier to getting service in restaurants, hotels, and even decent transportation and housing. Non-white diplomats and other traveling guests were caught up in the mesh of American racial discrimination.

Compounding the situation were the horror stories these diplo-mats read about the ongoing black struggle. Among other stories that they heard, the diplomats read and saw images of lynching, the Montgomery bus boycott, police brutality against peaceful demon-strators, the Emmett Till lynching, and the mockery trial and ac-quittal of his murderers, and the government's censorship of W. E. B. DuBois and Paul Robeson.[124] Frustrated Secretary of State John Foster Dulles described the situation as "ruining our foreign policy. The effect of this in Asia and Africa will be worse for us than Hungary for the Russians."[125] In anticipation of such damaging events, the State Department drastically changed its handling of instances of discrimination against foreigners after World War II. Some examples are illustrative.

In 1943, when an Indian visitor to the United States was denied service in a Virginia restaurant and complained to the State Depart-ment, the State Department decided that "transmitting the com-plaint to the Governor of Virginia would not be effective in pre-venting similar incidents . . . but would serve only to irritate the Governor."[126] When a similar incident involving a Jamaican digni-tary took place in a Miami airport restaurant in 1945, the American consul general in Jamaica informed the State Department that the incident caused an uproar of anti-American sentiment. Jamaican leaders described the United States as "devoid of any decency, devoid of any culture, and devoid of any of that human feelin[g] that makes for a respectful citizenry." The American consul general further stated that as far as the Jamaican people were concerned, the United States could not buy respect, it had to earn it.[127]

While the government could have certainly chosen to ignore incidents of discrimination targeting foreign visitors, it could not afford the negative publicity generated by each incident, especially after 1945.[128] Furthermore, the State Department had to respond to formal complaints filed by foreign embassies in the United States. Such was the case when the Haitian embassy formally complained that its secretary of agriculture, Francois Georges, was the target of discrimination in Biloxi, Mississippi. The National Association of Commissioners, Secretaries, and Directors of Agriculture invited Georges to attend its conference in Biloxi. Upon his arrival, Georges was told that for "reasons of color" he could not stay in the hotel. When Georges pressed his claim to a room, the hotel manager offered him "servants' quarters" and informed him that his meals would be served in his room. Georges left at once for Washington, where Haiti's president, Estime ordered him home. In the presence of Haiti's president who "remained gloomy throughout," Georges told the U.S. ambassador to Haiti that he should understand "how I would not wish to visit your country soon again." The U.S. ambassador told the State Department that it was "unfortunate that we should have lost an honest and influential friend in this way."[129]

In Washington, the assistant secretary of state met with the Haitian ambassador, who told him that the treatment of Francois Georges "does not well accord with the policy of sympathy" that the United States has been preaching around the world. He informed the State Department of his government's decision to decline all invitations to events in the United States "where our delegates would be exposed to slights not to be endured by the representatives of a sovereign and friendly country."[130]

The 1947 Biloxi incident made headlines in Haitian newspapers. Editorials mocked the "defenders of American democracy" who had before their eyes "the brutal fact of what this democracy is." Editorials asked how could "serious people still speak of American democracy" and pointed out that Biloxi reinforced the "unhappy opinion held throughout the world of the stupid color prejudice rotting certain southern states of the United States."[131]

The consequences of the humiliation Francois Georges suffered in the United States were not lost on American business firms. One businessman wrote Secretary of State George Marshall that at a time when U.S. international relations "not only presuppose[d] but require[d] the utmost tact," incidents of this nature should be deplored.[132]

American firms conducting business with Asian nations were outraged by the treatment some of their visitors endured while in the United States. Indians, in particular, were the victims of many ugly experiences. Morris Rosenthal, a prominent New York executive, wrote Under Secretary of State Dean Acheson that an Indian business associate was refused cafeteria service at the Washington National Airport and had filed a formal complaint with the Indian embassy. Rosenthal asked Acheson how such an incident could take place in a country where nations of all races were invited to meet. "If such treatment is to be accorded to them in our national capital, the world at large will soon lose respect for our democracy and feel that we are guilty of many of the sins against which we ourselves fought during the war."[133] Rosenthal also wrote letters to Senators Arthur Vandenberg and John Connally because they attended many international settlements that they "should be keenly aware of this problem," and therefore could see to it that racial discrimination be eliminated at home if we [are to] have proper influence among the nations of the world."[134]

The State Department alerted the airport authorities that it had received a formal complaint from the Indian embassy. Department officials said that when foreigners were mistreated at the airport of the nation's capital, "resentments are created that seriously affect our relations with friendly and important countries." The department recognized that the airport was applying the segregation laws of the Commonwealth of Virginia, but argued that "concessions must be made to avoid similar incidents."[135]

Enforcement of racial segregation at airport facilities became a frequent problem for the State Department. A dark-skinned man refused service at the airport restaurant in Houston in 1955 turned out to be the ambassador from India. Route 40 leading to Washington, D.C., was the scene of many embarrassing incidents.[136] State Department officials had to take action. In a series of meetings, department officials urged airport administrators to take measures to prevent segregation of foreigners. It justified its interest in an otherwise local matter by the commitment "this government had made in agreeing to have the capital of the U.N. in this country."[137] Airport officials agreed to bring in arbitrators who would work with local commissioners, hotels, airports, railroads, and chambers of commerce. They also agreed to bypass Senate representatives lest the problem might become "a political or jurisdictional issue."[138]

It was not very long before the Indian embassy was provoked again into protest. Mohandas Ghandhi's personal physician was barred from a restaurant during a visit to the United States. The embassy filed another complaint with the State Department. The incident was reported in every newspaper in Bombay, Gandhi's hometown.[139] Years later, the Indian ambassador, G. L. Mehta, was separated from a group of diplomats at the Houston Airport dining room. This time Secretary of State John Foster Dulles and the mayor of Houston extended their apologies.[140]

It was not uncommon for American companies stationed in India to send their employees to the United States for training. These visits "turned out to be disastrous . . . because the representatives were treated as Negroes in the United States and often returned with deeply entrenched anti-American feelings."[141] In an effort to avoid such embarrassing episodes, American companies advised their Indian employees to always wear turbans when traveling in the United States.[142] At the time that Indian visitors were experiencing discrimination in the United States, India gained its independence from Great Britain after a fierce civil rights struggle and became an active member of the United Nations. Thus, there was a sad irony in Indians confronting discrimination in the United States. Discrimination toward them felt like the sting from salt rubbed in their healing wounds.[143]

In 1948, when Ras Imru, the Ethiopian minister to the United States, was asked to leave his seat at Constitution Hall and move to the "Negro section," the Indian press exploited the incident to vent its opinions of U.S. hypocrisy. This incident was unique in that it happened in the presence of President Truman, who was addressing the American Association for the Advancement of Science, to which Imru had been invited. Describing the United States as the country that claimed modern superiority in the world, editorials lashed out at America's talk of democracy abroad and its practice of the worst kind of racial fascism at home.[144] An Indian official was appalled that "such an outrage on civilized behavior should have been perpetrated in the capital city of the U.S., at a meeting of the American savants and in the presence of President Truman." He criticized Truman for tacitly acquiescing in this arrangement of discrimination by agreeing to address a segregated audience.[145]

The Ethiopian government filed a formal protest stating that it considered the offense as "grave and prone to create serious implications especially [because] the incident happened in the presence of the President of the United States." The State Department formally apologized and the Ethiopian legation formally rejected the apology. Moreover, the legation demanded that the U.S. government take appropriate measures to ensure such incidents would not happen in the future.[146]

The Council on African Affairs chairman, Paul Robeson, accused the U.S. government of insulting Ethiopia, saying that such "disgraceful occurrences" would never happen if the government did not preserve and foster racial discrimination and segregation practices in its own capital. Robeson noted that the minister of Ethiopia was not the only foreign diplomat to fall victim to prejudice while a guest in the United States and warned that "you may be sure that these incidents do not go unnoticed in the world outside America."[147] He suggested that as long as visitors could be humiliated in the United States, "and they will continue to be as long as fifteen million Negro Americans are discriminated against," it was useless for Americans to talk about world democracy.[148]

Another incident that confronted the State Department involved a group of Malaysian labor representatives touring the United States on a leadership grant sponsored by the department. A Washington, D.C., drugstore refused to serve the group. In turn, the Federation of Government Administrative and Clerical Unions complained to the State Department that its members were "greatly shocked . . . and [the incident] is bound to cause very unfavorable reactions among our unions especially at a time when the U.S. is looked upon as champion in [the] cause of freedom and justice."[149] The U.S. embassy in Kuala Lumpur expressed the "utmost concern and deep regret of the U.S. government" to the Malaysian Federation over the incident. Embassy officials told the State Department that the incident had aroused reaction in the local press and among labor leaders, damaging the prestige of the United States as well as the State Department's exchange program. The embassy concluded that while the incident would die a natural death, labor leaders would continue to be apprehensive and suspicious.[150] Not surprisingly, the Malaysian Trade Union Council exploited the incident to vent anti-American sentiment. It accused the United States of trying "to strangle Malaysian workers by manipulation of tin and rubber prices and now adds insult to injury by refusing to serve us food . . ."[151] The council subsequently refused to nominate candidates for future State Department programs in the United States.[152]

Although sponsoring Africans at American universities was an integral part of the State Department's program of indoctrinating students on democracy and political and economic development, African students were not spared incidents of discrimination. They were shocked by segregation not only in the South but also in the North.[153] A survey of four hundred African students in forty-three American colleges and universities reported that racial segregation was perceived to be the greatest problem for them.[154]

Another site of racial segregation of African students visiting the United States was the YMCA. A newspaper editor from Uganda studying in the United States on a State Department grant was excluded from the recreational facilities at the YMCA where he was staying. The State Department intervened by warning YMCA officials that its segregation policies injured U.S. foreign policy in Uganda and the rest of Africa, and that the YMCA's operations throughout Africa would also suffer from news of such incidents.[155]

Incidents of violence against African students did not go unnoticed. When a Nigerian student attending a college in Terrell, Texas, was ordered to the back of a bus and then beaten by a police officer, the African Student Union of the Americas told Secretary of State John Foster Dulles and Texas Governor Price Daniel that such incidents should not occur in a civil society:

We at the Union deeply regret incidents of this type, especially since, as foreign students, we come to America with such high regard for her democratic way of life and her reputed hospitality. . . . That any American law enforcement officer should behave in this manner seems shocking to us. . . . It is very difficult for the African to grasp the idea that, in American society, he has a "certain place." Perhaps you will realize something of the impression which [the student] will carry back to his country . . . [we] firmly believe that relations between the American and African peoples can be cordial only through mutual respect for each other . . . realizing the gravity of this incident and that it may have far-reaching repercussions for the future relations, harmony and peace between the American and African people . . . we hope that you will take such measures as will prevent its recurrence to any of our students.[156]

African students were not the only victims of segregation in the United States. In 1951, a group of fifty-three foreign exchange students declined an invitation to tour the Tennessee Valley Authority, as part of their program of orientation to the United States, after two dark-skinned Panamanian colleagues were barred from a hotel in Knoxville.[157] A *Crisis* editorial commented, "What a strange way of teaching democracy to foreigners."[158]

Incidents of racial discrimination against foreign dignitaries and foreign students in the United States put additional pressures on the Truman Administration to pursue race reforms. The State Department reached several unavoidable conclusions: racial discrimination against foreign visitors resulted in "ill-will, misunderstanding, and even hostility," it created detrimental effects on foreign relations, it exposed America's hypocrisy and produced embarrassing incidents, and finally it provided the [C]ommunist governments with "skillful propaganda to the detriment of the United States."[159]

Conclusion

In this chapter, I have argued that racial segregation in the United States was a primary target of international criticism and pressure. In addition to the rising power of the black vote and the peaking of the civil rights movement, the atmosphere of the Cold War and the rise of independent Africa and Asia pushed the federal government to become an active partner in the struggle against segregation. Civil rights activists stressed the international dimension of their struggle. Friends and foes around the world utilized the opportunities that segregationist policies provided in order to advance their causes in their own countries and in the international arena.

The United States could not champion its support for human rights and equality unless it was showing progress and setting an example. The timing of successful desegregation efforts is no coincidence. They went hand in hand with international events and the makeover of Asia and Africa – a makeover the United States wished to mold. Fortunately, Southern defiance to the interests of "global" America opened the United States even more to world spectators,[160] to international criticism and pressure, and, consequently, to an increasingly active federal government.

The practical needs of both domestic and foreign policies focused attention on racial conditions that the nation had, for so long, been able to ignore. Only within these circumstances was the government prepared to accept both the legal and moral obligations to uphold the principles of equality. It is crucial to consider the broader international context in which the government sponsorship of race reforms occurred. Without such context, the change in the government's position toward black America may appear to consist of interesting but disconnected events. Domestic pressures had to be accompanied by an international environment that would not tolerate institutionalized discrimination in the United States. The pressures on both fronts constitute a period where, for the first time since Reconstruction, African Americans received so much attention from the federal government.

CHAPTER FIVE

Conclusion

The world has not yet sounded or measured the immense power of mere publicity. I do not mean advertisement in newspapers; I mean the knowledge that your actions are to be known and discussed, and particularly that you will have to answer questions about them face to face with your questioner. Publicity is the only new weapon which the [League of Nations] possesses, but if properly used it may well prove to be about the most powerful weapon that exists in human affairs.[1]

American exceptionalism was explained largely as the outcome of moral superiority, not the result of a favored geopolitical position.[2]

In June of 1961, Lyndon B. Johnson received an emergency call from the State Department. A diplomatic crisis was about to unfold. In the vice president's home state of Texas, Ghana's ambassador to the United States had been denied a room in the Dallas Hilton Hotel. Ironically, the ambassador had been invited to Dallas to address the American Bar Association. Although accompanied by a State Department representative, the ambassador was told the hotel was segregated and that his room reservation could not be honored.[3] In desperation, the State Department contacted Johnson for help. In a revealing telephone conversation, the vice president told a Hilton official that "these people have 20 odd votes in the United Nations. . . . It is going to be explosive internationally. We are outnumbered 17 to 1, black to white in this world." The Hilton official then asked if the ambassador was "the type who will go into the dining room?" Johnson answered,

Yes. . . . You will have to do just like we did when we were in Africa. The Presidents wanted Mrs. Johnson to sit next to them at the head table. She did. . . . The Russians had to sit at the end of the table after that . . . treat him like you would treat any head of state. Bow to him if necessary. I had a big dinner here a few nights ago for the President of Congo, he is just as black as he can be. But these people are right at the crossroads . . . they don't know where they are going. This little country of Ghana isn't as big as Houston. . . . But if this gets out that [Dallas] has refused him, we will have Freedom Riders all over the town. They will pick at me at the Waldorf when I go tomorrow.[4]

Johnson stressed the economic implication of Hilton's policy of segregation: "if you have a hotel in Ghana, you can't afford to hurt [the ambassador's] feelings . . . it would take a lot of white people to fill up a hotel in Ghana. . . . If word gets out that the Hilton Hotels are segregated, Hilton Hotels all over the world are in trouble . . . the Jews, etc., all of them won't like it."

The Hilton official inquired if the ambassador would want to go swimming. Johnson replied, ". . . if he did, I would let him and if necessary, go down there with him. . . . Hilton has hotels in every country. We have a lot of people in Africa . . . oil, etc."[5] Johnson's argument is revealing in two ways. On the one hand, it clearly spells out the dynamics between racial discrimination, segregation, and U.S. foreign policy interests. On the other, Johnson's fears that segregation of a non-white foreign dignitary might provide political opportunities for civil rights advocates such as the Freedom Riders and other critics of America's race policy also became clear.

The Hilton Hotel incident crystallizes the thrust of this book. It summarizes the three major themes that run through the entire project: civil rights leaders' strategy to mobilize international attention and pressure; international pressure exerted on the Executive branch to reform race policy; and the Executive branch's reaction to outside pressure. As we have seen in Chapter Two, although the civil rights struggle had an international dimension from at least the early 1800s, it was not until World War II that the strategy of reaching out bore fruit. The racist ideology of and subsequent genocide practiced by the Third Reich discredited racial discrimination in international politics as never before. The rationalization of racial oppression expressed in the United States and the racist ideology displayed in the South led civil rights advocates at home and abroad to compare racism in the United States to Hitlerism in Nazi Germany.[6] These activists were able to point out the hypocrisy involved in fighting a world war against an enemy who preached a master race ideology, while supporting racial segregation and ideas of white supremacy at home. As Thomas Borstelmann put it, "explicit racial domination had lost its legitimacy in the gas chambers of the German holocaust."[7] The Holocaust impelled the Western nations, including the United States, to proclaim their opposition to racism in every form. The Holocaust and World War II also provided opportunities and reasons for activists who wished to press for racial reform. It taught African Americans and people of color all over the world at least two important lessons. On the one hand, Germany's racist policies were widely seen as morally reprehensible. On the other hand, oppressed people saw clearly the logic of resisting discrimination against them. These included African American soldiers, who quite logically reasoned that if they could fight racism abroad, then they should also fight it at home.

The creation of the United Nations provided the international platform African Americans have been waiting for. As A. Philip Randolph stated in 1945, "Since the reaction of the American system to an issue is conditioned by the world attitude . . . we should develop techniques to focus world opinion on the [discrimination and segregation] problem."[8] And civil rights leaders, as we have seen in the preceding chapters, did precisely that.

The United Nations had shown a spotlight on the disjuncture between the practice of racism at home and the rhetoric of democracy and equality in the international arena.[9] The new international organization provided an open forum for debating issues of discrimination, human rights, and protection of minorities. It also became the stage where both superpowers aired each other's dirty laundry. Institutionalized racism was America's Achilles heel. It did not help that three African American organizations petitioned the United Nations in 1946, 1947, and 1951 for protection from their own government. What made the United States' government even more vulnerable was that the international organization's headquarters was in New York, where non-white foreign dignitaries were not spared, and indeed frequently experienced, de facto segregation. The numerous public relations disasters that occurred in and around the nation's capital created a heightened sense of urgency where ending segregation was concerned. Discrimination against non-white diplomats, foreign officials, and visiting students was even worse in the South, where de jure segregation still defined all facets of life. Denial of accommodation to a Ghanaian official visiting Dallas was just one incident among many.

The second major theme of this book is the pressure that foreign government and non-government entities exerted on the Executive branch, especially the State Department. Two global developments granted leverage to the international community and made its criticism of the United States effective: the wave of independence in Asia and Africa, and the Cold War competition between the United States and the Soviet Union to fill the power vacuum created by the crumbling of colonialism.

The dismantling of colonial empires that began after the end of World War II forced the United States to change its racial policies in order to cultivate allies in the recently independent African and Asian nations. With each country's independence, the non-white people of Africa and Asia would offer additional reminders of the centrality of the race issue in world politics. The birth of these nations changed the power configurations in world politics. American racism inhibited the ability of the U.S. government to influence these countries: segregation "cast a shadow on its moral position . . . [and] raised doubts about its ability to rally to its cause the increasingly important and politically active non-white segment of the world's population."[10]

The implications of this wave of independence were numerous. Decolonization abroad energized African Americans in their own struggle for racial reforms. The U.S. civil rights effort could be seen as part of the worldwide struggle against colonialism and racism. It is not a coincidence that the African American struggle caught fire at the same time that other nations from across the racial spectrum were negotiating and gaining their independence. Finally, although the United States had taken a principled stand in opposition to colonialism (yet had been harshly criticized for not taking stronger stands against colonialist allies like France in the case of Algeria),[11] its racist policies at home prevented U.S. officials from rigorously espousing anticolonialism abroad. As Assistant Secretary of State George McGhee wrote in 1950 about a North Africa conference held in Tangier, "for the French our conference must have been comparable to their holding a meeting in Mobile, Alabama, to examine the status of black American citizens in the south. . . . I came away from the meeting with deep foreboding."[12]

Foreign governments and non-government entities used America's race policy to exert pressure on the federal government and they were effective. Foreign critics targeted unjust court rulings as in the cases of Rosa Lee Ingram, Jimmy Wilson, and the murderers of Emmett Till, among others. Foreign critics targeted the federal government in the Autherine Lucy and Little Rock incidents. They protested the treatment of non-white foreign officials such as Haiti's secretary of agriculture, Ethiopia's minister to the United States, Malaysia's labor union leaders, Ghana's finance minister, minister of labor, and head of civil service among many other dignitaries. Foreign critics kept the State Department on constant alert. According to Secretary of State John Foster Dulles, America's race problem was ruining the country's foreign policy and damaging its efforts of global leadership.[13] Through embassies, consulates, public opinion surveys abroad, and news coverage, foreign criticism of the gap between America's preaching and practice regarding race issues filled the air. There were times when the race issue "all but dominated the incoming cable files, and in the words of one high official 'it interlards almost everything we do in the State Department and the United States Information Agency'."[14]

The Communist bloc effectively used American racism to discredit the United States in the eyes of the non-white officials of Asia and Africa that they sought – often successfully – to befriend.[15] The United States, as the emerging heir to Western power, and as a country that segregated and discriminated against one-tenth of its own population, had a bleak image in the minds of non-white people. The importance of improving relationships and establishing allies within the Third World was underscored with the "loss" of China in 1949. This vital expansion of Communism's reach was a hard blow for the United States government.

Racial prejudices at home hindered U.S. ambitions in the Cold War. In particular, segregation and discrimination made it difficult for the United States to court the new non-white nations as allies in the struggle against the Soviet Union and Communism. World opinion of U.S. policies took on new importance with the end of America's isolation and its postwar global aspirations. U.S. officials were fully aware that other countries could not be dominated; they had to be persuaded, and that meant a high moral standing in addition to military and economic superiority. Government officials appreciated the significance of packaging and marketing the country in the cloth of justice and principles of humanity, equality, equal opportunity, democracy, and freedom. In turn, the Soviet Union had to be identified as totalitarian and as a violator of civil rights, especially as regards its discrimination against its own national minorities. This attempt to shape perceptions was, however, dampened by the realities of race policy at home.

Both the Soviet Union and the United States needed the votes of new United Nations members, especially in the General Assembly. In the wake of the Bandung Conference of 1955, for instance, the Asian and African votes forced issues such as Algeria's freedom from France and condemnation of the Apartheid policies of South Africa onto the agenda. In order for the United States to court these new nations, it had to capitulate to some of their demands and adequately respond to some of their criticism. Racism, as we have seen, was at the top of the critics' list.

The third and final theme addressed in these pages is the examination of the concrete steps taken by the Executive branch in the face of foreign criticism. During the Truman and Eisenhower Administrations, the nation responded to international pressures and sometimes took preemptive measures to avoid further damage to U.S. foreign policy goals. Consider the following as an early example of government response to international pressure and a damage-control measure: Truman's 1947 Civil Rights Committee and its report. In 1946, the United Nations Commission on Human Rights was established followed by the Subcommission on the Prevention of Discrimination and Protection of Minorities. In the words of Dean Rusk, future secretary of state,

[The] first session of the Subcommission is a very important one to the United States, principally because it deals with a very difficult problem affecting the internal affairs of the United States. United States' problems concerning relationships with minority groups have been fully treated in the press of other countries. This Subcommission was established on the initiative of the U.S.S.R., and there is every indication that country and others will raise questions concerning our domestic problems in this regard.[16]

These civil rights reform initiatives were undertaken despite a hostile domestic climate – a challenge that affected Truman in particular because of the friction within his own Democratic Party. The State Department, its diplomatic corps, and United States Information Agency personnel were instrumental in the government's effort to end discrimination and segregation of African Americans. As detailed in Chapter Three, the impact of the State Department was clear in the work of both the 1947 Civil Rights Committee and the 1957 Civil Rights Commission. It was also clear in Truman's and Eisenhower's executive orders and in the latter's decision to intervene in Little Rock. The State Department's participation in the Supreme Court's push for desegregation decisions on the grounds of national security and world peace is obvious. Instead of intervening at different fronts of discrimination, the federal government focused on the area that had received the harshest international criticism. Segregation, for example, was a practice to which many non-white foreign dignitaries had been subjected. Thus, the government took speedy steps towards chipping down the wall of segregation, beginning with public accommodations in busy entry ports such as Miami and Washington, D.C. As Plummer put it: "In undertaking these reforms, the United States had done what it had to do to maintain internal order and external credibility. U.S. officials, those charged with foreign as well as domestic policies, had indeed been influenced by black activism during the era. Their ultimate response, however, derived principally from reasons of the state."[17] In other words, to be able to attract and lure countries away from Communism, to be able to pursue its ideological and economic aspirations, to be able to occupy the position of influence that Britain and France had in Asia and Africa and not be looked at as a colonialist but rather a liberator, the United States had to clean its own house.

Until recently, most studies of American civil rights have lacked a systematic examination of the international context of the civil rights movement and the impact of international pressures on U.S. race policy. This book explains the reasons behind the American administration's decision to promote civil rights reforms beginning in 1946, although the administration had previously delegated matters of race to state and local governments. The timing of the federal government's intervention in race policies was a reflection of international as well as domestic factors. Indeed, the shift in the government's position to reform race policy can be fully appreciated and understood only when examined from a global perspective.

Implications of This Study

This study identifies a number of limitations in traditional social movement theory, which generally examines only the domestic realm of social change. In contrast, this book consistently shows how civil rights advocates marshaled international factors to provide leverage and new political opportunities for their cause.[18] The four dimensions of political opportunity structure, namely the openness of the institutionalized political system, divisions among elites, the emergence of new allies, and the state's capacity and propensity for repression, were all influenced by international events. First, the end of America's relative isolation meant the opening of its institutions, especially the Executive branch, to the international community. As a democratic country that hoped to influence the policies of others, the United States found its domestic policies exposed to inspection by other nations. Race policies were no exception. America's race problem, once considered a domestic issue, became an international concern. Second, under President Truman, international factors contributed to the split between the Executive branch and Congress. While members of Congress looked after their regional and state interests, the president was looking after the national interest, national security, America's diplomatic relations, and its international prestige. It was the president who had to mediate domestic and international pressures. Third, international factors converted neutral if not hostile persons into some of the most active allies of civil rights reform. Those included sympathetic State Department officials as well as members of the diplomatic corps whose change of heart was a result of changes in international political configurations. In addition to finding new support at home, civil rights leaders found support from around the world. Fourth, the decline of violence toward African Americans, especially in the South, was partly because such violence aggravated and invited criticism from the rest of the country as well as from the international community. Savvy politicians knew that supremacist violence against African Americans encouraged various kinds of unwanted federal intervention. As discussed in Chapter Four, there was very strong international reaction to unjust Southern court rulings against African Americans as well as lynching incidents such as the 1955 Emmett Till murder. Even the federal government's repression of world-famous personalities such as Paul Robeson and W. E. B. DuBois caused a wave of criticism from many countries.

Social movements do not only find their political opportunities enhanced by international conditions. As I have demonstrated in Chapters One and Two, framing strategies and resource mobilization, two other ingredients of successful social movements, are also susceptible to global influence, and civil rights advocates deliberately framed their struggle in terms of international events and processes. First, civil rights activists tactfully highlighted the similarities between the U.S. civil rights struggle and the anticolonial struggle of peoples and nations of Asia and Africa. In addition, as the Cold War dominated the policy discourse, civil rights leaders skillfully argued that an end to institutionalized racism would bolster the U.S. anti-Communist effort. Second, resources available for mobilization by members of a social movement are not limited to those within national boundaries. Civil rights advocates systematically widened their circle of appeal to the international community to garnish support in helping put pressure on the United States government. The support for the African American plight as well as criticism of the U.S. government following the three petitions to the United Nations illustrate the savvy tactic of resource mobilization by the civil rights movement's leaders.

In sum, social movement scholars need to recognize the role international factors may play in shaping new opportunities for collective action, in affording new resources for mobilization, and in providing international framing of domestic issues that attracts new allies and widens the base of support for social movements. Social scientists could benefit from a perspective that locates national political issues in an international context. They need to be less parochial and more international. They need to focus less on the obvious moments of change and look more at the pressures both within and outside state institutions that made the change possible. As the case of civil rights policies demonstrates, the Executive and Judicial branches, significantly driven by international factors, influenced Congress to change, beginning with the 1957 Civil Rights Act.[19]

But aren't at all parallel

As more government archives become available, it will be interesting to examine how international influences impacted other United States domestic policies. Environmental issues, trade and labor unions, and women's rights are possible candidates for the intersection of domestic and international spheres.

A Final Thought

We will never know how far or how fast the American political system and American society would have moved by themselves toward equality and full citizenship of African Americans. We will never know what the substance of freedom would have been if the world scene were not drastically altered and brought white supremacy down so abruptly. We will never know if civil rights reforms would have taken just years, as it did, or generations.

What we know is that domestic discrimination was a liability to American objectives abroad. We know that the government's efforts in fighting legal discrimination were secondary to its fight against Communism. Instead of genuinely addressing problems of discrimination, violence, and the denial of rights to black America, the federal government directed its resources to glazing over problems and trying to change, through public relations, the world's perception of American race relations. Instead of government officials attacking racism as wrong, illegal, and immoral, officials attacked race policies as being detrimental to the United States' fight against Communism. Moreover, to sell reforms, civil rights advocates had to package their plight with international appeals.

Nothing could undermine the importance of the civil rights struggle, which has been consistent since the founding of this nation. However, this study casts a shadow on the motives behind the U.S. government's advocacy of civil rights. It is crucial to acknowledge that the federal government could both strengthen and limit possibilities of change. For many decades, the federal government chose the latter. However, it is hard to imagine the same degree of civil rights advances, in the two decades following World War II, without the Executive branch's rigorous actions. The two questions that will remain forever unanswered are: How sincere were U.S. officials in their advocacy of equal rights? More importantly, could today's economic and social disparities between whites and blacks be partially due to the lack of sincerity of our political leadership in past years?

Notes

Chapter One. Introduction

1. An editorial in a Shanghai newspaper, quoted in despatch No. 452, American Consulate General, Shanghai, China to Secretary of State, May 10, 1948, record group 59, decimal file 811.4016/5-1048, National Archives, Washington, D.C. The State Department files of record group 59 are all at the National Archives, Washington, D.C. Therefore, it will suffice to footnote record group 59 sources as such, without citing the location. Members of the U.S. House of Representatives also emphasized the importance of moral leadership versus scientific and material advances. For example, James Roosevelt, representative from California, told his colleagues that "the world is not looking to the United States for leadership in material advances. It knows that we have scientific knowledge, the technological knowledge, and the business knowledge to put us in the forefront of material progress. What the world is looking for is some indication that we are able to supply the moral and spiritual leadership for free men everywhere. . . . The struggle will not be won by atomic ships or by huge military reserves, but by an adherence to a philosophy of life that recognizes the inherent dignity of each individual, without regard to such superficial factors as race or color." Civil Rights Hearings before the Subcommittee on the Judiciary, House of Representatives, Eighty-fourth Congress, second session, *Congressional Record* (Washington, DC: U.S. Government Printing Office, 1956), 198.

2. The Japanese newspaper, *Hochi*, in a 1919 issue. Quoted in Paul Gordon Lauren, *Power and Prejudice: The Politics and Diplomacy of Racial Discrimination* second edition (Boulder, CO: Westview Press, 1996), 106.

3. Indian news agency, quoted in despatch No. 619, American Consulate, Calcutta, India, to Department of State, March 13, 1956, record group 59, decimal file 811.411/3-1356.

4. Absent in 1946 was the massive campaign of civil disobedience and the protest movement that ignited in the 1950s and 1960s and that would attract national and world attention. Advances in mass media, especially television, played a crucial role in increasing the visibility of the black struggle. Television showed the whole world how the white majority op-

pressed African American citizens. Television afforded Martin Luther King, Jr., a worldwide audience and an opportunity to both nationalize and internationalize the civil rights movement. The whole world could watch African Americans boycott the buses in Montgomery and the nine black students, with incomparable courage and dignity, be screamed at and attacked in Little Rock. But television did not play a role in the 1940s and early 1950s. For the impact of television on the civil rights movement, see Aldon Morris, "A Man Prepared for the Times: A Sociological Analysis of the Leadership of Martin Luther King, Jr.," in *We Shall Overcome: Martin Luther King, Jr., and the Black Struggle*, Peter Albert and Ronald Hoffman, eds., (New York: Pantheon Books, 1990); and George M. Fredrickson, *Black Liberation: A Comparative History of Black Ideologies in the United States and South Africa* (New York: Oxford University Press, 1995), 270–5.

5. Civil rights for African Americans were virtually ignored until 1941, when A. Philip Randolph threatened President Roosevelt with a mass "March on Washington" one-hundred thousand black people strong. Roosevelt, in response to Randolph, issued Executive Orders 8802 in 1941 and 9346 in 1943, by which he established the FEPC. Until 1944, the FEPC was financed from the President Emergency Fund. Congress curtailed the president's use of that fund in 1944. That year Congress appropriated $500,000 for the FEPC. In 1946, Congress cut off funding. Donald R. McCoy and Richard T. Ruetten write that Roosevelt established the FEPC "only under extreme pressure at a delicate time . . . in the face of intense, widespread racial violence in 1943, he had said nothing and done little." Donald R. McCoy and Richard T. Ruetten, *Quest and Response: Minority Rights and the Truman Administration* (Lawrence, KS: The University Press of Kansas, 1973), 53. The 1941 March on Washington has been described as a "landmark in the history of black protest, because it was the first successful effort to mass mobilization in the streets, or at least the threat of it, to change government race policy." Fredrickson, 217.

6. See David McCullough, *Truman* (New York: Simon & Schuster, 1992), 588; McCoy and Ruetten, 14; Alonzo L. Hamby, *Liberalism and Its Challengers: FDR to Reagan* (New York: Oxford University Press, 1985), 66. Michael H. Hunt writes that Truman's early correspondence was rich with racist references such as "Greaserdom" for Mexico, and "bohunks" for Slavic peoples. But the "nigger" and the "Chinaman" occupied the lowest ranking. The only foreigners Truman praised were the British. Michael H. Hunt, *Ideology and U.S. Foreign Policy* (New Haven: Yale University Press, 1987), 163.

7. Some have argued that Truman's Contract Compliance Committee contributed to the rise of the median family income of non-whites from $1,671 in 1950 to $2,357 in 1963. Donald R. McCoy and Richard T. Ruetten "The Civil Rights Movement: 1940–1954," *The Midwest Quarterly* 11 (October 1969), 11–34.

8. V. O. Key, *Southern Politics: In State and Nation*, New Edition (Knoxville: University of Tennessee Press, 1984), 332. The opposition to Truman's civil rights crusade was not limited to the avowed white supremacists. Republi-

can organizations, especially in the South, denounced Truman's efforts as "a glaring example of invasion of the rights of the states and of curtailment of the freedom of individual citizens – all in violation of the Constitution of the United States." Key, 290. The Southern Democratic and Northern Republican coalition that opposed civil rights, although for different reasons, was solid throughout the 1940s and beyond. That is why attempts to pass civil rights legislation failed repeatedly. James L. Sundquist, *Politics and Policy* (Washington, DC: Brookings Institution, 1968), 222–3.

9. The fragmentation of "power in Congress that facilitated legislative independence, in combination with seniority systems used to elect committee chairmen in Congress and the one party system character of Southern politics until the 1960s, provided an institutional power base for [S]outherners within the national government." Arend Lijphart, Ronald Rogowski, and Kent Weaver, "Separation of Powers and Cleavage Management," in *Do Institutions Matter? Government Capabilities in the United States and Abroad*, R. Kent Weaver and Bert A. Rockman, eds. (Washington, DC: Brookings Institution, 1993), 318.

10. Southern Democratic leaders who called for unity behind Truman's bid for the presidency in 1948 explained this strategy. They feared that party disunity might lead to a Republican presidential victory. But they agreed that once Truman was elected, "[Southerners] will let [their] congressmen and senators beat him down when he needs beating." Key quotes Cameron Morrison, former governor of North Carolina. Key, 336.

11. Arthur M. Schlesinger, *The Politics of Upheaval* (Cambridge, MA: Houghton, Mifflin, 1960), 437–8.

12. Henry Lee Moon, *The Balance of Power: The Negro Vote* (Garden City, NY: Doubleday, 1948), 11–12, 213–4; Harvard Sitkoff, "Harry Truman and the Election of 1948: The Coming of Age of Civil Rights in American Politics," *Journal of Southern History* 37 (1971); Richard Dalfiume, *Desegregation of the U.S. Armed Forces: Fighting on Two Fronts, 1939–1953* (Columbia, MO: University of Missouri Press, 1969); Barton J. Bernstein, "The Ambiguous Legacy: The Truman Administration and Civil Rights," In *Politics and Policies of the Truman Administration*, Barton J. Bernstein, ed. (Chicago: Quadrangle Books, 1970); and Steven F. Lawson, *Black Ballots: Voting Rights in the South, 1944–1969* (New York: Columbia University Press, 1976).

13. Key, 625–33; Lawson, 45–50. Doug McAdam writes, "To fully appreciate the daunting challenge that confronted the civil rights movement, one has to understand the depths of black powerlessness on the eve of the struggle. In 1950, fully two-thirds of all blacks continued to live in the southern United States. Yet, through a combination of legal subterfuge and extralegal intimidation, blacks were effectively barred from political participation in the region. Less than 20 percent of all voting age blacks were even registered to vote in 1950. In the states of the so-called 'Deep South,' the figure was several times lower. In Mississippi, for example, barely 2 percent were registered in 1950. Fear kept more from trying to register. Small wonder, as late as 1955 two blacks were killed in Mississippi for refusing to remove their

names from the voting rolls." Doug McAdam, "The framing function of movement tactics: Strategic dramaturgy in the American civil rights movement," in Doug McAdam, John D. McCarthy, and Mayer N. Zald, eds., *Comparative Perspectives on Social Movements: Political Opportunities, Mobilizing Structures, and Cultural Framings* (Cambridge, MA: Cambridge University Press, 1996), 345. Of black enfranchisement in the South in 1948, O. Douglas Weeks commented that although the 1944 *Smith v. Allwright* Supreme Court decision "judicially ended" the white primary, the remaining hurdles could be removed only by legislation and more litigation. O. Douglas Weeks, "The White Primary: 1944–1948," *American Political Science Review* 55 (1948), 510.

14. Robert Martin, "The Relative Political Status of the Negro in the United States," in Harry A. Bailey, Jr., ed., *Negro Politics in America* (Columbus, OH: Charles E. Merrill Books, 1967), 27. These figures reflect potential rather than actual voters.

15. *Conference of Scholars on the Truman Administration and Civil Rights,* April 5–6, 1968, the Truman Library, Independence, Missouri, 102–3.

16. Martin, 31. Nevertheless, some have argued that African Americans in urban areas of the North provided the margin of victory in key states. See, for example, McCoy and Ruetten, *Quest and Response,* 43–7; McCullough, 712–3; Sitkoff, 613–4.

17. Summarizing the status of African American enfranchisement in the South in 1948, O. Douglas Weeks wrote that although increasing number of blacks were admitted to the Democratic primaries of 1944 and 1946, "the remaining suffrage requirements, registration restrictions, and election provisions, and the political and administrative methods of applying them" represented tremendous hurdles. Weeks concluded that under the present political environment, the potential of wide-scale black suffrage in the near future was not clear. Weeks, 500–10.

18. Franklin Frazier, *Black Bourgeoisie: The Rise of a New Middle Class* (New York: The Free Press, 1957).

19. John Hope Franklin, *From Slavery to Freedom: A History of Negro America,* 3rd ed. (New York: Knopf, 1967), 620; Peter B. Levy, *The Civil Rights Movement* (Westport, CT: Greenwood Press, 1998), 5, 43.

20. Key, 674–5.

21. David S. Meyer, "Political Opportunity and Nested Institutions," paper delivered at the Annual Meeting of the Midwest Political Science Association, April 14, 1994, Chicago, 2.

22. The civil rights struggle has been grouped with other social movements in the United States, such as the peace movement, the women's movement, the environmental movement, and the gay rights movement. I disagree with this grouping. Not only did all other American social movements, to a significant extent, ride on the coattails of the civil rights movement, but the civil rights struggle was unique in a very important, but overlooked, way. The international implications of the black struggle for democracy on U.S. foreign policy interests and the international attention and pressures

for U.S. racial reform set the civil rights movement apart from other movements.

23. Lauren, 371, footnote 93.

24. Mary L. Dudziak's "Desegregation as a Cold War Imperative," *Stanford Law Review* 41 (November 1988): 61–120, is the earliest work this author found that explicitly links civil rights advances during the Truman Administration and Cold War U.S. foreign politics. Dudziak demonstrates how America's image abroad and its new role as a world leader were instrumental in bringing about civil rights reforms. Most of the comprehensive works that examine the profound effect of race on international politics are by historians. For example, Paul Gordon Lauren's *Power and Prejudice* traces the revolutionary development of the global approach to the principle of racial equality, from Japan's unfruitful efforts at the League of Nations to the successful international pressures on South Africa to end Apartheid. Thomas Borstelmann's *Apartheid's Reluctant Uncle: The United States and Southern Africa in the Early Cold War* (New York: Oxford University Press, 1993) links the United States' reluctance to condemn Apartheid to its need for South African uranium, the main component in atomic weapons. In addition, the South African government's stringent anti-Communist stands made a precious ally too difficult to criticize. Brenda Gayle Plummer's *Rising Wind: Black Americans and U.S. Foreign Affairs, 1935–1960* (Chapel Hill, NC: University of North Carolina Press, 1996) explores the important connections between race and U.S. foreign policy, stressing the efforts of black Americans to influence that policy. Gerald Horne's *Black and Red: W. E. B. DuBois and the Afro-American Response to the Cold War, 1943–1963* (Albany, NY: State University of New York Press, 1986) is an elaborate account of DuBois' international prominence, his struggle for racial equality for all colored people, and his efforts to expose America's hypocrisy to the world. In addition, there are works on both Paul Robeson and Malcolm X that briefly examine the activists' efforts to mobilize the international community. See Martin Duberman, *Paul Robeson* (New York: Knopf, 1988), 434–64, and Alex Haley, *The Autobiography of Malcolm X* (New York: Ballantine Books, 1965), Chapter 19. See also Carol Anderson, "From Hope to Disillusion: African Americans, the United Nations, and the Struggle for Human Rights, 1944–1947," *Diplomatic History*, Vol. 20, No. 4 (Fall 1996), 531–63.

25. As Paul Gordon Lauren states, "This external pressure from the Cold War began to play a monumental role in creating a new beginning for racial equality within the United States." 201. For a discussion of the dominance of the Cold War in U.S. domestic and foreign policy, see Bernard A. Weisberger, *Cold War, Cold Peace: The United States and Russia Since 1945* (New York: American Heritage, 1984); and David Caute, *The Great Fear: The Anti-Communist Purge under Truman and Eisenhower* (New York: Simon & Schuster, 1978).

26. Godfrey Hodgson, *America in Our Time* (New York: Doubleday & Company, 1976), 71.

27. The State Department attempted to expose racism in the countries of its critics. In an informal inquiry, U.S. embassies were asked to report on "any outstanding incidents of discrimination" that might be used as ammunition. Embassies reported the presence of racism in the Soviet Union, China, Mexico, Brazil, Canada, Australia, New Zealand, and South Africa. On the other hand, U.S. embassies could not find "dirt" to expose in Cuba, Luxembourg, the Philippines, Iraq, Sweden, and most of the countries of the Middle East. Lauren, 203. The problem for U.S. officials was that they were the ones who were striving to sell their social and economic order and win friends and influence people. Other countries, such as India with its caste system or the Soviet Union with its oppressive regime, were not claiming leadership based on moral superiority.

28. For Communist exploitation of U.S. race policies, see Exploitation of American Racial Incidents, Report 174-62, December 3, 1962, record group 306, National Archives, Suitland, Maryland. The United States Information Agency files of record group 306 are all at the National Archives, Suitland, Maryland. Therefore, it will suffice to footnote record group 306 sources as such without citing the location.

29. David Guerin, *Negroes on the March: A Frenchman's Report on the American Negro Struggle* (New York: George L. Weissman, 1956), 23.

30. Fredrickson, 237.

31. The NAACP thirty-fourth annual meeting, New York City, January 4, 1943, NAACP papers, quoted in Plummer, 77.

32. Rayford Logan, ed., *What the Negro Wants* (Chapel Hill, NC: 1944), 1.

33. The term *international community*, throughout this work, refers to official and unofficial foreign entities including universities, nonprofit organizations, the private and public business sectors, and press and media channels. In some countries, the press was the government's mouthpiece. It is important to note that because of the secrecy and sensitivity that surrounds international diplomacy, the international responses to the U.S. race problem were often subtle, as when foreign dignitaries spoke off the record or when foreign government officials leaked public opinion surveys of anti-American sentiment to State Department officials.

34. Doug McAdam, "Conceptual Origins, Current Problems, and Future Directions," in *Comparative Perspectives*, 34.

35. By political opportunities I refer to the favorable conditions that were seized by civil rights advocates and foreign critics of the U.S. government and transformed into opportunities to promote change in race policies. These opportunities result from shifts in political configurations like alignments, conflicts among the opposition, the openness of political institutions, and availability of new allies. Throughout the book I argue that neither the opportunities nor the shifts that make them possible are limited to national boundaries.

36. Although the study of social movements is interdisciplinary, it is a field that has been dominated by sociologists. But aside from sociologists, the community of historians, American institutions scholars, international relations

specialists, as well as public policy analysts should address, where appropriate, the dynamics of domestic and international factors behind collective action and policy shifts that result from pressures on political institutions.

37. Earlier accounts of political opportunity structure appeared in the work of political process theorists who stressed the broader political system in which opportunities or constraints could be found. See, for example, Charles Tilly, *From Mobilization to Revolution* (Reading, MA: Addison-Wesley, 1978); Doug McAdam, *Political Process and the Development of Black Insurgency 1930–1970* (Chicago: University of Chicago Press, 1982); and Sidney Tarrow, *Struggling to Reform: Social Movements and Policy Change during Cycles of Protest.* Western Societies Program Occasional Paper No. 15 (Ithaca, NY: New York Center for International Studies, Cornell University, 1983).

38. The earliest proponents of resource mobilization theory are John D. McCarthy and Mayer N. Zald. See *The Trend of Social Movements in America: Professionalization and Resource Mobilization* (Morristown, NJ: General Learning Press, 1973) and "Resource Mobilization and Social Movements: A Partial Theory," *American Journal of Sociology* 82 (6): 1212–41. Charles Tilly documented the critical role of grassroots setting in the success of collective action. See Charles Tilly, Louis Tilly, and Richard Tilly, *The Rebellious Century 1830–1930* (Cambridge, MA: Harvard University Press, 1975), and Tilly, *From Mobilization to Revolution.* Studying the U.S. civil rights case, Aldon Morris and Doug McAdam analyzed the mobilization role played by black churches and black colleges in the emergence and development of the movement. See Aldon Morris, "The Black Southern Sit-In Movement: An Analysis of Internal Organization," *American Sociological Review* 46, 1981: 744–67, and *The Origins of the Civil Rights Movement: Black Communities Organizing for Change* (New York: Free Press, 1984); and McAdam, *Political Process.*

39. It was David Snow and his colleagues who coined the phrase *framing process.* See David A. Snow, E. Burke Rochford, Jr., Steven K. Worden, and Robert D. Benford, "Frame Alignment Processes, Micromobilization, and Movement Participation," *American Sociological Review* 51 (1986), 464–81. While using different terminology to refer to the function of framing in social movements, others have discussed what McAdam called "cognitive liberation" or the "conscious strategic efforts by groups of people to fashion shared understandings of the world and of themselves that legitimate and motivate collective action." *Political Process,* 6.

40. The first account of political opportunity structure could be found in Peter Eisinger's article "The Conditions of Protest Behavior in American Cities," *American Political Science Review* 67 (March 1973): 11–28. Eisinger examines the frequency and intensity of protest behavior in forty-three American cities in 1968. He concludes that protest behavior is related to the city's political structure.

41. Ibid., 28.

42. William Gamson and David Meyer, "Framing Political Opportunity," paper prepared for the Conference on European/American Perspectives on So-

cial Movements, Washington, DC, August 13–5, 1992, 3; and Sidney Tarrow, *Power in Movement: Collective Action, Social Movements and Politics* (Cambridge, MA: Cambridge University Press, 1994), Chapter 5.

43. Gamson and Meyer, 2.

44. McAdam, "Conceptual Origins," *Comparative Perspectives,* 27.

45. Supreme Court rulings that were favorable to African Americans rose from 1946–50 and rose even more in the period 1951–5. Doug McAdam, *Political Process,* 83.

46. These figures exclude the antilynching bills proposed in Congress. Virginia A. Pratt, *The Influence of Domestic Controversy on American Participation in the United Nations Commission on Human Rights, 1946–1953* (New York: Garland Publishing, 1986), 96.

47. *A Record of the March of Events of 1948* (Chicago: Encyclopaedia Britannica, Inc., 1949).

48. As the implications of the U.S. integration in international politics and membership in the United Nations on U.S. constitutional issues became clear in the early 1950s, a bitter partisan debate took place in Congress. The attraction of isolationism was strong in a country unaccustomed to the mantle of world leadership. The Bricker Amendment in 1952–4, the most serious attempt to restrict the president's foreign policy powers, began with a resolution in 1951 expressing the Senate's opposition to the proposed U.N. Human Rights Charter. Some senators perceived the Charter as an invasion of state sovereignty. Among the supporters of the Bricker Amendment were those who opposed civil rights legislation. They feared the U.N. provisions, as those on human rights, could readily become the basis for civil rights legislation. Pratt, 207. The Bricker Amendment failed to pass by a one-vote margin.

49. Plummer, 80.

50. The seven states are New York, New Jersey, Pennsylvania, Ohio, California, Illinois, and Michigan. McAdam, *Political Process,* 79–80.

51. Anthony Oberschall, "Opportunities and Framing in the Eastern European Revolts of 1989," in *Comparative Perspectives,* 94.

52. *New York Times,* June 30, 1947, 1:4, and 3:1–5.

53. The Dixiecrat revolt cost Truman thirty-nine electoral votes.

54. National opinion polls reveal the lack of strong consensus that poor race relations at home undermine the country's foreign policies. See Hazel Erskine, "The Polls: World Opinion on U.S. Racial Problems." *Public Opinion Quarterly* 32 (Summer 1968): 299–312.

55. Martin Smith, *Pressure, Power and Policy: Autonomy and Policy Networks in Britain and the United States* (London: Harvester Wheatsheaf, 1993), 95.

56. McAdam, *Political Process,* 109.

57. Allan Morrison, "The Secret Papers of FDR," *Negro Digest* 9 (January 1951): 4, 5, 9, and 12.

58. Lauren, 152.

59. Allida M. Black writes, "No other noted white American of her stature spoke out so consistently, so eloquently, and so brazenly on [the racial justice]

issue or encountered such vicious public ridicule for this stand than Eleanor Roosevelt." *Casting Her Own Shadow: Eleanor Roosevelt and the Shaping of Postwar Liberalism* (New York: Columbia University Press, 1996), 85. For a fascinating account of Eleanor Roosevelt's civil rights activities during World War II, see Doris Kearns Goodwin, *No Ordinary Time: Franklin and Eleanor Roosevelt: The Home Front in World War II* (New York: Simon & Schuster, 1994).

60. Fredrickson, 213.
61. Lauren, 149.
62. Borstelmann, 38.
63. In contrast with the new support the Supreme Court lent to the civil rights struggle is the Court's history of construing the Thirteenth, Fourteenth, and Fifteenth Amendments. By narrowly interpreting these amendments, the Supreme Court was unsupportive of African Americans.
64. John T. Elliff, *The United States Department of Justice and Individual Rights, 1937–1962* (New York: Garland Publishing, Inc., 1987), 134.
65. Ibid., 147
66. Ibid., 151.
67. Frank Coleman, "Freedom from Fear on the Home Front," 29 *Iowa Law Review* (1944), 415–6.
68. Elliff, 251.
69. Ibid., 323–6. Perlman's argument enraged some congressmen on the House Appropriations Committee. In response to their criticism, he said that his duty was to represent the interests of the United States and that it would be a poor solicitor general who would condone the violation of his country's constitution. In October 1948, Acting Attorney General Perlman was instrumental in pressuring Commerce Secretary Charles Sawyer and Civil Aeronautics Administrator D. W. Rantzel to end segregation at Washington International Airport on December 27, 1948. McCoy and Ruetten, *Quest and Response*, 151.
70. Ibid., 333.
71. Ibid., 392. Some have argued that civil rights progress during the Eisenhower Administration was less a testament to the president's efforts than those of Brownell. Richard Polenberg, *One Nation Divisible: Class, Race, and Ethnicity in the United States Since 1938* (New York: The Viking Press, 1980), 159.
72. Ibid., 340–2. Brownell's bold tactics in supporting civil rights reforms led to unfavorable situations with his boss, President Eisenhower. On more than one occasion, Brownell jeopardized his own office and his own job.
73. Harold Ickes to the Secretary of State, June 8, 1945, in Minutes of the Sixty-sixth Meeting of the United States Delegation, June 8, 1945, Department of State, *Foreign Relations*, 1945, 1206. It is interesting to note that racist beliefs were so embedded at the time that even a civil rights advocate such as Ickes had a condescending view of African Americans. In his secret diary, Ickes describes Marian Anderson's concert at the base of the Lincoln Memorial on April 15, 1939. He writes, "This was one of the most impressive affairs I

have ever attended. Marian Anderson is unmistakably a Negress, for which I was glad – about three-fourths blood I would say – *but* she is a person of dignity and power." *The Secret Diary of Harold L. Ickes,* Volume II: *The Inside Struggle 1936–1939* (New York: Simon & Schuster, 1954), 614 (emphasis my own).

74. Plummer, 146. It is ironic that Ickes' son, Harold Ickes, Jr., who was active in the 1960s civil rights movement, was beaten so badly in Louisiana by white segregationists that he lost a kidney as a result. *Vanity Fair,* September 1997, 192.

75. Borstelmann, 141.

76. Doug McAdam identifies the diplomatic corps as the first to feel the international condemnation of American racism, followed by high-placed State Department officials and then the White House. Doug McAdam, "On the International Origins of Domestic Political Opportunities" in *Social Movements and American Political Institutions,* Anne Costain and Andrew McFarland, eds. (Lanham, MD: Roman and Littlefield, 1998).

77. Nigerian House of Representatives resolution and communication to the U.S. Congress in response to the Congress' joint resolution of greetings to the Gold Coast and Nigeria. Despatch No. 97, American Consul General, Lagos, Nigeria, to Department of State. January 19, 1955, record group 59, decimal file 745H.00/1-1955.

78. Chester Bowles, *Ambassador's Report* (New York: Harper, 1954), 305–7. Bowles discovered that "in any Asian press conference, or forum, the number one question was, 'What about America's treatment of the Negro?'" 31. The ambassador concludes his report by stating that, "Over and over again in this book I have emphasized the painful sensitivity of all Asian peoples on [racial discrimination] and the fantastic success which Communist propaganda has had in creating anti-American feeling. . . . I have not exaggerated. It is impossible to exaggerate." 395–6.

79. Of the Western European countries, France, England, Denmark, and Sweden were among the harshest critics of U.S. racial policies, as the following chapters will show.

80. There is no doubt that the antiracism rhetoric was used to divert attention away from other issues of domestic and international concerns. But an examination of the motives behind these international pressures is beyond the scope of this study. It does, however, provide fertile grounds for future research.

81. Harold Isaacs, "World Affairs and U.S. Race Relations: A Note on Little Rock," *Public Opinion Quarterly,* Vol. 22, No. 3 (Fall 1958), 365.

82. James Button has argued that one of the benefits of the unprecedented electoral access and the consequent rise in the number of black elected officials in the South has been the marked decline in the use of violence against blacks in that region. James W. Button, *Blacks and Social Change* (Princeton, NJ: Princeton University Press, 1989). It is important to note that the threat of losing one's livelihood was used in substitute of physical violence. As William H. Chaffe writes, "all a white person needed to do to

keep blacks in line was to send them on a vacation. Credit lines were canceled, sharecroppers were evicted from the land, and food and seed were withheld." William H. Chaffe, "Postwar American Society: Dissent and Social Reform," in *The Truman Presidency*, Michael J. Lacey, ed. (New York: Cambridge University Press, 1989), 166.

83. The average number of lynchings in each of the four years following World War I, for example, was sixty, while the total number of lynchings in the four years following World War II was eleven. McAdam, *Political Process*, 89. There are differing accounts as to how many blacks died at the hands of white segregationists following World War II. Borstelmann, for example, writes that "at least sixty African Americans died violently at the hands of whites in areas strongly influenced by the Ku Klux Klan during 1945 and 1946; Southern police officers, an important element in Klan organization, were directly implicated in two-thirds of those cases." Borstelmann, 62–3. See also Harold Preece, "Klan 'Murder, Inc.,' in Dixie," *Crisis* 53 (October 1946), 299–301; Robert L. Zangrando, *The NAACP Crusade against Lynching, 1909–1950* (Philadelphia: Temple University Press, 1980); Bernard C. Nalty, *Strength for the Fight: A History of Black Americans in the Military* (New York: The Free Press, 1986).

84. McCoy and Ruetten, *Quest and Response*, 55. The publicizing of violence against blacks by the national press and the international press must be considered when comparing incidents of such violence at different time periods. For example, while there were 130 lynchings in 1900, they attracted far less attention and did less to arouse angry response than a few lynchings in the decades following World War II. See Robert Cushman, "Our Civil Rights Become a World Issue," *New York Times Magazine*, January 11, 1948, 12.

85. Richard Valelly, "Party, Coercion, and Inclusion: The Two Reconstructions and the South's Electoral Politics," *Politics and Society*, Vol. 21, No. 1, March 1993, 55. While President Roosevelt refused to endorse proposed antilynching legislation because it was a "state sovereignty" issue, he was the first president to declare that lynching is murder. See *Crisis*, January 1934, 20.

86. Trudell and Lewis, both fourteen years old, were sentenced to death in Jackson, Mississippi, for the murder of their employer. International appeals, headed by the British, failed to save them. Telegram No. 195, from London to Secretary of State, January 10, 1946, record group 59, decimal file 811.4016/1-1047 and 811.4016/1-1647; despatch No. 3662, U.S. Embassy, London to Secretary of State, February 6, 1947, record group 59, decimal file 811.4016/2-647.

87. Rosa Lee Ingram and two of her twelve children were sentenced to death, in Georgia, for the murder of her white neighbor who had harassed her for many years. When he attacked her, her children killed him in self-defense. An international campaign was organized for the Ingrams' defense. Petitions to the United Nations were presented. Memorandum of Conversation, United States Mission to the United Nations, August 29, 1949, record group 59, decimal file 811.4016/8-2949; Office memorandum, October 10,

1949, record group 59, decimal file 811.4016/10-1049; Petition to the U.N. General Assembly, November 16, 1955, record group 59, decimal file 811.411/11-1655; Guerin, 56–77. As Herbert Shapiro writes, "Clearly, the execution of a black mother and her two teenage sons, in circumstances where there was strong reason to believe the prisoners had acted in self-defense, would have damaged the American world image." Herbert Shapiro, *White Violence and Black Response: From Reconstruction to Montgomery* (Amherst, MA: The University of Massachusetts Press, 1988), 362. The death sentence was commuted to life imprisonment. The Ingrams remained in prison until they were granted parole in 1959.

88. An international campaign to save McGee, convicted of raping a white woman, failed. He was executed on May 8, 1951. Telling is the statement of Mississippi's Supreme Court Chief Justice Harvey McGehee. In response to the argument of the defense that something was hidden in the case, the justice said, "if you believe, or are implying that any white woman in the [S]outh, who was not completely down and out, degenerate, degraded and corrupted, could have anything to do with a Negro man, you not only do not know what you are talking about, but you are insulting us, the whole South." Shapiro, 395. Several international figures joined the protest in the Willie McGee case. Among them were Albert Einstein and William Faulkner. Shapiro, 399. There are numerous files in State Department records that document the international attention to McGee's case. See, for example, despatch No. 376, American Embassy in Paris to Department of State, February 9, 1951, record group 59, decimal file 811.411/2-951; communication No. 51 from the United States Mission to the U.N. to the Department of State, February 9, 1951, record group 59, decimal file 811.411/2-951.

89. The Jimmy Wilson case received the most overseas publicity. In 1958, Wilson was sentenced to death for stealing $1.95 from a white woman. Appeals on his behalf came from the six continents of the world. Leaders such as Prime Minister Nkrumah of Ghana contacted President Eisenhower. The State Department was bombarded as was Alabama Governor James Folsom. Finally, Secretary of State John Foster Dulles told Folsom that U.S. diplomatic missions around the world had reported widespread revolt over the Wilson sentence. The governor said he received one thousand letters daily, most from abroad. Folsom commuted Wilson's sentence, he said, to put an end to the "international hullabaloo" over the case. There are several folders in the State Department records on the Jimmy Wilson case. See, for example, outgoing telegram, John Foster Dulles to James Folsom, September 4, 1958, record group 59, decimal file 811.411/4-558; incoming telegram, Folsom to Dulles, September 5, 1958, record group 59, decimal file 811.411/9-558.

90. Till, fourteen years old, was kidnapped and tortured to death in Mississippi by two white men allegedly because he hissed at the wife of one of them. Till's mother insisted on leaving his coffin open, "so the world could see what they did to my son." The murderers were acquitted by an all-white jury,

who was told by the defense lawyer, "I am sure that every last Anglo-Saxon one of you will have the courage to free these two men." Levy, 60. Black newspapers proclaimed the day of acquittal, September 23, 1955, as Black Friday. Major rallies took place in Baltimore, Chicago, Cleveland, Detroit, New York, and Los Angeles. The international response to the murder and the verdict was tremendous. See, for example, despatch No. 244, American Embassy in Bern, Switzerland, to Department of State, September 28, 1955, record group 59, decimal file 811.411/9-2855; despatch No. 668, American Embassy, Paris, to Department of State, October 5, 1955, record group 59, decimal file 811.411/10-555; *Crisis*, December 1955, 596–602.

91. *Crisis*, December 1955, 599. John A. Salmond gives three reasons why the Emmett Till murder and the trial of his murderers should be considered "one of the symbolic energizing events of the entire civil rights movement." It received national attention, including that of more than one hundred newspapers and television reporters, and therefore the Southern way of life and justice system were brought under a national microscope; Emmett Till's uncle demonstrated bravery in identifying, in court, his nephew's killers; and finally the murder had a "long-term impact no one could possibly have foreseen. A generation of black teenagers . . . recognized themselves in his bloated and mutilated body." John A. Salmond, *"My Mind Set on Freedom": A History of the Civil Rights Movement, 1954–1968* (Chicago: Ivan R. Dee, 1997), 23.

92. *Baltimore Afro-American*, September 10, 1955.

93. Many have argued that the Red Scare and the Cold War were detrimental to the civil rights struggle. It drew cleavages between African Americans and labor organizations. It also divided African Americans, suppressed them, and diverted their attention from racial reforms. Fredrickson, for example, writes that "the civil rights movement was not, as is sometimes supposed, on a steady upward trajectory from the March on Washington to the Civil Rights Act of 1964–1965. The onset of the Cold War and the anti-radical hysteria personified by Senator Joseph McCarthy put a damper on militant protest movements of all kinds . . . [civil rights leaders] were often accused of being 'reds' by people who shared the common belief that only Communists believed in racial equality." Fredrickson, 236. See also Manning Marable, *Race, Reform, and Rebellion* (Jackson, MS: Mississippi University Press, second edition, 1991), 13–39; Gerald Horne, "Who Lost the Cold War? Africans and African Americans," *Diplomatic History*, Vol. 20, No. 4 (Fall 1996): 613–26; Robert Korstad and Nelson Lichenstein, "Opportunities Found and Lost: Labor, Radicals and the Early Civil Rights Movement," *Journal of American History*, Vol. 75, No. 3, December 1988; George Lipsitz, *Rainbow at Midnight: Labor and Culture in the 1940s* (Chicago: University of Illinois Press, 1994); Michael K. Honey, *Southern Labor and Black Civil Rights* (Chicago: University of Illinois Press, 1993); and Barbara S. Griffith, *The Crisis of American Labor: Operation Dixie and the Defeat of the CIO* (Philadelphia: Temple University Press, 1988). Nevertheless, I argue that although the Cold War dealt severe blows to civil liberties and may have diverted the

public's attention away from racial reforms, it did give impetus to the call at home and abroad for African American equality. International pressures and international considerations of the American state continued throughout the Red Scare. Despite intimidation and persecution at home, federal officials were not able to dismiss the linkage that foreign critics and civil rights advocates made between racial discrimination at home and the country's foreign policy goals. International politics continued to feed domestic issues and challenge traditional race policy. In addition, as my empirical data indicates, repression of African Americans during the McCarthy era caused further criticism abroad of the racial situation at home.

94. Edwin P. Hoyt, *Paul Robeson: The American Othello* (Cleveland: World Publishing Co., 1967), 212.
95. McAdam, *Comparative Perspectives*, 34.
96. Oberschall, 95.
97. McAdam, *Comparative Perspectives*, 3–5
98. Ibid., 3.
99. Dieter Rucht, "The Impact of National Contexts on Social Movement Structures: A Cross-Movement and Cross-National Comparison," *Comparative Perspectives*, 185. It is interesting to note that by "broader political environment," Rucht is referring to national politics. I am extending his point to the international political environment.
100. Franklin, 601, 647.
101. Ronald Segal, *The Race War* (London: Jonathan Cape, 1966), 270.
102. Many scholars have recognized the effective use of Cold War rhetoric by civil rights advocates and foreign critics of U.S. racism. Those scholars argue that, because of the status of African Americans, the United States was scrutinized with extreme care and that the presence of non-white diplomatic representatives was not lost on the White House and congressional members as they debated segregation policies in the 1940s and 1950s. But based on these accounts, one is led to believe that the pressures for racial reforms that the government faced were self-imposed rather than explicitly exerted by the international community. In addition, the conclusions reached by most scholars have generally relied on Cold War rhetoric and American media sources and are not based on research or documentation of the explicit international pressures exerted on the United States government. See, for example, C. Vann Woodward, *The Strange Career of Jim Crow*, 3rd rev. ed. (New York: Oxford University Press, 1974), 130–2; Franklin, preface; William C. Berman, *The Politics of Civil Rights in the Truman Administration* (Athens, OH: Ohio University Press, 1970), Chapter Two; Frances Fox Piven and Richard A. Cloward, *Poor People's Movements: Why They Succeed, How They Fail* (New York: Vintage Books, 1977), 206–8; Derrick A. Bell, Jr., "*Brown v. Board of Education* and the Interest-Convergence Dilemma," *Harvard Law Review* 93 (1980): 518–33; and McAdam, *Political Process*, 83. More precisely, as this study shows, international pressures caused the government to be more than just con-

cerned. They influenced and pressured the timing, content, and process by which racial policy reforms became public policy.

103. The fifteen years following World War II saw "800 million people in forty new countries free themselves from colonial bondage, followed by the creation of another twenty-five new nations, mostly in Africa, in the first half of the 1960s." Borstelmann, 12. At its creation in 1945, the United Nations consisted of fifty-one nations, of whom two were African, three Asian, and seven from the Middle East. In 1965, white Western nations were in the distinct minority in the international organization. By 1971, there were 132 member states, seventy percent of whom belonged to "Third World" countries. Hugh Tinker, *Race, Conflict and the International Order: From Empire to United Nations* (New York: St. Martin's Press, 1977), 61.

104. *Frame extension* is a term introduced by David A. Snow and his colleagues. They define it as "the movement attempting to enlarge its adherent pool by portraying its objectives or activities as attending to or being congruent with the values or interests of potential adherents." 472.

105. Isaacs, 365.

106. U.S. Senate Hearings, Subcommittee of the Committee on the Judiciary 1949, Testimony of Roy Wilkins and Thurgood Marshall of the NAACP, *Congressional Record* (Washington, DC: U.S. Government Printing Office), 37.

107. President's Committee on Civil Rights, *To Secure These Rights* (Washington, DC: U.S. Government Printing Office, 1947), 146–8.

108. *Conference of Scholars, on the Truman Administration and Civil Rights,* 82.

109. Brief for the United States as amicus curiae, *Brown v. Board of Education,* 374 U.S. 483, 7–8.

110. Incoming telegram No. 38, from Ankara, Turkey, to Secretary of State, September 12, 1956, record group 59, decimal file 811.411/9-1256.

111. Despatch No. 45, American Consulate General, Amsterdam, the Netherlands to Secretary of State, September 16, 1957, record group 59, decimal file 811.411/9-1657.

112. Despatch No. 37, American Consulate, Kampala, Uganda, to Department of State, October 3, 1957, record group 50, decimal file 811.411/10-357.

113. Hearings before the Committee on the Judiciary, U.S. Senate, Eighty-fourth Congress, April, May, June, 1956, *Congressional Record* (Washington, DC: U.S. Government Printing Office), 13.

114. Civil rights hearings on S.1725 to establish a commission on civil rights among other measures. Subcommittee of the Committee on the Judiciary, United States Senate, June 17, 1949, *Congressional Record* (Washington, DC: U.S. Government Printing Office), 12.

115. *Atlanta Constitution,* September 2, 1955.

116. Civil rights hearings, Subcommittee on Constitutional Rights of the Committee on the Judiciary, U.S. Senate, February 14, 1957, *Congressional Record* (Washington, DC: U.S. Government Printing Office), 415–9.

117. David Snow and his colleagues define *frame bridging* as "the linkage of two

or more ideologically congruent but structurally unconnected frames regarding a particular issue or problem." 467.

118. Despatch No. 45, American Consulate General, Amsterdam, the Netherlands, to Secretary of State, September 16, 1957, record group 59, decimal file 811.411/9-1657.

119. *Pittsburgh Courier,* January 10 and January 8, 1942, quoted in Dalfiume, 96–97.

120. Gamson and Meyer remind us that, "Movements often have a range of actors pursuing numerous strategies in both institutional and extrainstitutional venues." "Framing Political Opportunity," in *Comparative Perspectives,* 283. To treat the black struggle for equal rights as a single entity is both misleading and incomplete because it distorts our understanding of what was actually a varied, decentralized effort. Yet, focusing on the political and economic ideologies of the different sectors of the struggle is beyond the scope of this work. Although I recognize that there were fundamental divisions between "mainstream" and "radical" civil rights advocates, these divisions were on the methods rather than the objectives of the struggle. Between the early 1940s and 1964, there was a general consensus among the different civil rights activists on the goal of the struggle that was to end institutionalized racism. In addition, by the end of World War II, Black American leaders saw their struggle in a larger international context. The longstanding debates between integration and separation were absent in these years of heightened expectations. While the NAACP and other moderate organizations and individuals accepted the U.S. claim to be the legitimate leader of the free world as part of their strategy to push their civil rights agenda, DuBois and Robeson, among others, were harsh critics of America's foreign policy and its hypocrisy in dealing with colored people, including African Americans. Nevertheless, the new and rapidly changing role of the United States in the global political economy was used by all to pressure the federal government into change. Moderates framed their efforts in anti-Communist rhetoric. But non-conformists also framed their efforts in Cold War politics and the new political configurations that accompanied the decline of Western colonialism. There were a few African Americans who rejected the linkage between racism at home and America's international aspirations. George Schuyler, for example, supported the appointment of segregationists Senator John J. Sparkman of Alabama and former Secretary of State James Byrnes to the U.S. delegation to the United Nations. He justified his position by saying that "carrying our domestic quarrels into the highly charged international arena does not benefit the U.S.A., nor the fifteen million Negroes who rise or fall with it." George Schuyler, "Byrnes U.N. Appointment," *Atlanta World,* October 18, 1953. I would argue that the diversity of strategies adopted by the "mainstream" and the "radicals" was necessary to end institutionalized discrimination. As in earlier years, the different tactics of the civil rights movement in later years have been credited with the success of the movement. See Herbert H. Haines, *Black Radicals and the Civil Rights Mainstream,*

1954–1970 (Knoxville: University of Tennessee Press, 1988); Michael Lewis, "The Negro Protest in Urban America," in Joseph R. Gusfield, ed., *Protest, Reform, and Revolt* (New York: John Wiley & Sons, 1970), 149–90; Doug McAdam, "Tactical Innovation and the Pace of Insurgency," in *We Shall Overcome,* David J. Garrow, ed., Vol. 2, (Brooklyn, NY: Carlson Publishing, 1989), 617–36; and Daniel W. Wynn, *The Black Protest Movement* (New York: Philosophical Library, 1974).

121. Paul Robeson to *The New York Times,* April 12, 1947, 4.

122. The order in which I pose the research questions is indicative of the causal relation between international pressures and government response. Because civil rights leaders were instrumental in using the international community to bring pressure on the U.S. government, it is logical to begin the next chapter with that part of my research.

123. Leaders in Africa and Asia exploited the U.S. vulnerability on the race issue during various conflicts. Examples of such exploitation during international debates include the discussions in the late 1940s of the proposed U.N. Human Rights Charter when the U.S. delegation expressed opposition to some of the Charter's provisions; the 1955 debates over the admission of China to the United Nations and the U.S. government opposition on the grounds of China's human rights violations; and the 1955–6 negotiations between the U.S. government and Gamal Abdel Nasser of Egypt over the financing of the Aswan High Dam.

124. African American leadership primarily fought for the equality of opportunities, including that of education, employment, and political participation. They also fought for antilynching legislation. The NAACP invested much of its resources in the legal battle for equal rights through desegregation cases. What I argue here is that the federal government's efforts against segregation were partly motivated by the government's foreign policy agenda: the embarrassing incidents involving foreign dignitaries and students, and the fact that much of the international attention was focused on U.S. segregation.

125. In Chapter Four, I cover several diplomatic crises that resulted from segregation policies. The U.S. media consistently covered the bleak conditions of segregation and poverty in Washington, D.C. See, for example, Robert Cushman, "Our Civil Rights Become a World Issue," *New York Times Magazine,* January 11, 1948, 12, 16; Howard Whitman, "Washington–Disgrace to the Nation," *Woman's Home Companion* 77 (February 1950): 34, 45–6, 48.

126. Bert B. Lockwood, Jr., "The United Nations Charter and United States Civil Rights Litigation: 1946–1955," *Iowa Law Review* 69 (1984): 901–56; see also Robert L. Harris, Jr., "Racial Equality and the United Nations Charter," in *New Directions in Civil Rights Studies,* Armstead L. Robinson and Patricia Sullivan, eds. (Charlottesville, VA: University of Virginia Press, 1991), 126–148. The United Nations Charter was a revolutionary development. It was the first international document to include the term *human rights.*

127. Brief for the United States as Amicus Curiae, *Brown v. Board of Education,* 374 U.S. 483 (1954), 6.

128. Dennis Chong uses rational choice models to demonstrate the change in the federal government's role in race issues and its response to the civil rights movement. Yet Chong overlooks the government's response to civil rights demands as part of the country's foreign policy ambitions after the war. He fails to see that the government, as a rational actor, had no choice but to respond to the mounting international criticism of American racism. Dennis Chong, *Collective Action and the Civil Rights Movement* (Chicago: University of Chicago Press, 1991).

129. E. E. Schattschneider, *The Semisovereign People: A Realist's View of Democracy in America* (New York: Holt, Rinehart and Winston, 1960), 2.

130. A possible reason for this oversight could be that most scholarship marks the beginning of the modern civil rights movement with either the 1954 *Brown* decision or the Montgomery bus boycott of 1955–6. Therefore, the distinctive dynamics of domestic policies and international politics behind the launching of racial reforms in the 1940s remain underdeveloped. McAdam applies the "*political process*" to the New Deal era and the changing socio-economic-political dynamics of racial policy; see also Piven and Cloward, Chapter Four; and August Meier and Elliot Rudwick, *From Plantation to Ghetto* (New York: Hill and Wang, 1976).

Chapter Two. Mobilizing and Utilizing International Pressure: A Strategy of U.S. Civil Rights Leaders

1. W. E. B. DuBois presenting the National Association for the Advancement of Colored People petition to the United Nations, October 23, 1947.

2. Paul Robeson to the *New York Times*, April 12, 1947.

3. St. Clair Drake, "The International Implications of Race and Race Relations," *The Journal of Negro Education* 20 (Summer 1951), 263. Drake comments in his work that the extreme form of racism to which Hitler resorted shocked the Western world: "Exterminating Bushmen and Tasmanians was one thing; exterminating fellow Europeans 'of a different race' was quite a different matter." 263, footnote 10.

4. For the advantageous position the Soviet Union enjoyed among the oppressed people of Africa and Asia, see Bowles, 215–9; Noam Chomsky, "A View from Below," in *The End of the Cold War: Its Meaning and Implications,* Michael J. Hogan, ed. (New York: Cambridge University Press, 1992), 142.

5. Going back to the Civil War, for example, the institution of slavery had detrimental implications for the Confederacy. Slavery deprived the South of European support during the Civil War. When Abraham Lincoln committed himself to abolishing slavery in 1863, he defended the Emancipation Proclamation on two grounds, one of which was international. First, he asserted that freeing the slaves was a war measure that would weaken the Southern economy and force Jefferson Davis to divert more soldiers to security against state rebellion. Second, Lincoln believed the Emancipation Proclamation would give the Union war effort a moral purpose that would make it impossible for European powers to support the Confederacy.

W. E. B. DuBois, *Black Reconstruction in America* (New York: Russell & Russell, 1935), 85–7.

6. DuBois, 90. See also Samuel Bernstein, "The Opposition of French Labor to American Slavery," FSN SC 004,578-5, Schomburg Center Clipping File, Schomburg Collection, New York Public Library.

7. Paul Robeson, *Here I Stand* (Boston: Beacon Press, 1958), 67–70. It was Douglass who, in 1845, said, "So long as my voice can be heard on this or the other side of the Atlantic, I will hold up America to the lightning scorn of moral indignation. In doing this, I shall feel myself discharging the duty of a true patriot; for he is a lover of his country who rebukes and does not excuse its sins." Quoted in Duberman, 434.

8. Douglass traveled to England partly to avoid being captured and sent back to slavery. He did not return to the United States until his British admirers raised $711 to give Hugh Auld, who agreed to sell Douglass's manumission. Douglass arrived in Boston in April 1847, a free man.

9. Some four hundred thousand African Americans went into the armed services in World War I, with fifty thousand of them serving abroad. For the conditions and racial discrimination against black soldiers during and after World War I, see Roi Ottley, *"New World a-Coming": Inside Black America* (New York: Arno Press and *New York Times*, 1968), Chapter 21; Nalty, Chapters 8–9; Logan, *The Betrayal of the Negro*, 369–70.

10. Arthur E. Barbeau and Florette Henri, *The Unknown Soldiers: Black American Troops in World War I* (Philadelphia: Temple University Press, 1974), 114–5.

11. General George Marshall confidentially told reporters in August 1943 that "he would rather handle everything that the Germans, Italians, and Japanese can throw at me, than to face the trouble I see in the Negro Question." John W. Dower, *War without Mercy: Race and Power in the Pacific War* (New York: Pantheon Books, 1986), 173. Marshall also feared that "[w]e are getting a situation on our hands that may explode right in our faces." Quoted in Polenberg, 77.

12. *New York Times*, April 12, 1944, 7. During World War II, the British Home Office issued a directive throughout the United Kingdom that, "There is no color bar in the United Kingdom and none will be permitted." Walter White, *A Rising Wind* (New York: Doubleday, Doran and Company, 1945), 27. World War II afforded new opportunities for African Americans in government employment and overseas technical positions with non-government organizations. An example of the private sector employment is the Red Cross, which had 560 African Americans overseas with a payroll of $1.94 million. Plummer, 121.

13. White's *A Rising Wind* is rich with detailed stories of racial clashes between white and black military personnel overseas as well as both official and unofficial reaction of their host countries. White also includes stories of white soldiers and officers who fought segregation and discrimination. See also Graham Smith, *When Jim Crow Met John Bull: Black American Soldiers in World War II Britain* (London: I. B. Tauris, 1987), 218–9. In 1952, Danish newspapers condemned U.S. military police for ordering restaurants in

Copenhagen to refuse service to black patrons. "The American race conflict shall not be fought out on our soil," concluded one editorial. At the same time in France, American white and black servicemen clashed over mixed race dating and integrated public facilities. Plummer, 207.

14. DuBois' papers include correspondence with many prominent figures and organizations worldwide. For example, in 1932 DuBois wrote to Mussolini that many people had told him that the Italian prime minister expressed "keen interest in the Negro problem in America." DuBois expressed gratitude for this interest and asked if, like Einstein, Gandhi, and other distinguished world leaders, Mussolini would like to write a statement for the NAACP publication, the *Crisis*. Reel 38, #526, W. E. B. DuBois Papers; hereafter DuBois.

15. See Imanuel Geiss, *The Pan-African Movement* (London: Methuen & Co, 1968), 229–62.

16. For the origins and goals of the NAACP, see Frazier, 100–4.

17. Plummer, 12.

18. Philip S. Foner, ed., *W. E. B. DuBois Speaks: Speeches and Addresses 1890–1919* (New York: Pathfinder, 1970), 188.

19. Woodrow Wilson was the first president to introduce segregation into the departments of the federal government. See Nancy J. Weiss, "The Negro and the New Freedom," in Allen Weinstein and Frank Otto Gatell, eds., *The Segregation Era, 1863–1954* (New York: Oxford University Press, 1970), 129–42; Hunt, 130–1; Shapiro, 153. Even when Wilson, in a public statement in 1918, denounced lynching as a "disgraceful evil," the president's words "had merely the effect of keeping news of lynchings out of the press." Shapiro, 145.

20. Reel 7, #114, DuBois papers. DuBois was not the only one to address President Wilson. In an open letter to Woodrow Wilson, Professor Kelly Miller of Howard University wrote, "You are the accepted spokesman of world democracy . . . but a chain is no stronger than its weakest link. A doctrine that breaks down at home is not fit to be propagated abroad. One is reminded of the pious slaveholder who became so deeply impressed with the plea for foreign mission that he sold one of his slaves to contribute liberally to the cause. . . . Why democratize the nations of the earth if it leads them to delight in the burning of human beings after the manner of Springfield, Waco, Memphis, and East St. Louis, while the nation looks helplessly on? . . . The outrages complained of against the Belgians become merciful performances by gruesome comparison. Our frantic wail against the barbarity of Turk against Armenian, German upon Belgian, Russian upon Jew are made of no effect. . . ." See Kelly Miller, "The Disgrace of Democracy, an Open Letter to President Woodrow Wilson, August 4, 1917," in V.F. Calverton, ed., *Anthology of American Negro Literature* (New York, 1929); see 363–78 for the complete text of the open letter.

21. Reel 7, #115, DuBois papers.

22. For an account of confrontations at the League of Nations, see Harold Nicolson, *Peacemaking 1919* (New York: The Universal Library, 1965).

23. Nicolson, 145–6. It is interesting to note that U.S. senators expressed "fears that a racial equality clause in the League of Nations Covenant might seriously threaten domestic jurisdiction within the United States." Lauren, 96. It was the same fears that prevented the United States from supporting some of the clauses of the United Nations Charter in post–World War II. Since the United Nations formation meeting in 1945, the United States government opposed any U.N. human rights program. John P. Humphrey, *Human Rights and the United Nations: A Great Adventure* (New York: Transnational Publishers, 1984), 176.

24. Lauren, 108.

25. DuBois expressed that opinion in one of a series of letters, in 1922, to Leonard Hobhouse, chairman of the proposed British Committee on the Negro Problem. Reel 10, #1160, DuBois papers.

26. Cedric J. Robinson, *Black Marxism: The Making of the Black Radical Tradition* (London: Zed Books, 1983), 270. As they continued to be rejected by white America, African Americans found refuge in recollecting the "homeland" of Africa and in black nationalist movements. The dividing question among black intellectuals was whether African Americans should return to Africa or remain and struggle for racial equality. The Harlem Renaissance of the 1920s produced a wealth of artistic and literary talent among African Americans, which helped raise the national consciousness about the contributions and capabilities of the black population. African American poets and writers such as DuBois, James Weldon Johnson, Alain Locke, Claude McKay, Langston Hughes, Walter White, and many others captured a wide audience. The most celebrated new talents included Richard Wright, James Baldwin, and Ralph Ellison. African American artists who developed international reputations include singer and actor Paul Robeson, jazzman Duke Ellington, musician Louis Armstrong, and singers Billie Holiday and Marian Anderson. The flame that fueled Harlem's Renaissance somehow bridged some of the distance between the worlds of white and black. It was also influential in bringing African Americans in contact with Africa. Harlem became what historian James Weldon Johnson called "the intellectual and artistic capital of the Negro world" for the very reason that New York City was the intellectual and cultural capital of the white world in America. Howard University and Lincoln University played an important role in the intellectual outreach to Africa and other parts of the world. African students, including future nationalist leaders, studied in black colleges in America and interacted with civil rights activists. Lincoln University alumni, for example, include Kwame Nkrumah and Ako Adjedi of Ghana, Nnamdi Azikiwe of Nigeria, and Jomo Kenyetta of Kenya. For the importance of Harlem as "the Negro capital," see Ottley, Chapters 1–5.

27. For an account of Back-to-Africa movements, see Edwin S. Redkey, *Black Exodus: Black Nationalist and Back-to-Africa Movements, 1890–1910* (New Haven: Yale University Press, 1969).

28. Geiss, 263–82.

29. Lauren, 115.

30. Robinson, 297. George Padmore described Garvey as the man who first made blacks conscious of themselves and made the world conscious of them as a force to be reckoned with in world politics. Padmore also wrote that "one of the reasons why Garvey was so unceremoniously bundled out of the U.S. in 1926 was the fact that the Japanese Government had been trying to make arrangements to finance his back-to-Africa movement. They wanted to embarrass and disrupt the imperialist empires in Africa." C. L. R. James, *Notes on the Life of George Padmore* (Chicago: University of Chicago Press, 1972), 9–11; also see Tony Martin, *Race First: The Ideological and Organizational Struggles of Marcus Garvey and the Universal Negro Improvement Association* (Westport, CT: Greenwood Press, 1976), introduction; and Edmund David Cronon, *Black Moses: The Story of Marcus Garvey and the Universal Negro Improvement Association* (Madison, WI: University of Wisconsin Press, 1969). On a much smaller scale, there were the Rastafarians, inspired by Garvey and by Ethiopia, the only purely indigenous African country to retain independence from Western colonialism until it fell to Italy in 1936; and also the Forty-Niners movement of the 1930s, which proposed that all African Americans move to a state in the blackbelt and have their own nation. The Nation of Islam adopted the Forty-Niners' proposal.

31. Schattschneider argued that the audience of a conflict determines the outcome of that conflict. Schattschneider, 2.

32. *Pittsburgh Courier,* September 9, 1939.

33. Ibid., September 2, 1939. See also *Chicago Defender* editorials, May 25 and June 15, 1940.

34. "Lynching and Liberty," *Crisis,* 47, July 1940 (emphasis in original).

35. Walter White mentioned this advertisement in a letter to Hollywood producer David Selznick. The letter is deposited in the Humanities Research Collection, Theater Arts Collection, University of Texas at Austin, the Selznick Collection, Box 331, folder 3. In an NAACP report entitled "The Threat to Negro Soldier Morale," a Southern black soldier was quoted as saying he hoped Hitler would win the war because "if he does and comes over here, he will treat American white people the way they treat us. They will know what it feels to be treated like dogs; they will understand how we feel. Then we can all get somewhere." Reel 12, #0384, A. Philip Randolph papers, hereafter Randolph.

36. Alain Locke, "The Unfinished Business of Democracy," *Survey Graphic* 31 (November, 1942).

37. *Pittsburgh Courier,* March 22, 1941, 3.

38. Horace Cayton, "The American Negro – A World Problem," *Social Education* 8 (May 1944), 206. The term United Nations referred to the Allied nations.

39. Ibid., 206–7. Langston Hughes expressed his dismay at the violence against blacks during the war years in the following poem excerpts:

You tell me that [H]itler
Is a mighty bad man.
I guess he took lessons

From the Ku Klux Klan.
You tell me [M]ussolini's
Got an evil heart.
Well, it mus-a been in Beaumont
That he had his start.
Cause everything that [H]itler
And [M]ussolini do
Negroes get the same
Treatment from you.
You [J]im crowed me
Before [H]itler rose to power –
And you're still [J]im crowing me
Right now, this very hour.
Yet you say we're fightin
For democracy.
Then why don't democracy
Include me?
I ask you this question
Cause I want to know,
How long I got to fight
BOTH HITLER–AND JIM CROW.

Langston Hughes, "Beaumont to Detroit, 1943," *Common Ground,* Fall 1943, p. 104.

40. *Crisis,* December, 1938, 393; March 1941, 7; November 1942, 343.
41. Ibid., October 1942, 311–13.
42. Sean Dennis Cashman, *African Americans and the Quest for Civil Rights 1900–1990* (New York: New York University Press, 1991), 72.
43. Ibid.
44. Walter White, *A Man Called White* (New York: Viking Press, 1948), 190. The impact of the March on Washington Movement was tremendous. It captured the imagination of the masses, it pushed other African American organizations into a style of militancy, and it resulted in the flourishing of the NAACP. In 1940, the NAACP had 355 branches and a membership of 50,556. By 1946, it grew to 1,073 branches and a membership of approximately 450,000. Dalfiume, 99–100.
45. Morrison, 9, 10, 12.
46. Reel 28, #0011, Randolph papers. Randolph made this statement while addressing the thirty-second Annual Conference of the NAACP in Houston in 1941. In April 1941, thirty-one youth leaders were invited to the White House to discuss matters of concern. The only African American among the group was James Farmer, who challenged President Roosevelt's description of France and Britain as champions of democracy. FDR's response was, "In which country would you rather live today – France or Nazi Germany?" James Farmer, *Lay Bare the Heart: An Autobiography of the Civil Rights Movement* (New York: Arbor House, 1985), 69.

47. Reel 1, #278, Randolph papers.
48. Reel 28, #0029, Randolph papers. India's distrust of the United States also stemmed from the immigration exclusion. Like other ethnic groups, Indians faced tremendous immigration restrictions.
49. W. E. B. DuBois, *The Souls of Black Folk* (New York: Penguin Books, 1903), 2.
50. *Crisis,* August/September 1949, 246; see also Lawrence Neal, "Black Power in the International Context," in *The Black Power Revolt,* Floyd B. Barbour, ed. (Boston, 1968), 136–7.
51. Reel 54, #1, DuBois papers. White wrote DuBois that the British ambassador told him in confidence that the British agreed with White's suggestion. Lord Halifax, the British ambassador, himself wrote that Roosevelt's administration "is seriously worried about feeling among the coloured population, which according to every survey is apathetic to the war, which it considers a white man's conflict." Cited in Christopher Thorne, *Allies of a Kind: The United States, Britain and the War Against Japan, 1941-1945* (New York: Oxford University Press, 1978), 142. See also "FDR, Churchill Asked to Consider Color Problems," *Baltimore Afro-American,* August 28, 1943, 9.
52. Thomas E. Hachey, ed., *Confidential Dispatches: Analyses of America by the British Ambassador, 1939–1945* (Evanston, IL: New University Press, 1973), 208.
53. The number of blacks, for example, employed in manufacturing rose from 0.5 million to 1.2 million. Chaffe, 164.
54. President's Committee on Civil Rights, *To Secure These Rights,* 59–61. As soldiers and sailors were demobilized after the war, African Americans and other minority groups had to compete with them for jobs.
55. Peter B. Levy, *Let Freedom Ring: A Documentary History of the Modern Civil Rights Movement* (New York: Praeger, 1992), 251; William Harris, *The Harder We Run: Black Workers Since the Civil War* (New York: Oxford University Press, 1982), 123–46; Chaffe, 165.
56. President's Committee Report, 57; Levy, 250.
57. If nothing else, the Federal Employment Practices Committee was a big step in the right direction. Not only did it initiate the tactic of mass mobilization to force government intervention, but it also signifies the first time ever that the government used its authority to combat job discrimination. It was the first decisive act on behalf of African Americans by the federal government since Reconstruction; see Ottley, Chapter Twenty.
58. Lee Finkle, *Forum for Protest: The Black Press during World War II* (London: Associated University Press, 1975), 97; Chaffe, 165.
59. Lauren, 149.
60. Outrageously violent crimes in particular are said to have had a dramatic impact on the Truman Administration. In 1946, two African American couples were lynched together in Monroe, Georgia. During the same year, Sergeant Isaac Woodward was brutally beaten, then blinded in both eyes by the Chief of Police in Aiken, South Carolina. White, *A Man Called White,* 322–3; *Conference of Scholars,* 12.
61. Woodward, 132–3.

62. Because of political instability, many European cities were excluded from consideration to host the United Nations.

63. Edmund Davison Soper, *Racism: A World Issue* (Abingdon, NY: Cokesbury Press, 1947), 252.

64. *New York Times,* November 12, 1946, 28. Dean Acheson, then assistant secretary of state, also opposed the location of the United Nations. He disliked New York City, "a crowded center of conflicting races and nationalities." Dean Acheson, *Present at the Creation* (New York: Norton, 1969), 99–101.

65. Plummer, 163.

66. See, for example, the *New York Times* for incidents involving India, July 25, 1947, 3, August 24, 1955, 4; Haiti, November 13, 1947, 20; and Ethiopia, September 16, 1948, 1, September 17, 1948, 17, 24, September 18, 1948, 8, September 21, 1948, 10.

67. Testimony of Marie S. Klooz. Unpublished U.S. Senate Hearings, Committee on District of Columbia Affairs, 1951, 20.

68. *New York Times,* March 19, 1959, 50.

69. J. Irving Scott and Helen Ruth Scott, "Foreign Students in Negro Colleges and Universities in the United States of America, 1951–1952," *Journal of Negro Education* 22 (Fall 1953), 489.

70. U.S. Senate Report, Executive Committee of the Committee on Foreign Relations, Eighty-fifth Congress, 1958, *Congressional Record* (Washington, DC: United States Government Printing Office), 235. The administration's goal to indoctrinate foreign students in the American way through American universities was made clear in a 1958 report by the U.S. Senate Executive Committee on Foreign Policy Review, a subcommittee of the Senate Committee on Foreign Relations. The report resulted from a series of meetings of senators headed by William Fulbright with a group of noted personalities such as Henry Luce of Time-Life, Inc. and Robert Bowie of Harvard University. The role of American universities was described as "crucial" in getting hold of future leaders in the newly independent countries of Africa.

71. For the fascinating account of the early U.N. debates and resolutions introduced to end race discrimination, see Lauren, 178–94.

72. African American leaders were encouraged by the discussion and the 1946 vote on a resolution addressing the treatment of Indians by the South African government. The resolution stated that the South African government had to comply with international obligations and that Indian and South African officials needed to discuss these issues and report back to the U.N. General Assembly. As Lauren puts it, "If the United Nations could focus attention on discrimination in South Africa, might it not also look at racial discrimination in the United States?"183–4. For the Indian–South African dispute in the United Nations, see H. Lauterpacht, *International Law and Human Rights* (Archon Books, 1968), 192–9.

73. It is appropriate to discuss the third petition in the section on Paul Robeson for two reasons. First, Robeson coauthored the 1951 document. Second, I prefer to keep the chronology of events intact.

74. Reel 55, #475, DuBois papers.

75. Reel 12, #414, Randolph papers.

76. The NAACP was one of forty-two organizations that were appointed by the government to act as consultants to the U.S. delegation. Some have argued that it was the presence of African Americans, as consultants and observers, that "effectively placed and kept human rights, racial equality, and decolonization on the table. The [U.N.] charter statements on human rights, vague as they were, would not have appeared without pressure placed on the major players to insert them." Plummer, 152; Humphrey, 13.

77. White, *A Man Called White*, 294–8.

78. The National Negro Congress, as did DuBois decades earlier, argued that the future of blacks in the United States was intertwined with the future of all the colored people of the world. Walter White memorandum to the NAACP Board of Directors, August 1, 1944, Papers of the NAACP, Library of Congress, Pt. 1, reel 6.

79. *New York Times,* June 2, 1946, 33; "The First Petition to the United Nations from the Afro-American People," in Herbert Aptheker, *Afro-American History: The Modern Era* (New York: Citadel Press, 1971), 301–11; Abner W. Berry, "Rough, Tough and Angry," *New Masses,* June 18, 1946, 17–9.

80. Herbert Aptheker, ed., *The Correspondence of W. E. B. DuBois,* Vol. 3 (Boston: University of Massachusetts Press, 1978), 155–6.

81. Reel 59, #616, DuBois papers.

82. *Chicago Defender,* November 2, 1946, 1.

83. Reel 80, #993, DuBois papers.

84. Reel 60, #1080, DuBois papers.

85. Office Memorandum, November 4, 1947, record group 59, decimal file 501.BD Human Rights/11-447.

86. Commission on Human Rights, Subcommission on Prevention of Discrimination and Protection of Minorities, Draft Resolution proposed by Mr. A. P. Borisov, United Nations, E/CN.4 SUB .2/24, December 1, 1947, original in Russian. The Soviet position, not only toward African Americans but also its anticolonial proclamations at United Nations meetings, worried the State Department. The Soviet Union was taking over America's historic role as champion of freedom. "Russia, I fear, may appear before the world as the champion of all dependent peoples," declared Acting Secretary of State Joseph Grew, "[Soviet Foreign Minister Vyacheslav] Molotov's move may confirm in the minds of the people of Asia their already strong suspicion that the Anglo-American powers are not their real champions and will turn to Russia as their more outspoken friend and spokesman." Joseph Grew, Acting Secretary of State, to Secretary of State Edward R. Stettinius, May 8, 1945, Department of State, *Foreign Relations,* 1945, 1:652; *The Documents of the United Nations Conference on International Organization,* Vol. 4 (Washington, DC: U.S. Government Printing Office, 1946).

87. Incoming telegram from Geneva to Department of State, November 29, 1947, record group 59, decimal file 501.BD Human Rights/11-2947.

88. Commission on Human Rights, Subcommission on the Prevention of

Discrimination and the Protection of Minorities, First Session, Summary Record of the Thirteenth Meeting, Geneva, December 2, 1947, E/CN.4/Sub.2/SR/13, p. 7; see also the *New York Times*, December 3, 1947, 11 and December 4, 1947, 6. There were ugly exchanges between Daniels and A. P. Borisov, the head of the Soviet delegation, each accusing the other of the use of human rights in political propaganda. Daniels expressed regret that political propaganda had to be injected into proceedings of an expert group, and said that such remarks came with poor grace from a country that achieved equality by uniformly suppressing human rights, that refused to allow wives of alien husbands to leave the Soviet Union, that used minorities as puppets, and that concealed information about internal conditions. Borisov retaliated with an explanation of the democratic character of the Soviet Constitution. He criticized the lack of free press in the United States and asked why the U.S. did not free Soviet citizens from concentration camps in Germany. Incoming Airgram from Geneva to Secretary of State, December 3, 1947, record group 59, decimal file 501.BD Human Rights/12-347.

89. Office Memorandum, November 25, 1947, record group 59, decimal file 501.BD Human Rights/11-2547.

90. A few months earlier, the Department of State informed the president that racial discrimination is a handicap for the government's relations with other countries. See the next chapter for a detailed account of correspondence between the State Department and Truman's committee. As Alexander DeConde states, "The problem had become so acute that Truman created a special body, the President's Committee on Civil Rights, to investigate it." Alexander DeConde, *Ethnicity, Race, and American Foreign Policy: A History* (Boston: Northeastern University Press, 1992), 130.

91. Reel 63, #336, DuBois papers.

92. For the importance of the role of India in the early years of the United Nations sessions, see Lauren, 166–74.

93. Vijaya Lakshmi Pandit was one of India's first female politicians. She was a Congress Party activist and later a diplomat. She and her brother, Jawaharlal Nehru, were lifelong friends of Paul Robeson and his wife Eslanda. Pandit later recalled that during her 1945 visit to the United States, she saw the notices "For Whites" and "For Colored." These signs, "took me back through the years to the time in my country when benches marked 'For Europeans Only' had been a familiar sight. I could hardly believe my eyes." Pandit refused to address segregated crowds while on tour. Vijaya Lakshmi Pandit, *The Scope of Happiness* (New York: Crown Publishers, 1979), 191–2.

94. Reel 60, #125, DuBois papers. In response to DuBois' letter, Pandit wrote back that she "shall certainly do what she can to help you place this before the Assembly." Reel 60, #129, DuBois papers.

95. Eleanor Roosevelt was described as the most important person in the United Nations human rights program. Humphrey, 4. It is interesting to note that unlike Eleanor Roosevelt, who resigned from the Daughters of the American Revolution when they refused to rent Constitution Hall to

Marian Anderson, Bess Truman had no objection to being honored by the same group although days earlier they refused to rent Constitution Hall to Hazel Scott, once more because of race. Adam Clayton Powell scorned Bess Truman as "the last lady." Bernstein, 273.

96. Aptheker, *The Correspondence*, 189.

97. India, Haiti, Liberia, and the Soviet Union had offered to present the NAACP petition to the United Nations.

98. Aptheker, *The Correspondence*, 189. Eleanor Roosevelt wrote the NAACP that the United States mission refused to receive the organization's petition because the Soviet Union refused to accept complaints directed against its government. Shapiro, 509–10, footnote 3.

99. Genna Rae McNeil, *Groundwork: Charles Hamilton Houston and the Struggle for Civil Rights* (University of Pennsylvania Press, 1983), 198.

100. Reel 80, #937, DuBois papers.

101. Ibid.

102. Ibid., #938.

103. Reel 60, #190, DuBois papers.

104. Ibid. Clark was clear about his views concerning the petition when he declared, "No act of accidental injustice, let alone those of calculation, will go unobserved by our enemies. Lip-service to our ideals will be seen for the mockery that it is." Ronald Segal, *The Race War* (New York: Viking Press, 1966), 223.

105. White, *A Man Called White*, 358. Whereas White took credit for much of the publicity the petition generated, he increasingly distanced himself from the document as he geared the NAACP toward more conservative methods of working closely with President Truman and his administration.

106. Reel 60, #279, 286, 699, 706, DuBois papers.

107. White, *A Man Called White*, 358–9; Horne, *Black and Red*, 15, 78.

108. *The Nation*, December 13, 1947, 645.

109. Ibid.

110. Reel 60, #788, DuBois papers.

111. Ibid.

112. For the black press's attack on Communism, see Earl Ofar Hutchinson, *Blacks and Reds: Race and Class in Conflict 1919–1990* (East Lansing: Michigan State University Press, 1995). For a critique of the black press, see Frazier, 174–94.

113. James Roark, "American Black Leaders: The Response to Colonialism and the Cold War, 1943–1957, "*African Historical Studies* 4 (June 1971), 253–70.

114. Among the works on the role of the black press during and after World War II are Beth Bailey and David Ferber, "The 'Double-V' Campaign in World War II Hawaii: African Americans, Racial Ideology, and Federal Power," *Journal of Social History* (Summer, 1993), 817–43; Lee Finkle, "The Conservative Aims of Militant Rhetoric: Black Protest During World War II," *Journal of American History*, 692–713; Richard L. Beard and Cyril E. Zoerner II, "Associated Negro Press: Its Founding, Ascendency and Demise," *Journalism Quarterly* 46 (Spring 1969), 47–52; and Phyl Garland,

"The Black Press: Down but Not out," *Columbia Journalism Review* 21 (September/October 1982), 43–50.

115. U.S. Senate Hearings, Subcommittee of the Committee on Labor and Public Affairs 1952, *Congressional Record* (Washington, DC: U.S. Government Printing Office), 142–6.

116. *Crisis,* January 1954, 22. In 1950, Sampson became the first black American to join the American delegation at the United Nations. The *Chicago Defender* applauded her appointment, stating that ". . . President Truman could hardly have chosen a more able foe of the Communists or a more courageous fight for a just cause. . . . The Russian delegates will never have the last word as long as Mrs. Sampson has a chance to get the floor." *Chicago Defender,* September 16, 1950. Time and time again, Sampson highlighted Soviet oppression, stating that "We Negroes aren't interested in Communism. . . . We were slaves too long for that. Nobody is happy with second-class citizenship, but our best chances are in the framework of American democracy." Quoted in Helen Laville and Scott Lucas, "The American Way: Edith Sampson, the NAACP, and African American Identity in the Cold War." *Diplomatic History,* Vol. 20, No. 4 (Fall 1996), 575. In 1959, Sampson admitted that her approach to racial redress was faulty. She said, "We were mistaken. No, we were wrong. Ours was not the only way. It was not even the best way. . . . If only it were possible to start all over again. . . . There were so many missed opportunities that this time I'd seize and exploit. There are so many things that I lacked the courage to try, so many things I did badly because I hadn't the wisdom to do them well." Laville and Lucas, 578–9.

117. *Crisis,* April 1952, 237.

118. Mercer Cook, "Race Relations as Seen by Recent French Visitors," *Phylon* 15, No. 2, 1954, 121–38.

119. Frank M. Snowden, "The Italian Press Views America's Attitude toward Civil Rights and the Negro," *Journal of Negro Education* 21 (Winter 1952), 20–6.

120. *Crisis,* March 1947, 73. When Secretary of State James Byrnes, a South Carolinian, demanded free elections in Bulgaria, black educator Horace Mann Bond sent him the following poem quoted in Borstelmann, 218, footnote 7.

Dear Mr. Byrnes, we doff our hats, in humblest admiration;
Your latest note has thrown the Reds in utmost consternation.
The echo sounds throughout the world – "Free Ballots for the
 Bulgar!"
And none would raise a sour note – except, of course, the vulgar . . .
When you have time, dear Mr. Byrnes, from your high tasks
 dramatic,
Please raise your voice in your own State, in accents as emphatic.
There's Barnwell, and there's Bluffton, and there's Ballentine and
 Bowman,
We love to see the Bulgars vote; now how about the Black man?

121. Ibid., April 1947, 105.
122. Ibid., October 1950, 578. Bunche was awarded the Nobel Peace Prize for his role in the division of Palestine between Arabs and Jews. In the late 1940s, Bunche had turned down the job of assistant secretary of state, opting to work for the United Nations in New York, partly because he did not "relish the prospect of life in segregated Washington." Brian Urquhart, *Ralph Bunche: An American Life* (New York: W. W. Norton, 1993), 135.
123. Ibid., October 1951, 510.
124. Dalfiume, 91; Polenberg, 76.
125. Finkle, *Forum for Protest*, 150.
126. Reel 13, #541, Randolph papers. It is ironic that Winston Churchill's son Randolph used the same language in a 1946 meeting with journalist Walter Lippmann. "Why do you worry about our niggers?" asked Randolph Churchill. "We don't worry about yours." Quoted in Plummer, 128.
127. Reel 12, #527, Randolph papers. For example, in 1949, Randolph accompanied by Joe Louis, led a March of Silence to protest segregated drafts. Randolph said the march was to teach America that the problem of minorities was no longer exclusively their own. "How we treat that problem is no longer our own affair. Three quarters of the people of the world are colored. It is inconceivable to imagine, and stupid to believe, that they would place their hopes in a nation which tolerates the twin evils of segregation and discrimination." Reel 13, #0059.
128. Reel 12, #476, Randolph papers.
129. Ibid.
130. Ibid., #528.
131. Reel 13, #1960, Randolph papers.
132. See Nalty, Chapter 15; and Philip A. Klinker, "Fighting the Jim Crow Army," *American Legacy* (Fall 1998), 20–6.
133. C. L. R. James summed up this viewpoint when he stated that "[o]bviously the conscience of mankind or growing enlightenment was not going to abolish Negro slavery in America. These forces in the heart of man had not abolished slavery for 250 years. . . . What we are really witnessing here is not that sudden change in the conscience of mankind so beloved of romantic and reactionary historians, but the climax of a gradual transformation of world economy." C. L. R. James, *A History of Pan-African Revolt* (Chicago: Charles H. Kerr Publishing, 1995), 57–69.
134. Editors of *Freedomways, Paul Robeson: the Great Forerunner* (New York: Dodd, Mead & Company, 1978), 9.
135. *New York Times,* September 24, 1946, 60.
136. Editors of *Freedomways,* 8; Duberman, 307.
137. Philip S. Foner, ed., *Paul Robeson Speaks: Writings, Speeches, Interviews, 1918–1974* (New York: Brunner Mazel Publishers, 1978), 176–8.
138. Duberman, 389–91.
139. *New York Times,* August 5, 1950, 4.
140. Editors of *Freedomways,* 127; *Daily Worker,* August 25, 1950, 5.
141. *Freedom,* November 1952, 1.

142. *Rockwell Kent v. John Foster Dulles,* 357 U.S. 116 (1958).

143. Hoyt, 212.

144. Editors of *Freedomways,* 115. In 1946, Robeson was described by the *Gold Coast Observer* as "the voice of Africa outside of Africa to the native African . . . Mr. Robeson represents all their hopes and aspirations." Quoted in Penny M. Von Eschen, *Race against Empire: Black Americans and Anticolonialism 1937–1957* (Ithaca, NY: Cornell University Press, 1997), 67.

145. *Chicago Defender,* December 12, 1944, 1.

146. *New York Age,* September 10, 1949, 2.

147. *Afro-American,* July 23, 1949, 4.

148. *New York Times,* April 24, 1949, 37.

149. Robeson, 41–2.

150. *New York Times,* April 21, 1949, 6.

151. See Duberman, 342–50 for the response of African American leaders to Robeson's Paris speech.

152. Civil rights activist Bayard Rustin summed up this point by saying, "There's a sort of unwritten law that if you want to criticize the United States you do it at home; it's corollary of the business where you're just a nigger if you stand up and criticize colored folks in front of white folks – it's not done." Quoted in Duberman, 344.

153. Gerald Horne, *Communist Front?: The Civil Rights Congress, 1946–1956* (Rutherford, NJ: Fairleigh Dickinson University Press, 1988), 172–4.

154. *Daily Worker,* December 15, 1951, 1.

155. *New York Times,* December 18, 1951, 13; Hutchinson, 205–11.

156. In 1949, six black men were convicted of murdering a white storeowner in Trenton. The NAACP was successful in reversing the conviction and gaining a new trial. In 1951, four of the six were freed, while two were convicted. The Martinsville case involved seven black men convicted for the rape of a white woman. The seven were executed in Richmond, Virginia, on February 2, 1951. Shapiro, 395.

157. *Civil Rights Congress, We Charge Genocide: The Historic Petition to the United Nations for Relief from a Crime of the United States Government against the Negro People,* William Patterson, ed. (New York: International Publishers, 2nd ed., 1970), vii, xiv–xvi, xvii–xviii, 58–187; *New York Times,* December 18, 1951, 13.

158. Patterson, 27–8.

159. William L. Patterson, *The Man Who Cried Genocide: An Autobiography* (New York: International Publishers, 1971), xvi, xviii; Shapiro, 418–28.

160. Louis Lomax, *The Negro Revolt* (New York: Harper & Row, 1962), 258.

161. *Freedom,* July–August 1955, 1.

162. *Crisis,* May 1977, 184–9.

163. Roeslan Abdulgani, *The Bandung Connection: The Asia-Africa Conference in Bandung in 1955* (Singapore: Gunung Agung, 1981), 88; H. W. Brands, *The Specter of Neutralism: The United States and the Emergence of the Third World, 1947–1960* (New York: Columbia University Press, 1989), introduction.

164. Richard Wright, *The Color Curtain: A Report on the Bandung Conference* (New York: World Publishing, 1956), 83.

165. John Foster Dulles, "The Cost of Peace," *U.S. Department of State Bulletin* 34 (June 18, 1956): 999–1000. For the secretary of state's reaction to the Bandung Conference, see Brands, 110–13.

166. Lauren, 227.

167. Robeson, 45–6. DuBois also sent a message that was read at the conference. He stated that "because of my 50 years of service in the cause of 25 million colored peoples of America I venture of my own initiative to address you in their name, since the United States will not allow me to attend this meeting." Reel 71, # 935, 936, DuBois papers.

168. Quoted in Duberman, 431.

169. Richard Wright, 85.

170. Ibid., 86.

171. The African American response to the Bandung Conference and the black press coverage of it were included in the *Far Eastern Reporter*, May 1955. See also Charles Hamilton, *Adam Clayton Powell, Jr.: The Political Biography of an American Dilemma*, 242–5.

172. James L. Hicks, "Dark Nations Assert Power," *Baltimore Afro-American*, October 8, 1955, 1.

173. James L. Hicks, "Says Battle to End Colonialism Won at Bandung Conference," *Baltimore Afro-American*, October 15, 1955, 8.

174. At Bandung, Congressman Powell denied that segregation existed in the nation's capitol, adding that African Americans were no longer second-class citizens in their own country. Many African Americans criticized Powell. *Baltimore Afro-American* reflected the general sentiment that, "The better way to answer propaganda is simply by reciting the untarnished truth, certainly not by restoring patent falsehood." *Baltimore Afro-American*, April 30, 1955.

175. When *U.S.S. Midway* disembarked in Capetown, South African authorities, with the acquiescence of the U.S. consul and the ship's captain, attempted to segregate the Asian American and African American members of the crew. After protests from the NAACP and the American Committee on Africa, the segregation plan was aborted. Plummer, 238.

176. Unpublished U. S. Senate Hearings, Committee on Foreign Affairs 1955–6, 7–9.

177. Abdulgani, 164.

178. Pratt, 23.

179. Plummer, 103.

180. Robeson, 71.

Chapter Three. Civil Rights Commissions: A Vehicle of Government Response to International Pressure

1. Letter to Robert Carr from Secretary of State George Marshall, July 20, 1947, record group 59, decimal file FW 501.BD Human Rights/7-2047.

2. President Truman's special civil rights message to Congress, February 2, 1948.

3. *Conference of Scholars*, 21.
4. Lauren, 199.
5. Some have described Truman's civil rights efforts as halfhearted, occasional, and ambiguous; and that like FDR, Truman did not emphasize the nation's obligation to its black citizens. See, for example, Bernstein, 273.
6. *To Secure These Rights* has been described as "one of the most outspoken and impressive documents of all time bearing upon human rights." Lauterpacht, 157.
7. J. W. Anderson, *Eisenhower, Brownell, and the Congress: The Tangled Origins of the Civil Rights Bill of 1956–1957* (University of Alabama Press, 1964), 12.
8. McCoy and Ruetten, *The Civil Rights Movement: 1940–1954*, 21.
9. In 1946, the British notified the U.N. General Assembly that it would place several of its African colonies under authority and grant independence to several others.
10. Some members of Congress pointed out the hypocrisy of American democracy. Representative Mary T. Norton, arguing for anti–poll tax legislation, asked her colleagues how they "can in all honesty insist on free elections by others when we do not hold them ourselves." United States, *Congressional Record*, Eighty-first Congress, second session, July 25, 1949, 10098.
11. Lauren, 200.
12. Ibid., 201.
13. The committee represented business, labor, education, law, and the general public. Charles Wilson, president of General Electric Corporation, chaired it. The committee included Charles Luckman, president of Lever Brothers; Rev. Francis J. Haas, bishop of Grand Diocese; Rev. Henry K. Sherrill, presiding bishop of the Protestant Episcopal Church; Sadie T. Alexander, assistant city solicitor of Philadelphia; James B. Carey, secretary treasurer of the CIO; Boris Shishkin of the American Federation of Labor; Rabbi Roland B. Gittelsohn of the Long Island Rockville Center; Frank P. Graham, president of the University of North Carolina; John S. Dickey, president of Dartmouth College; Dr. Channing H. Tobias, Director of the Phelps-Stokes Fund; Franklin D. Roosevelt, Jr., New York attorney; M. E. Tilly of the Methodist Episcopal Church South in Atlanta; Morris Ernst, civil liberties activist; and Francis P. Matthews, former head of the Knights of Columbus.
14. *To Secure These Rights*, vii–ix.
15. Letter to Secretary of State George Marshall from Robert Carr, May 23, 1947, record group 59, decimal file 811.4016/5-2347.
16. Office memorandum to Secretary of State from Dean Rusk, July 15, 1947, record group 59, decimal file FW 501.BD Human Rights/6-547.
17. Ibid.
18. Letter to Robert Carr from Secretary of State George Marshall, July 20, 1947. The Department of State also sent the committee foreign press items on racial discrimination from Scandinavia, the Soviet Union, India, and Greece. Record group 59, decimal file FW 501.BD Human Rights/7-2047.

19. Letter from Robert Carr to Dean Rusk, August 11, 1947, record group 59, decimal file 811.4016/8-1147.
20. President's Committee Report, 147–8.
21. Ibid., 148 (emphasis in original).
22. Ibid., 146–7.
23. William C. Berman, *The Politics of Civil Rights in the Truman Administration* (Columbus, OH: Ohio State University Press, 1970), 85.
24. Ibid.
25. Richard Neustadt, "Congress and the Fair Deal: A Legislative Balance Sheet," in Richard Abrams and Lawrence W. Levine, eds., *The Shaping of Twentieth Century America* (Boston: Little, Brown, 1965), 574.
26. McCullough, 588. Because he was closely associated with Southern racists, the NAACP refused to endorse Truman when he ran for county judge in Jackson, Missouri, in 1924. Some argue that Truman decided early on to put his personal "Southern" feelings aside for the sake of his political aspirations, and later on as president, for the sake of the national interest. One of Truman's early pro-civil rights actions came in 1938 when he, as senator from Missouri, voted for cloture on an antilynching bill. *Conference of Scholars*, 77–80.
27. Quoted in Lauren, 205.
28. Public opinion surveys between 1945 and 1955 indicate less than overwhelming support for racial reform. See, for example, Plummer, 167–8.
29. These briefs and cases will be discussed in detail in Chapter Four.
30. The first African American to serve in the U.S. Congress in the twentieth century was Oscar DePriest. A Republican, DePriest was elected to the House of Representatives in 1928. In 1934, Arthur Mitchell of Illinois defeated DePriest and became the first African American Democrat to be elected to the House. Mitchell declined to run in 1942. William Dawson was elected in 1944 to represent the same congressional district DePriest and Mitchell served. Dawson became the first African American to chair a major congressional committee, the Government Operations Committee.
31. Members of the Supreme Court validated these arguments with their own personal experiences overseas. For example, Justice William Douglas stressed the domestic-international angle of U.S. race relations. During his travels in India in 1950, he wrote that "the attitude of the United States towards its colored minorities is a powerful factor in our relations with India" and that *"Political alliances of an enduring nature will be built not on the power of guns or dollars, but on affection."* William O. Douglas, *Strange Lands and Friendly People* (New York: Harper & Brothers, 1951), 296, 326 (emphasis in original). Chief Justice Earl Warren traveled to England, Sweden, Denmark, and Norway in 1953. Earl Warren, *The Memoirs of Earl Warren*. (Garden City, NY: Doubleday, 1977). See also Robert H. Jackson, *The Supreme Court in the American System of Government* (New York: Cambridge University Press, 1955). Justice Jackson served as prosecutor in the Nuremberg trials in Germany. These travels coincided with prominent coverage of U.S. racial discrimination all over the world. It is hard to argue that members of

the Supreme Court during these visits could have escaped the international attention to race relations in the United States. Although the Supreme Court said nothing about foreign affairs in its decisions, the Court did not reject as immaterial the arguments of those who did make such references.

32. Civil rights hearings on S.1725 to establish a commission on civil rights among other things. Subcommittee of the Committee on the Judiciary, United States Senate, Friday, June 17, *Congressional Record* (Washington, DC: U.S. Government Printing Office, 1949), 12.

33. Ibid., 13.

34. Ibid.

35. Ibid., 37.

36. U.S. Senate Hearings, Subcommittee of the Committee on the Judiciary, June 17, *Congressional Record* (Washington, DC: U.S. Government Printing Office, 1949), 37. Testimony of Roy Wilkins and Thurgood Marshall of the NAACP.

37. Amending Interstate Commerce Act (Segregation of Passengers), Committee on Interstate and Foreign Commerce, House of Representatives, May 13, 1954, *Congressional Record* (Washington, DC: U.S. Government Printing Office, 1954), 57–9.

38. Hearings before the Subcommittee of the Committee on the Judiciary, House of Representatives, Eighty-fourth Congress, first session, July 27, 1955, 237–9.

39. Hearings before the Committee on the Judiciary, U.S. Senate, Eighty-fourth Congress, April, May, June, 1956, 13.

40. Ibid., 73.

41. Ibid.

42. Civil rights hearings, Subcommittee on Constitutional Rights of the Committee on the Judiciary, U.S. Senate, February 14, 1957, *Congressional Record* (Washington, DC: U.S. Government Printing Office, 1957), 122.

43. Ibid., 415–19.

44. Testimony of David Scull. Unpublished U.S. Senate Hearings, Committee on District of Columbia Affairs, 1951, 18.

45. Ibid., 108.

46. Ibid., 154.

47. In 1962, civil rights advocates were still making the same arguments. Mennen Williams, assistant secretary of state for African affairs, and Angier Duke, the State Department's chief of protocol, testified to Congress about the difficulties non-white diplomats experienced in finding homes in Washington, D.C. "This image of the American way of life and this violation of our principles of equality of opportunity [are things] the diplomat will carry with him when he returns to his native land – and we might say, that diplomat may turn out to be the next Foreign Minister or Prime Minister of his own country." Foster Rhea Dulles, *The Civil Rights Commission: 1957–1965* (East Lansing, MI: Michigan State University Press, 1968), 160.

48. U.S. Senate Hearings, Subcommittee of the Committee on Labor and Public Affairs, *Congressional Record* (Washington, DC: U.S. Government Printing

Office, 1952), 1942–6. Walter White did not limit such statements to congressional hearings. In 1950, he organized a conference to which he invited many prominent government officials and cabinet members, politicians, civil rights activists, trade unionists, media executives, and educators. White briefed the group on the "shrinkage of U.S. prestige, particularly in Asia, Africa, and the Caribbean," that he witnessed while traveling around the world. White stressed the propaganda the Russians were spreading in Korea using America's race problem. *Conference of Scholars*, 21. It is important to note that the American government's choice to drop the first atomic bombs over Hiroshima and Nagasaki, while sparing Caucasians the terrible devastation of nuclear war, indicated to many the inequality of race in the minds of the West. Canadian Prime Minister Mackenzie King aggravated the fears and speculations of Africans and Asians when he said, "it is fortunate that the use of the bomb should have been upon the Japanese rather than upon the white races of Europe." Quoted in Lauren, 176.

49. At present, the ninety-six-year-old Thurmond still represents South Carolina in the U.S. Senate.

50. Civil rights hearings before the Subcommittee on Constitutional Rights of the Senate Committee on the Judiciary, Eighty-fifth Congress, first session, February 21, *Congressional Record* (Washington, DC: U.S. Government Printing Office, 1957), 667.

51. Ibid.

52. Civil rights hearings before the Committee on Rules – House of Representatives, May 14, 1957, Eighty-fifth congress, first session: H.R. 6127: a bill to provide the means of further securing and protecting the civil rights of persons within the jurisdiction of the United States, 148.

53. On the home front, the Supreme Court's *Brown v. Board of Education* decision followed by the 1955–6 Montgomery bus boycott marked the beginning of what many scholars term the modern civil rights movement. The successful launching of the African American civil disobedience campaign in the South, aided by television, forced white America to confront the country's ugliest problem, a problem it was able to sweep under the national rug for centuries. Finally, Americans had to address what Gunner Myrdal, a decade earlier, termed "The American Dilemma."

54. During his first term, Eisenhower had issued executive orders to accelerate the desegregation of the military and to integrate public facilities in the nation's capital.

55. The commission was authorized to investigate allegations that U.S. citizens were being deprived of the right to vote due to color, race, religion, or national origin; to collect information on legal developments that constituted a denial of the equal protection of the law; to appraise the laws and policies of the federal government in the whole field of civil rights; and, within two years, to report its findings and recommendations to the president and Congress.

56. John A. Hannah, president of Michigan State University, chaired the com-

mission. He stated that he accepted his appointment only because of his conviction that race relations were the most important problem facing the United States, ". . . from the standpoint of long-time relationships with the uncommitted areas of the world that are so vital to the long-time well-being of the country." Dulles, 20. Commission members included Robert G. Storey, Dean of Southern Methodist University Law School; John S. Battle, former governor of Virginia; Father Theodore M. Hesburgh, president of Notre Dame; J. Ernest Wilkins, assistant secretary of labor; and Doyle E. Carleton, former governor of Florida. The committee was politically balanced, with three Democrats, two Republicans, and an independent. Wilkins was the only African American.

57. Letter to Christian Herter from Gordon Tiffany, Commission on Civil Rights, May 28, 1958, record group 59, decimal file 811.411/5-2858.

58. Ibid. It was reported in the early 1950s that between eighty to ninety percent of the Soviet propaganda against the United States pertained to America's race problem. *Conference of Scholars,* 22.

59. Because of the significant impact of this report on the final recommendations of the 1957 Civil Rights Commission, I quote extensively from the State Department's report. Since I discuss foreign news coverage in Chapter Four, here I focus on the State Department assessment of the impact of U.S. racism on U.S. relations with other countries, which is entitled "Part One" of the report.

60. Memorandum for the White House from the State Department, *Concerning Request from the Civil Rights Commission – "Treatment of Minorities in the United States – Impact on Our Foreign Relations."* December 1958, record group 59, decimal file 811.411/12-458, Part A. Summary Review, 1.

61. Ibid., 25.

62. Ibid.

63. Ibid., 1.

64. Ibid., 2–3.

65. Ibid., 2.

66. It was from the 1958 Accra Conference that Frantz Fannon, a Martinique-born psychiatrist who joined the Algerian National Liberation Front, emerged as a celebrity revolutionist. His 1961 book *The Wretched of the Earth* became a textbook for revolutionaries as well as human and civil rights advocates all over the world.

67. Memorandum for the White House 2–6. Part One, There was a widespread sentiment in Asia and Africa that South Africa's segregationists drew strength for their Apartheid policies from U.S. segregationists. The noninterventionist attitude the U.S. government adopted toward South Africa caused the newly independent countries to question the depth of U.S. commitment to the principles of equality and democracy. Frenise A. Logan, "Racism and Indian – U.S. Relations, 1947–1953: Views from the Indian Press," *Pacific Historical Review,* 1985, 76. It is interesting to note that the Federation of Rhodesia criticized efforts to integrate schools in the United

States. These efforts infuriated Rhodesian officials because of their own conservative racial policies. They viewed the American efforts as too "pro-African."

68. Ibid., 3
69. Ibid.
70. Ibid.
71. Ibid.
72. Ibid., Part B: Area Review, 1–35.
73. Ibid., 1.
74. Ibid.
75. Ibid.
76. Ibid.
77. Ibid., 3.
78. Ibid., 1.
79. An illustrative example of a racial incident that turned into anti-American sentiment is the following. In 1950, a Nigerian scientist, who was refused service at a Washington, D.C., restaurant, "ten minutes away from the State Department and close to Truman's White House," told the Nigerian press that Nigeria "had nothing spiritually, ethically, or morally to learn from the United States"; that the American civilization was "as bankrupt as any civilization built on purely materialistic lines." Despatch No. 385, American Embassy, Lagos, Nigeria, to Department of State, September 21, 1950, record group 59, decimal file 811.411/9-2150.
80. Part B: Area Review, 2.
81. Ibid. At the Summit Meeting of Independent States in Addis Ababa, Ethiopia, in 1963, delegates singled out racial discrimination in the United States as "intolerable malpractice which is likely to seriously deteriorate relations between African peoples and governments on the one hand, and African people and the government of the United States on the other." Martin Minogue and Judith Molloy, eds., *African Aims and Attitudes: selected documents* (London: Cambridge University Press, 1974), 258.
82. It is important to note that W. E. B. DuBois was one of Nkrumah's mentors. Nkrumah referred to DuBois as the father of Pan-Africanism. Nkrumah criticized the U.S. government's failure to issue DuBois a passport to attend Ghana's independence celebrations in March 1957. Nkrumah personally invited prominent members of the African American community to the independence ceremonies, including Ralph Bunche, A. Philip Randolph, Adam Clayton Powell, Channing H. Tobias (the chairman of the board of the NAACP), John Johnson (editor of *Ebony*), Horace Bond (president of Lincoln University, where Nkrumah went to school), Roy Wilkins, and Thurgood Marshall. Despatch No. 242, American Embassy, Accra, Ghana, to Department of State, record group 59, decimal file 74J.00/3-557; despatch No. 197, American Embassy, Accra, Ghana, Department of State, record group 59, decimal file 745K.13/1-2657.
83. Part B: Area Review, 3–4. While the report does not elaborate, it is clear that

Nkrumah was keen on criticizing the United States to enhance Ghana's leadership within Africa.

84. Ibid., 4.
85. It is said that while Nixon was in Ghana attending its independence celebrations, he sat next to a black man at dinner. The vice president asked his neighbor how it feels to be free, and the answer was, "I wouldn't know. I'm from Alabama." Tinker, 84.
86. Part B: Area Review, 4. This situation was rescued by President Eisenhower's "masterstroke, and nothing short of this would have done." Eisenhower sent his personal apology to the finance minister, followed by a breakfast invitation to the White House. Nevertheless, U.S. officials in Nigeria warned that similar incidents in the future would be detrimental to U.S.-African relations. Despatch No. 115, American Consulate, Lagos, Nigeria, October 14, 1957, record group 59, decimal file 811.411/10-1457.
87. Ibid. Besides Ghanaian dignitaries, Ghanaian students in the U.S. were personally familiar with U.S. racial problems. Some 160 Ghanaian students were in the United States in 1956–7. *Foreign Relations of the United States, Africa 1955–1957* (Washington, DC: U.S. Government Printing Office, 1989) 379.
88. Ibid.
89. In early 1961, the State Department established a special section within its office of protocol to deal with problems of African diplomats. In addition to lending assistance to the diplomats and their families, the Special Protocol Services Section was to prevent any embarrassing international incidents involving non-white foreign dignitaries.
90. Memorandum for the White House, Part B: Area Review, 5.
91. Ibid., 6.
92. Ibid., 10.
93. Ibid., 12.
94. Ibid., 14–16.
95. Ibid., 20–1.
96. Ibid., 23–4. For an account of how the Japanese used racial conflicts in its propaganda against the United States, see Ottley, Chapter Twenty-two, "Made in Japan."
97. Ibid., 35.
98. Ibid.
99. Ibid.
100. Ibid., 26.
101. Ibid., 27.
102. *New York Times,* January 28, 1950, 21.
103. Memorandum for the White House, Part B: Area Review, 27.
104. Ibid., 28.
105. Ibid., 27–8.
106. Ibid., 30.
107. The report was widely circulated. It was sent to U.S. embassies, the Justice Department, and the U.S. delegation to the United Nations.

108. Report of the United States Commission on Civil Rights (Washington, DC: U.S. Government Printing Office, 1959), 549.
109. Ibid., 548.
110. Quoted in McCullough, 639; also see Dewey W. Grantham, *The United States Since 1945: The Ordeal of Power* (New York: McGraw-Hill Book Company, 1976), 40.

Chapter Four. International Pressure and the State's Response to Racial Segregation

1. Letter from Secretary of State Dean Acheson to Attorney General James P. McGranery, December 2, 1952, record group 59, decimal file 811.411/11-1352.
2. Despatch 218, American Embassy, San Jose, Costa Rica, to Department of State, October 4, 1957, record group 59, decimal file 811.411/10-457.
3. Eisenhower's address to the nation on his decision to intervene in the Little Rock crisis, *Crisis*, November 1957, 533.
4. Despatch No. 284, American Consulate General, Madras, India, to Department of State, September 30, 1948, record group 59, decimal file 701.8411/9-3048.
5. Elliff, 155–6. The safe areas for federal intervention, the Justice Department stated, included the industrial field and "programs to enforce equal pay for equal work, and to train and upgrade Negroes." Quoted in Elliff, 156.
6. Ibid., 156.
7. One of the logical and legal starting points for civil rights reform, one would assume, would be voting rights. While state rights could prevent Congress from intervening in many issues such as suffrage qualifications for voting in state elections, Congress could have protected African Americans' rights to vote in federal elections. That is one of the rights of U.S. citizenship, which Congress may protect by law against violence and state discrimination.
8. Following the *Brown* decision, Autherine Lucy registered to attend the University of Alabama, which caused violent outbursts in the white community and marked the first clash between federal and state law enforcement agencies over the issue of school segregation. A U.S. district judge ordered the University of Alabama to protect Lucy, but the university trustees permanently expelled her because of charges she made against the university. Although Lucy appealed to the federal courts, her expulsion was not overruled. For more details on Autherine Lucy's background, see Salmond, 32–3.
9. Little Rock Central High School was to begin integration in September 1957. On September 4, Governor Faubus of Arkansas sent in the National Guard to keep the school segregated by preventing nine African American students from entering the school. On September 25, President Eisenhower federalized the Arkansas National Guard and sent in one thousand

paratroopers to restore order and to escort nine black students who were to attend Central High.

10. It is interesting to note that from 1945 to 1955, Africa received less than two percent of the $46.1 billion the United States dispensed in grants. Africa secured $186.1 million of the $34.7 billion that the United States dispensed in military assistance worldwide between 1948 and 1965. Rupert Emerson, *Africa and United States Policy* (Englewood Cliffs, NJ: Prentice-Hall, 1967), 36–7.

11. Arthur M. Schlesinger, Jr., *A Thousand Days: John Kennedy in the White House* (Greenwich, CT: Fawcett Publications, 1965), 322.

12. Quoted in Lauren, 206.

13. Before 1948, the Supreme Court ruled in favor of African Americans in several domains (as stated in Chapter One). While it is certain that the Court was aware of the international implications of racism on U.S. foreign policy, the arguments and briefs in court cases before 1948 made no reference to such issues.

14. Berman, 74; Hamby, 67.

15. Philip Elman, "The Solicitor General's Office, Justice Frankfurter, and Civil Rights Litigation, 1946–1960: An Oral History." Interview by Norman Siber, *Harvard Law Review* 100 (1987), 819.

16. Brief for the United States as Amicus Curiae, *Shelly v. Kraemer,* 334 U.S. 1 (1948), 19.

17. Berman, 75. The brief quoted from the letter Acting Secretary Acheson wrote to the FEPC in 1946, detailed in Chapter Three.

18. The U.N. Charter, as a binding agreement, was used repeatedly in court cases. One of the earlier cases was in 1946 when a group of African American homeowners appealed to California's Supreme Court for permits to live in Hollywood. The plaintiffs' case cited the U.N. Charter's guarantee against discrimination in housing based on race. *New York Times,* October 3, 1946, 38.

19. U.S. Brief, 97–8. The National Association of Real Estate Boards filed a brief on behalf of Kraemer that argued that the U.S. "could not be considered, by the [U.N. Charter] treaty, to have changed any State law. [The government] has agreed to take steps *within its power as the Federal Government* to support vaguely economic and social ends" (emphasis in original). Brief for the National Association of Real Estate Boards, *Shelly v. Kraemer,* 334 U.S. 1 (1948), 8–9. The government's amicus brief cited the U.N. Charter in *Henderson v. United States, Sweatt v. Painter,* and *Bolling v. Sharpe,* a companion case to *Brown v. Board of Education.*

20. Berman, 20; Richard Kluger, *Simple Justice: The History of Brown v. Board of Education, the Epochal Supreme Court Decision That Outlawed Segregation, and Black America's Century-Long Struggle for Equality under the Law* (New York: Vintage Books, 1977), 588.

21. Despatch No. 112, American Consulate, Madras, India, to Secretary of State, May 6, 1948, record group 59, decimal file number 811.4016/5-648. State Department despatches had wide circulation within the U.S. government.

For example, Congress discussed this despatch from India. See *Congressional Record*, Eighty-first Congress, second session, May 9, 1950, 96: 6694.

22. Brief for the United States, *Henderson v. United States*, 339 U.S. 816 (1950), 60. The brief included a letter from the secretary of state. It is interesting to note that Arthur Mitchell, the first African American Democrat to be elected to the U.S. House of Representatives (1934), was the central figure in *Mitchell v. U.S.* of 1941, in which the Supreme Court issued a unanimous decision upholding black passengers' right to equal accommodations and treatment on interstate trains. Mitchell was forced out of his first-class seat in a Pullman car in 1937. Although the Court ruling was never interpreted as a mandate to integrate interstate passenger trains, the case paved the way for the *Henderson v. U.S.* case.

23. Ibid., 61.

24. Ibid.

25. Ibid.

26. Ibid., 62.

27. Ibid. The U.S. mission to the United Nations attempted to respond and to engage in similar political propaganda against the Soviet Union and its allies. Nevertheless, U.S. delegates were in a weak position because the accusations launched against the United States were unanswerable. They were true. In addition, none of America's critics claimed leadership of the democratic "free world" as did America. Thus the United States was held to a much higher standard when it came to human and civil rights. Statements (when heard) such as outlined above strengthened the resolve of civil rights advocates in the United States. Moreover, these statements tended to bind together non-Communist nations that suffered racial discrimination under colonial rule to take strong anti-American stands that went beyond racial issues.

28. Letter from Walter Kotsching to George T. Washington, November 4, 1948, record group 59, decimal file 501.BD Human Rights/11-3048.

29. G. W. McLaurin was admitted to the University of Oklahoma but was segregated within the university. He was segregated in the library, the classroom, and the cafeteria. The issue here, as the NAACP argued, was that different treatment on the basis of race violated the equal protection of the law under the Fourteenth Amendment.

30. Herman Marion Sweatt was denied admission to the University of Texas law school. The Texas Supreme Court ruled that the university's action was a violation of Sweatt's rights under the Fourteenth Amendment. The university system responded by opening a separate black law school, outside the University of Texas, with meager facilities and resources. The question here was whether the black law school was equal to the white law school. The NAACP argued that it was not and, therefore, was an unacceptable solution.

31. Memorandum for the United States as amicus curiae, 1–2, *McLaurin v. Oklahoma*, 339 U.S. 637 (1950), and *Sweatt v. Painter*, 339 U.S. 629 (1950).

32. Ibid., 9.
33. Ibid., 12. The brief referred to the government's brief in the *Henderson* case for "concrete illustrations of the extent to which the existence of racial discrimination in this country embarrasses the United States in the conduct of foreign affairs."
34. Ibid., 13.
35. In November 1951, President Truman vetoed a bill because it had a provision requiring schools in seventeen Southern states, which were operated and owned by the federal government, to be segregated to "the maximum extent practicable." In a White House press release, Truman explained his action by describing the proposed provision as a "backward step in the efforts of the [f]ederal [g]overnment to extend equal rights and opportunities to all our people. . . . We have assumed a role of world leadership in seeking to unite people of great cultural and racial diversity for the purpose of resisting aggression. . . . We should not impair our moral position by enacting a law that requires a discrimination based on race. . . ." Barton J. Bernstein and Allen J. Matusow, eds., *The Truman Administration: A Documentary History* (New York: Harper & Row, 1966), 113–4.
36. Brief for the United States as amicus curiae, *Brown v. Board of Education*, 374 U.S. 483, 6.
37. Ibid., 7.
38. Ibid., 7–8.
39. Ibid., 8.
40. Ibid., 4–5.
41. *New York Times*, May 18, 1954, 1. Representative Victor Anfuso of New York told the U.S. House of Representatives that "virtually the entire press of Western Europe reacted with enthusiastic approval of the *Brown* decision. Publications usually lukewarm to United States policies, or opposed to them joined in approval. These included in England, the Labor Party's *Daily Herald* and the highly respected *Observer;* in France, *Le Monde,* the spokesman for neutralist elements; in Switzerland, the *Tribune de Geneve;* and in Germany, the influential publication *Stuttgarter Zeitung.*" Civil Rights Hearings before the Subcommittee of the House Committee on the Judiciary, Eighty-fourth Congress, first session, 1955, 209.
42. Carl T. Rowan, *The Pitiful and the Proud* (New York: Random House, 1956), 19. Rowan, who served as head of the United States Information Agency in the 1960s, was the subject of a sad yet amusing racial incident. While mowing his lawn, a "lady" driving a Cadillac pulled up to the curb and asked, "Oh, Boy? Boy? What are they paying you to mow this grass?" Rowan's answer was that the lady of the house "lets me sleep with her." And off went the Cadillac.
43. Despatch No. 1498, American Embassy, Rio de Janeiro, Brazil to Department of State, June 2, 1954, record group 59, decimal file 811.411/6-24.
44. Despatch No. 248, U.S. Consul, Dakar, French West Africa, to Department of State, May 26, 1954, record group 59, decimal file 811.411/5-2654.

45. *Opinion about U.S. Treatment of Negroes,* Report 38, July 24, 1956, Office of Research, Public Opinion Barometer Reports, 1955–1962, Western Europe 1955–1956, Box 4, ii, 12, record group 306.
46. Communication No. 84 from the United States Mission to the United Nations (USUN), New York to the Department of State, August 6, 1956, record group 59, decimal file 811.411/8-656.
47. Lucy declined the offer, saying she wanted to fight the battle until the end.
48. Incoming telegram, American Embassy, Copenhagen, Denmark, to Secretary of State, February 9, 1956, record group 59, decimal file 811.411/2-956.
49. Ibid.
50. Despatch No. 660, American Embassy, Copenhagen, to Department of State, February 9, 1956, record group 59, decimal file 811.411/2-956.
51. Ibid.
52. Despatch No. 973, American Embassy, Stockholm, Sweden, to Department of State, March 7, 1956, record group 59, decimal file 811.411/3-756.
53. Ibid. Embassy officials worried about the high status Baker enjoyed in Sweden. At the above-mentioned event, the defense minister introduced Baker while the Swedish prime minister and his wife were in the audience. Because Baker had already given up her citizenship, the State Department could not impose travel restrictions on her, a measure it exercised on W. E. B. DuBois, Paul Robeson, and William Patterson, among others. Mary Dudziak has documented how the State Department harassed Baker and persuaded other governments to do the same and to limit her performances. See Mary L. Dudziak, "Josephine Baker, Racial Protest, and the Cold War," *Journal of American History* 81 (September 1984), 543–70.
54. Despatch No. 109, American Consulate, Nice, France, to Department of State, February 27, 1956, record group 59, decimal file 811.411/2-2756.
55. Incoming telegram No. 1194, from The Hague to Secretary of State, February 9, 1956, record group 59, decimal file 811.411/2-956.
56. Incoming telegram from Warsaw to Secretary of State, March 9, 1956, record group 59, decimal file 811.411/3-956.
57. Despatch No. 106, American Consulate General, Lagos, Nigeria, to Department of State, February 24, 1956, record group 59, decimal file 811.411/2-2456.
58. Despatch No. 109, American Consulate General, Lagos, Nigeria, to Department of State, February 27, 1956, record group 59, decimal file 811.411/2-2756.
59. Ibid.
60. Ibid.
61. *New York Times,* April 29, 1956.
62. It is interesting to note that a sold-out rally in Madison Square Garden to honor Autherine Lucy included Eleanor Roosevelt, Martin Luther King, Jr., Representative Powell, and other civil rights leaders. Addressing the racially mixed audience, the former First Lady urged the Northerners to have the courage to recognize that racial discrimination is as much a Northern problem as it is a Southern problem. Black, 116.

63. Incoming telegram No. 38, from Ankara, Turkey, to Secretary of State, September 12, 1956, record group 59, decimal file 811.411/9-1256.

64. Despatch No. 40, American Consulate General, Montreal, Canada, to Department of State, September 11, 1956, record group 59, decimal file 811.411/9-1156.

65. The act empowered the federal government to seek court injunctions against obstruction or deprivation of voting rights, among other things.

66. The actions of one of the nine, Minnie Jean Brown, exemplified how these black students stood their ground. Brown dropped a bowl of chili on a white boy in the school cafeteria when he blocked her path. For that she was expelled for three days. She was expelled again for calling a white girl "white trash" in response to this girl calling her "nigger bitch." All nine students received hundreds of letters from well wishers in countries they had never heard about. One girl told Harold Isaacs, "I take letters with me to school; they make me feel good. . . . I read them in school." Another girl added, "I read a letter every morning before I go to school, and it makes me feel good all day, and I read one when I come back. It lifts my spirits." Harold R. Isaacs, *The New World of Negro Americans* (New York: The John Day Company, 1963), 12.

67. A day after the crisis broke out, Eisenhower stated that he did not intend to propose federal intervention in Southern school disputes. Eisenhower viewed the presidency as a "place of moral leadership" but that segregation was not a moral issue. As Hamby puts it, "[Eisenhower's] support of black objectives was quite limited and resulted mostly from the urgings of his Department of Justice." 126–7.

68. In his memoirs, Chief Justice Earl Warren recalled that Eisenhower invited him to a White House dinner shortly before the *Brown* decision. The president told Warren that Southerners valued the chief justice's opinion. "The President . . . took me by the arm and as we walked along, speaking of the Southern states in the segregation cases, he said, 'these are not bad people. All they are concerned about is to see that their sweet little girls are not required to sit in school alongside some big overgrown Negroes. . . . ' Shortly thereafter, the *Brown* case was decided, and with it went our cordial relations." Earl Warren, "The Memoirs of Earl Warren." In Peter Woll, *American Government* (Boston: Little, Brown and Co., 1978).

69. Isaacs, "World Affairs and U.S. Race Relations: A Note on Little Rock," 367.

70. An open letter was sent to the American ambassador and the American community in Indonesia expressing "disgust" and questioning how Americans hoped to convince the Asian people of their championship of democracy "as long as there is still ill-treatment of Negroes such as happened again in Little Rock" and stating that photos of Little Rock spoke louder than words. The letter suggested that Southerners should go to Asia to learn something about tolerance. The U.S. embassy confirmed to the State Department that the writers of the letter were not Communists. Despatch No. 188, American Embassy, Djakarta, Indonesia, United States

Information Service to Department of State, October 7, 1957, record group 59, decimal file 811.411/10-757.

71. In Libya, the United States was bitterly criticized for calling itself "mother of liberty and democracy while permitting 16 million African Americans to be smashed under the soles of the white and live a life of humiliation." An editorial asked Americans why Libyans should believe their propaganda when they know the tragedies that are taking place in their country. Despatch No. 141, American Embassy, Tripoli, Libya, to Department of State, October 22, 1957, record group 59, decimal file 811.411/10-2257.

72. In Brazil, so-called American democracy was denounced. The American consul general in Sao Paulo told the State Department that Little Rock made the favorable side of Negro progress hard to present and that statements by Louis Armstrong and Eartha Kitt about Negro progress were not helpful at this time. Despatch No. 111, American Consulate, Sao Paulo, Brazil, to Department of State, September 23, 1957, record group 59, decimal file 811.411/9-2357. Because of Little Rock, Louis Armstrong abandoned a government-sponsored trip to the Soviet Union, declaring that "the way they are treating my people in the South, the Government can go to hell." Armstrong called Governor Faubus "an uneducated plow-boy" and President Eisenhower "two-faced" and stated that, "It's getting so bad a colored man hasn't got any country." "Louis Armstrong, Barring Soviet Tour, Denounces Eisenhower and Gov. Faubus," *New York Times*, September 19, 1957, 23. In Ecuador, leading papers carried editorials of condemnation. Despatch No. 256, American Embassy, Quito, Ecuador, to Department of State, October 10, 1957, record group 59, decimal file 811.411/10-1057. In Argentina, open letters were sent to President Eisenhower and various U.S. student bodies. Eisenhower was asked how he expected to convince Russia and the rest of the world about the advantages of democracy when he could not persuade Faubus to obey the law. Letter to Eisenhower from Buenos Aires, September 16, 1957, record group 59, decimal file 811.411/10-957; letter from the Federation of Free Students of Argentina to the students of the United States, October 10, 1957, record group 59, decimal file 811.411/10-1457.

73. Little Rock occupied front-page space "usually reserved for major domestic news." Despatch No. 151, American Embassy, Canberra, Australia, to Department of State, October 1, 1957, record group 59, decimal file 811.411/10-157.

74. *Public Reactions to Little Rock in Major World Capitals*, Special Report Series SR-8, October 29, 1957, 1, Office of Research, Box 1, record group 306.

75. Ibid., 5.

76. Ibid., 7.

77. Ibid., 8.

78. Incoming telegram No. 31 from Copenhagen, Denmark, to Secretary of State, September 5, 1957, record group 59, decimal file 811.411/9-557.

79. Despatch No. 255, American Embassy, Stockholm, Sweden, to Depart-

ment of State, September 10, 1956, record group 59, decimal file 811.411/9-1056.

80. Incoming telegram No. 31 from Bern, Switzerland, to Secretary of State, September 12, 1957, record group 59, decimal file 811.411/9-1257.

81. Ibid. It is interesting to note that in the wake of Eisenhower's intervention in Little Rock, Senator Herman Talmadge, a Georgia Democrat, played on the fears of anti-Communism. In a statement, he said "we still mourn the destruction of the sovereignty of Hungary by Russian tanks and troops in the streets of Budapest. We are now threatened with the spectacle of the President of the United States using tanks and troops in the streets of Little Rock to destroy the sovereignty of the State of Arkansas." *U.S. News & World Report*, October 4, 1957.

82. Ibid.

83. Despatch No. 45, American Consulate General, Amsterdam, the Netherlands, to Secretary of State, September 16, 1957, record group 59, decimal file 811.411/9-1657 (emphasis my own).

84. Ibid.

85. Despatch No. 115, American Embassy, Dublin, Ireland, to Department of State, September 23, 1957, record group 59, decimal file 811.411/9-2357.

86. Despatch No. 64, American Embassy, Luxembourg, to Department of State, September 24, 1957, record group 59, decimal file 811.411/9-2457.

87. Ibid.

88. Despatch No. 69, American Embassy, Luxembourg, to Department of State, September 30, 1957, record group 59, decimal file 811.411/9-3057 HBS.

89. Despatch No. 70, American Embassy, Luxembourg, to Department of State, October 1, 1957, record group 59, decimal file 811.411/10-157.

90. "Mike Wallace Asks Catherine Gavin: What Have the British Got against America?" *New York Post*, May 8, 1958.

91. Despatch No. 401, American Embassy, Brussels, to Department of State, October 8, 1957, record group 59, decimal file 811.411/10-857.

92. Despatch No. 462, American Embassy, Vienna, to State Department, November 5, 1958, record group 59, decimal file 811.411/11-558.

93. Telegram No. 23 from American Embassy, Paris, to Department of State, September 26, 1957, record group 59, decimal file 811.411/9-2657.

94. Quoted in Michael L. Kernn, "'Unfinished Business': Segregation and U.S. Diplomacy at the 1958 World's Fair," *Diplomatic History*, Vol. 20, No. 4 (Fall 1996), 593–4.

95. Incoming telegram No. 83, from Bonn, West Germany, to USIA, October 5, 1957, record group 59, decimal file 811.411/10-557.

96. Despatch No. 86, American Consulate, Dar es Salaam, to Department of State, September 28, 1957, record group 59, decimal file 811.411/9-2857.

97. Despatch No 96, American Consul, Nairobi, Kenya, to Department of State, October 2, 1957, record group 59, decimal file 811.411/10-257.

98. Despatch No. 31, American Consulate, Kampala, Uganda, to Department of State, October 4, 1957, record group 59, decimal file 811.411/10-457.

99. Despatch No. 37, American Consulate, Kampala, Uganda, to Department of State, October 3, 1957, record group 50, decimal file 811.411/10-357.

100. Despatch No. 31, American Consulate, Kampala, Uganda, to Department of State, October 4, 1957, record group 59, decimal file 811.411/10-57.

101. Despatch No. 115, American Consulate, Lagos, Nigeria, to Department of State, October 14, 1957, record group 59, decimal file 811.411/10-1457.

102. Ibid.

103. Ibid.

104. Despatch No. 155, American Consulate, Lagos, Nigeria, to Department of State, November 29, 1957, record group 59, decimal file 811.411/11-2957.

105. Despatch No. 59, American Consulate, Lourenco Marques, Mozambique, to Department of State, September 30, 1957, record group 59, decimal file 811.411/9-3057.

106. Ibid.

107. Despatch No. 11, American Consulate, Port Elizabeth, South Africa, to Department of State, November 13, 1957, record group 50, decimal file 811.411/11-1357.

108. Despatch No. 113, American Consulate, Johannesburg, South Africa, to Department of State, December 5, 1957, record group 59, decimal file 811.411/12-557.

109. Incoming telegrams 527, 532, The Hague, the Netherlands, to Secretary of State, September 26, 1957, record group 59, decimal file 811.411/9-2657.

110. Incoming telegram, Quito, Ecuador, to Secretary of State, September 28, 1957, record group 59, decimal file 811.411/9-2757.

111. Despatch 99, American Consulate, Dakar, French West Africa, to Department of State, October 30, 1957, record group 59, decimal file 811.411/10-3057.

112. See footnote 2 of this chapter.

113. Incoming telegram No. 415, Joint USIA-State, Rio de Janeiro, to Secretary of State, September 26, 1957, record group 59, decimal file 811.411/9-2657.

114. Communication No. 504 from U.S. United Nations mission, New York, to the Department of State, December 9, 1957, record group 59, decimal file 340.17/12-957.

115. Despatch 70, American Embassy, Luxembourg, to Department of State, October 1, 1957, record group 59, decimal file 811.411/10-157; despatch 59, American Consulate, Lourenco Marques, Mozambique, to Department of State, September 30, 1957, record group 59, decimal file 811.411/9-3057; despatch No. 401, American Embassy, Brussels, Belgium, to Department of State, October 8, 1957, record group 59, decimal file 811.411/10-857; despatch No. 96, American Consulate, Nairobi, Kenya, to Department of State, October 2, 1957, record group 59, decimal file 811.411/10-257; despatch No. 31, American Consulate, Kampala, Uganda, to Department of State, October 4, 1957, record group 59, deci-

mal file 811.411/10-457; despatch No. 313, American Embassy, Bogota, Colombia, to Department of State, October 7, 1957, record group 59, decimal file 811.411/10-757; Department of State, Instruction No. 1565 to American Embassy in London, November 17, 1957, record group 59, decimal file 811.411/11-1757.

116. Despatch 69, American Embassy, Luxembourg, to Department of State, September 30, 1957, record group 59, decimal file 811.411/9-3057 HBS.

117. Despatch 16, American Consulate, Cardiff, Wales, to Department of State, September 27, 1957, record group 59, decimal file 811.411/9-2757.

118. Incoming telegram No. 43 from Stockholm, Sweden, to Secretary of State, September 25, 1957, record group 59, decimal file 811.411/9-2557.

119. Office memorandum, July 18, 1958, S-11-58, Box 15, Office of Research, special reports 1953–63, record group 306.

120. *Post–Little Rock Opinion on the Treatment of Negroes in the U.S.*, Program and Media Series, PMS-23, 1, January 1958, Box 1, Office of Research, record group 306.

121. *New York Post,* June 4, 1958. For foreign opinion of American racial attitudes, see Hazel Erskine, "The Polls: World Opinion of U.S. Racial Problems." *Public Opinion Quarterly* 32 (Summer 1968): 299–312. Erskine reports that in the wake of Little Rock, the percent of the population who had a very bad opinion of the treatment of African Americans was as follows: sixty-seven in Brussels, eighty-two in Denmark, sixty-three in Finland, sixty-five in France, sixty-six in Great Britain, seventy-three in Iceland, sixty-one in Mexico, seventy-nine in the Netherlands, eighty-two in Norway, and eighty-seven in Sweden.

122. Memorandum for the White House from the State Department, *Concerning Request from the Civil Rights Commission – 'Treatment of Minorities in the United States – Impact on Our Foreign Relations.*" December 1958, record group 59, decimal file 811.411/12-458, Part A. Summary Review, 1. The 1958 World's Fair in Brussels provided an opportunity to counter the negative international public opinion following Little Rock. In an exhibit titled "Unfinished Business," the United States would, for the first time, exhibit its race problems and its efforts to solve them. See Kernn, 591–612.

123. I do not include the early 1960s school desegregation incidents that turned into international events. These would include the 1961 Alabama riots, the 1962 Mississippi crisis, and the 1963 confrontation at the University of Alabama. In the 1960s, race riots attracted extensive international response. For example, the Alabama riots of 1961 attracted worldwide attention and criticism. USIA reports assessed their impact as highly detrimental to America's image abroad, dealing a severe blow to U.S. prestige, which "might adversely [affect] our position of leadership in the free world as well as weaken the overall effectiveness of the Western alliance." *Worldwide Reaction to Racial Incidents in Alabama,* May 29, 1961, Report S-17-61, record group 306, 1.

124. Ambassadors often met with State Department personnel to protest and discuss racial incidents and racist comments by American officials. In

1963, for example, several ambassadors of Middle Eastern and African countries met with State Department officials regarding racist remarks made by Louisiana Senator Allen J. Ellender. Plummer, 322. See also Dean Rusk, *As I Saw It* (New York: W. W. Norton, 1990), 579–92.

125. Lauren, 220.

126. Letter to Department of State from Mr. Pereira, September 3, 1943, record group 59, decimal file 811.4016/707; Department of State, Division of Near Eastern Affairs, Memorandum, September 14, 1943, record group 59, decimal file FW 811.4016/707.

127. Letter from American Consul, Kingston, Jamaica, to the Secretary of State, September 12, 1945, record group 59, decimal file 811.4016/9-1245.

128. In 1958, a drugstore in Louisville, Kentucky, refused to serve the mayor of Jamaica who was visiting the U.S. as a guest of the State Department. Not only did the State Department formally apologize for the incident, the mayor of Louisville did so as well. *New York Times,* November 29, 1958, 19.

129. Letter from American Embassy, Port-au-Prince, Haiti, to Department of State, November 18, 1947, record group 59, decimal file FW 811.4016/11-1247; despatch No. 785, American Embassy, Port-au-Prince, Haiti, to Department of State, November 18, 1947, record group 59, decimal file 811.4016/11-1847.

130. Memorandum of conversation, Department of State, November 14, 1947, record group 59, decimal file FW 811.4016/11-1247; letter to State Department from the White House hotel in Biloxi, Mississippi, November 25, 1947, record group 49, decimal file 811.4016/11-2547. It is interesting to note that American tourists in Mexico requested that African Americans be barred from hotels they frequently occupied. The Mexican Hotel Association refused their request. *New York Times,* October 18, 1956, 41.

131. Airgram 3151, Port-au-Prince, Haiti, to Secretary of State, November 20, 1947 (quoting *La Nation,* and *Le Nouvelliste*), record group 59, decimal file 811.4016/11-2047.

132. Letter to Secretary of State George Marshall from Robert Holt, November 28, 1947, record group 59, decimal file 811.4016/11-2847.

133. Letters to Dean Acheson from Morris Rosenthal, February 11, March 17, April 14, 1947, record group 59, decimal file 811.4016/2-1147, 811.4016/3-1747, and 811.4016/4-1447.

134. Ibid.

135. Letter to Paul Steiner, assistant airport administrator, Washington National Airport, from Harold Minor, chief, Division of Middle Eastern and Indian Affairs, February 11, 1947, record group 59, decimal file 811.4016/2-1147. Desegregation of the Washington airport restaurants was a problem that received attention of both the departments of Commerce and Interior. Although the secretary of commerce was not "essentially a reformer of any kind," he was politically astute to the implications of racial segregation at the airport of the nation's capitol. *Conference of Scholars,* 18, 87.

136. Route 40 was a stretch of highway between Washington, D.C., and the United Nations in New York. The restaurants along the Maryland portion of the highway were infamous for refusing to serve many high-ranking diplomats. Maryland restaurants were desegregated when the state government passed public accommodations bills in March 1963. The State Department and the White House played a fundamental role in convincing Maryland legislators to support the measure. A State Department official explained the problem along Route 40 by saying, "I would like to put this in the clearest terms possible. . . . When an American citizen humiliates a foreign representative or another American citizen for racial reasons, the results can be just as damaging to his country as the passing of secret information to the enemy. . . . The Government needs your help in selling democracy to the world. It needs your help in eliminating a source of embarrassment to the Government of the United States and to the government of the state of Maryland." Statement by Pedro Sanjuan before the Legislative Council of the General Assembly of Maryland at Baltimore, Maryland, September 13, 1961. *Department of State Bulletin* 45 (October 2, 1961), 551–2.

137. Memorandum of conversation, May 22, 1947, record group 59, decimal file 811.4016/5-2247.

138. Ibid. Miami Airport, the site of many racial segregation incidents involving foreigners, continued to be a thorn in the State Department's side. Ten years after the meetings between department officials and airport administrators, a Jamaican dental surgeon was refused service at one of the airport's restaurants. Dr. M. B. Douglas was returning to his country after attending Ghana's Independence Day celebrations as the official representative of the West Indian Afro Welfare League. The British ambassador to the U.S. asked the secretary of state to inquire into the incident. The secretary of state contacted Florida Governor LeRoy Collins, who stated that the restaurant in question was privately owned and was not located on tax-supported property and therefore was not within his jurisdiction. Letter to the secretary of state from Governor LeRoy Collins from the acting assistant secretary of state, May 6, 1957, record group 59, decimal file 811.411/5-657; letter to Governor Collins from the Dade County Port of Authority attached to letter to Department of State from Governor Collins, May 27, 1957, record group 59, decimal file 811.411/5-2757.

139. *New York Times,* November 2, 1947, 17; also reported by Senator William Benton, *Congressional Record,* Eighty-first Congress, second session, May 9, 1950, 6694.

140. *Washington Evening Star,* August 23, 1955.

141. Airgram No. 953, American Consulate, Bombay, India, to Secretary of State, July 19, 1943, record group 59, decimal file 811.4016/654.

142. Ibid. The *New York Times* reported that African Americans, in an attempt to mock and at the same time avoid segregation laws, would also wear turbans and fake foreign accents. *New York Times,* November 19, 1947, 14. It is ironic that almost two decades later, this issue was still being discussed.

During his visit to Africa in 1964, Malcolm X urged African leaders to take the plight of black Americans to the United Nations. He warned the African people that unless they wore their national dress "at all times when you visit America, you may be mistaken for one of us and suffer the same psychological and physical mutilation that is an everyday occurrence in our lives." *The Militant,* August 24, 1964, 2.

143. U.S. Ambassador to India Chester Bowles frequently stressed how deeply Indians felt about U.S. racial segregation. The first question Indians asked Bowles was, "Why do Americans discriminate against, and segregate people simply because of the color of their skin?" In 1957, Bowles testified that, "America's prestige and popularity throughout the world has sunk so seriously since the war." *Crisis,* February, 1957, 92. At the wake of its independence, India became one of the most vocal international critics of American racial policies.

144. Despatch No. 1127, American Embassy, New Delhi, India, to Department of State, September 27, 1948, record group 59, decimal file 701.8411/9-2748 and 701.8411/9-1548; despatch No. 440, American Consulate General, Calcutta, India, September 24, 1948, record group 59, decimal file 701.8411/9-2448.

145. Despatch No. 284, American Consulate General, Madras, India, to Department of State, September 30, 1948, record group 59, decimal file 701.8411/9-3048.

146. Press Release No. 84, September 20, 1948, record group 59, decimal file 701.8411/9-2048. The State Department attempted to blame the incident on the Ethiopian minister's misunderstanding of the seating arrangement.

147. Letter to the Secretary of State from Paul Robeson, chairman of the Council on African Affairs, September 19, 1948, record group 59, decimal file 701.8411/9-1948.

148. Ibid.

149. Incoming telegram No. 48 from Kuala Lumpur to Secretary of State, August 29, 1952, record group 59, decimal file 811.411/8-2952.

150. Incoming telegram from Singapore to Secretary of State, August 31, 1952, record group 59, decimal file 811.411/8-3152.

151. Incoming telegram from Kuala Lumpur to Secretary of State, September 9, 1952, record group 59, decimal file 811.411/9-952.

152. Ibid.

153. *New York Times,* March 19, 1950, 50.

154. *Journal of Negro Education,* Fall 1953, 489.

155. Outgoing telegram No. 27, Department of State to American Consulate, Kampala, Uganda, December 16, 1958, record group 59, decimal file 811.411/12-1658.

156. Letter to John Foster Dulles from the All African Student Union of the Americas, Inc., September 23, 1957, record group 59, decimal file 811.411/9-2357. Patrons of the union included Nnamdi Azikiwe, future president of Nigeria, and Kwame Nkrumah, Ghana's president. The State

Department notified the union that the Justice Department was conducting a "complete investigation" of the unfortunate incident. The American consulate in Lagos warned the State Department that a wave of indignation welled up in Nigeria in the wake of recent incidents involving Ghana's finance minister and the beating of the Nigerian student in Texas and that Nigerians had reacted with restraint, which might not last much longer. Despatch No. 115, American Consulate, Lagos, Nigeria, October 14, 1957, record group 59, decimal file 811.411/10-1457.

157. *New York Times*, September 12, 1951, 30.

158. "Racial Incidents" editorial, *Crisis* 58 (October 1951), 530–1. Chester Bowles recalls in his *Ambassador's Report* that an Indian student attending medical school at the University of Minnesota wrote him that while visiting the South with other Indian friends during a winter vacation, he was refused hotel accommodations and discriminated against on trains and other public facilities. "I spent two years in correspondence with this one student and his friends in an effort to erase some of the early bitterness against America that that trip had created." Bowles, 319.

159. Record group 59, Box 4651, especially file 811.4016/5-847.

160. It is naive to view the USSR–U.S. rivalry over Asia and Africa as exclusively a struggle of ideology or a competition for votes at the United Nations. Asia and Africa possessed large quantities of strategic raw materials vital to both superpowers. These new nation states were also potential markets for the products and technology of the superpowers.

Chapter Five. Conclusion

1. Gilbert Murray, *Tradition and Progress* (Boston: Houghton Miffin, 1922), 199.

2. Kenneth Thompson, *Moralism and Morality in Politics and Diplomacy: The Credibility of Institutions, Policies, and Leadership* (New York: University Press of America, 1985), 12.

3. It is interesting to note that the State Department, while courting non-white foreign dignitaries on official visits, made every effort that these visitors not have any contacts with African Americans. One State Department official commented that the visitors were "herded off so fast it ain't even funny. The [State Department] officials bow and scrape to them, and take them on certain carefully arranged itineraries, where they are sure not to come in contact or conflict with any colored folks. I'm willing to bet you that of all the South Americans of Negro mixed blood and Negro extraction, not one of them knows there is such as thing as Howard University – unless they accidentally slipped up on it. The [State Department] folk see that they meet none of those Negroes, nor any others of consequence." Quoted in Plummer, 100.

4. Conversation of Vice President Lyndon Johnson with Porter Parrish, of Hilton Hotels, in Dallas, June 15, 1961. Administrative Files, 1960-1961, Lyndon B. Johnson Presidential Library, Austin, Texas.

5. Ibid.

6. The horrors of the Holocaust contributed to the death of theories of scientific racism and of the superiority of racial purity. These theories had enjoyed a degree of acceptability, if not respectability, in Western Europe and the United States before the war. For an account of the origins of these theories, see Lauren, introduction and 50–7, and Rayford W. Logan, *The Betrayal of the Negro: From Rutherford B. Hayes to Woodrow Wilson* (New York: Macmillan, 1954), Chapter 18. Ideological rationalization of racial oppression in the United States and the racist ideology displayed prominently in the South led civil rights advocates at home and abroad to compare the United States to Hitlerism in Nazi Germany. And "the hypocrisy and paradox involved in fighting a world war for the four freedoms and against aggression by an enemy preaching a master race ideology, while at the same time upholding racial segregation and white supremacy, were too obvious." Richard Dalfiume, "The Forgotten Years of the Negro Revolution," in *The Negro in Depression and War: Prelude to Revolution*, Bernard Sternsher, ed. (Chicago: Quadrangle, 1969), 298–316.

7. Borstelmann, 81.

8. Resolution adopted during a 1945 conference on campaigning for black civil rights in the postwar period. Reel 12, #414, Randolph papers.

9. At its creation in 1945, the United Nations consisted of fifty-one nations of whom three were African, three Asian, and seven from the Middle East. By 1965, predominantly white nations were in the distinct minority.

10. *New York Times,* January 28, 1950, 21. In contrast, from the onset of the Bolshevik revolution, Soviet leaders were able to claim concern for oppressed nations and national minorities, and to support struggles for freedom, equality, independence, and the right to self-determination. See Leon Trotsky, *Leon Trotsky on Black Nationalism and Self Determination* (New York: Pathfinder, 1978), 10; Allison Blakely, *Russia and the Negro: Blacks in Russian History and Thought* (Washington, DC: Howard University Press, 1986), 121. The oppressed, including those in America, perceived the Soviet Union (at least in theory) as the only one "among the big powers [to] render concrete aid, military and otherwise, to the colonized and semi-colonized world." Horne, *Black and Red*, 9.

11. America's allies also expressed anger with the United States when it opposed their colonialism, as was the case with the Portuguese in Mozambique and Angola. When the United States criticized them, they threatened to stop allowing the United States the use of the Azores Islands as a military base. See Peter J. Schraeder, *United States Foreign Policy toward Africa: Incrementalism, Crisis and Change* (New York: Cambridge University Press, 1994), introduction.

12. Plummer, 237–8.

13. Lauren, 220.

14. Isaacs, *Note on Little Rock*, 365.

15. In his diary, Truman wrote, "Propaganda seems to be our greatest foreign relations enemy. Russians distribute lies about us." Truman wrote this in

1945. Lee Nichols, *Breakthrough on the Color Front* (New York: Random House, 1954), 9.

16. Office Memorandum, November 4, 1947, record group 59, decimal file 501.BD Human Rights/11-447.

17. Plummer, 327.

18. A fertile area for future research is the impact of the end of the Cold War on U.S. civil rights policies. An excellent beginning is Gerald Horne's "Who Lost the Cold War? Africans and African Americans," *Diplomatic History*, Vol. 20, No. 4 (Fall 1996), 613–26. Horne argues that the disintegration of the Soviet Union has been economically detrimental to the African American community. One only needs to follow the actions since 1990 of local, state, and federal courts to see the backlash against civil rights issues, including affirmative action.

19. See Charles M. Payne, *I've Got the Light of Freedom: The Organizing Tradition and the Mississippi Freedom Struggle* (Berkeley: University of California Press, 1995).

Index